The Defiant Lady of Lathom

Defence of Lathom House

The Defiant Lady of Lathom
Accounts of Charlotte de la Trémoille, Countess of Derby & the English Civil War

The Life-Story of Charlotte de la Trémoille
Countess of Derby
Mary C. Rowsell

The Lady of Lathom
Madame Guizot de Witt

With an Account of the Siege of Lathom House
by Tho. Stanley

LEONAUR

The Defiant Lady of Lathom
Accounts of Charlotte de la Trémoille, Countess of Derby & the English Civil War
The Life-Story of Charlotte de la Trémoille Countess of Derby
By Mary C. Rowsell
The Lady of Lathom
By Madame Guizot de Witt
With an Account of the Siege of Lathom House by Tho. Stanley

FIRST EDITION

First published under the titles
The Life-Story of Charlotte de la Trémoille Countess of Derby
The Lady of Lathom

Leonaur is an imprint of Oakpast Ltd
Copyright in this form © 2021 Oakpast Ltd

ISBN: 978-1-915234-06-3 (hardcover)
ISBN: 978-1-915234-07-0 (softcover)

http://www.leonaur.com

Publisher's Notes
The views expressed in this book are not necessarily those of the publisher.

The Defiant Lady of Lathom
Accounts of Charlotte de la Trémoille, Countess of Derby & the English Civil War

The Life-Story of Charlotte de la Trémoille Countess of Derby

Mary C. Rowsell

The Lady of Lathom

Madame Guizot de Witt

With an Account of the Siege of Lathom House by Tho. Stanley

The Defiant Lady of Lathom
Accounts of Charlotte de la Trémoille, Countess of Derby & the English Civil War
The Life-Story of Charlotte de la Trémoille Countess of Derby
By Mary C. Rowsell
The Lady of Lathom
By Madame Guizot de Witt
With an Account of the Siege of Lathom House by Tho. Stanley

FIRST EDITION

First published under the titles
The Life-Story of Charlotte de la Trémoille Countess of Derby
The Lady of Lathom

Leonaur is an imprint of Oakpast Ltd
Copyright in this form © 2021 Oakpast Ltd

ISBN: 978-1-915234-06-3 (hardcover)
ISBN: 978-1-915234-07-0 (softcover)

http://www.leonaur.com

Publisher's Notes
The views expressed in this book are not necessarily those of the publisher.

The Life-Story of Charlotte de la Trémoille Countess of Derby

Contents

Peaceful Times	11
A Marriage of Convenience	19
Gathering Clouds	27
National Grievances	32
A Chapter of Correspondence	41
Cavaliers and Roundheads	45
Breast Laws and Deemsters	51
No More Peaceful Days at Lathom	57
More Ardour Than Discretion	63
Back at Lathom	69
Queen of Her Home	73
A Sad Massacre	83
A Lull in the Storm	91
Lord Derby Taken Prisoner	99
Peaceful Times at Knowsley	108

CHAPTER 1

Peaceful Times

Charlotte de la Trémoille was born at Thouars in Poitou in 1601. The fine old *château*, (now the *mairie*), in which the first days of her eventful life dawned upon her was the heritage of her ancestors, and now by right of birth belonged to her father, Claude de la Trémoille. The *château* is beautifully situated upon a hill, around whose base the River Thone runs so far as to give it the appearance of an island.

Charlotte was the second child of her parents, whose style and title are thus described in their contract of marriage signed at Chatelhéraut in 1598:—

Claude de la Trémoille, Duke de Thouars, peer of France, Prince de Tarente and de Talmont, with the very noble and gracious Dame Charlotte Brabantine de Nassau, daughter of William the Silent, Prince of Orange, and of his third wife, Charlotte de Bourbon Montpensier.

Thus, the noblest blood of France and of Nassau ran in the veins of the child who was destined to play such an heroic part in the land of her adoption, and whose romantic story stands enshrined in England's historic annals.

She was born in days of comparative peace: the Wars of the League were at an end, the accession of Henri IV. to the crown of France had silenced the clash of martial strife. Catholic and Calvinist no longer fought at the sword's point. The Edict of Nantes, extending liberty of conscience and civil rights to the Protestants, had brought at least outward tranquillity. The act of Henri IV. in abjuring the Reformed faith and entering the Roman Communion had justified the hopes of all moderate minds. The Reformed party, with Henri's lifelong friend and good genius—the minister Sully—at its head, had seconded the wishes of the Catholics, and advised him to the change.

The effect was magical, restoring tranquillity to distracted France. The ravaged fields and hillsides were once more clothed with growing grain and vines. Sully said:—

> Husbandry and pastures were the true treasures of Peru, and the paps which nourished the kingdom.

Claude de la Trémoille, a Huguenot by birth, had always concerned himself less about politics and polemics than fealty to his royal master. A certain sturdy, loyal singleness of mind seems to have been a distinguishing characteristic of his race. The duke was a born soldier. From the moment he could wield a sword, it had been employed for France and the king. Henri had need of his valiant subject, and did not forget to reward his services. It was after his brave fighting at Fontaine-Franchise, 1595, that the king raised the territory of Thouars to the rank of a peerage; and three years later, Claude de la Trémoille married the daughter of William the Silent.

Still, though peace and prosperity once more smiled upon the face of the country, the bitterness of religious difference rankled. Mutual jealousy further aggravated the soreness. The Catholics were arrogant in their triumph, and never lost sight of the fact that it was Henri's policy which had drawn him into their ranks. The Protestants, on the other hand, lost their inspiration when the king became a Catholic. Their allegiance to the sovereign remained; but their devotion to the man cooled. Theoretically, civil prerogative might be extended to them; but practically, their advice in the guidance of the State was not sought.

The court party was not slow to let them understand this fact, in defiance of the king's goodwill and affection which he never lost for his old co-religionists. Already the clouds of the sad and troubled future were beginning to gather for the Huguenots. Sullen and disappointed, their leaders retired from the court, and with them went the Duke de Thouars, to occupy himself exclusively with the affairs of his own estate and the interests of his family.

He had four children—two sons and two daughters. He lived in great state at Thouars; and when Monsieur de Rosny, the Duke de Sully, came to Poitou to assume the governorship of the province, he received him with great magnificence.

Still, though he had hung up his sword, the duke regarded it longingly, and at the smallest incitement was ready to take it down. The chance came before a very few years had passed. The great Protestant leader, the Duke de Bouillon, who, by his second marriage with a daughter of William the Silent, was the brother-in-law of the Duke de Thouars, had compromised himself in the matter of the Maréchal Biron's treasonable correspondence with Spain; and Biron's consequent disgrace with the king sorely troubled the peace of the family at Thouars.

The minister Sully, as full of goodwill towards de Thouars as of a desire to secure the services of so brave and tried a soldier, sent de Thouars a message to come to Paris, he wrote:—

> The king contemplates war, and has need of you to fight against the Spaniards.

De Thouars, who was still a young man of barely thirty-eight, had let fall to Sully a few words of dissatisfaction at his enforced inactivity, when the minister had been his guest at Thouars; and Sully now reminded him of these expressions, he wrote:—

> Henri liked to see his Protestant servants about him, and objected to such powerful lords remaining long at a time in their own provinces. They might be lending themselves to the hatching of plots.

Monsieur du Plessis Mornay, the great Huguenot leader and governor of Saumur, of which he had made a powerful Protestant stronghold, did his utmost to dissuade de la Trémoille from going to court, he said, "Excepting for those words which escaped you, I see no reason for your going."

"But if I can be employed?" rejoined the more than willing de la Trémoille.

Du Plessis replied only by a stern, half-scornful silence, and went back to his *château* at Bonmoy near Saumur; but hardly had he arrived there, than he received a letter from Madame de la Trémoille, informing him that her husband had been seized with gout in the arm, and praying that if there should be no speedy improvement in his condition, du Plessis would come to him. On the following night, she further wrote that if he desired to see his friend alive, he must come quickly.

Du Plessis immediately hastened to Thouars, to find Monsieur de la Trémoille exhausted with fever, and gasping with semi-suffocation. He, however, rallied sufficiently to evince great pleasure at the sight of Monsieur du Plessis, "uttering with effort a few words, in which he displayed all his ordinary sense and judgment." He was further able to recommend to his friend's care his wife and four children, who were thus losing him while still so young. But the distractions of this life were fast slipping away from the dying man, and it was chiefly upon his soul's welfare that Du Plessis conversed with him.

"It is not for me," said de la Trémoille, "to speak of anything but that"; and, unheeding all else, he mustered his remaining strength and speech to discuss the life to come—replying always with words that showed his courage in the face of death, the assurance of his faith in Christ, and displaying the sound judgment which had distinguished him in the days of his health.

While de la Trémoille was thus struggling in the agonies of death, his daughter Charlotte lay ill with an attack of smallpox; and the distracted duchess only left her husband's bedside to tend the suffering child.

In the midst of all this trouble a message was brought her that her sister-in-law, the Princess de Condé, desired to speak with her. The princess, she was told, had met with a mishap in the breaking-down of her coach upon the road near Thouars, and she asked her sister-in-law for the loan of her carriage. Little cordiality existed at this time between the princess and her brother. Damaging reports of her had recently circulated. She was suspected in the first place of having poisoned her husband. She had, moreover, found difficulty in establishing proofs of the legitimacy of the son born to her after the prince's death. In addition to this, she had forsworn the Reformed faith, and given up her son, the little Prince de Condé, into the hands of the king to be reared in the Catholic creed.

Whether the princess really wanted the coach in order to proceed on her journey, or whether she magnified the accident for the reason of the opportunity it afforded her of becoming reconciled to her brother, probably she alone knew; but in any case, her visit was too late for that. Monsieur de la Trémoille was already speechless. "I cannot see her," cried the duchess, and she piteously entreated Monsieur du Plessis not to allow the princess to enter the *château*.

Du Plessis hesitated. He knew that the poor wife's hopes that her husband might recover were vain. He thought it possible that the solemnity of the scene of her brother's deathbed might exercise a salutary effect upon his sister's mind; but the distress of the duchess conquered him; and he wrote a respectful letter to the princess begging her to defer her visit.

Thus, Madame de Condé continued her journey to Paris without coming to Thouars; but she laid the blame of the refusal on Monsieur du Plessis, who found some difficulty in clearing himself with the king, for the affront that she considered she had received.

In the meantime, the duke expired, aged only thirty-eight years. He left his wife and children under the guardianship of the *Elector-Palatine*, of Prince Maurice of Nassau, of the Duke de Bouillon, and of Monsieur du Plessis. He desired on his death-bed that his children should be brought up in the Reformed faith.

Scarcely was he in his grave than the fulfilment of these dying wishes was gravely imperilled. The Huguenots had sunk into almost complete disfavour at court. Death and disaffection had played sore havoc with the leaders of their party. Du Plessis was in disgrace; one reason for this, among others, being his close friendship with de Thouars, who, in his turn, was a connection of the Duke de Bouillon, still in rebellion. Why, demanded the court party, did he mix himself up with such persons? On the other hand, the disquiet of the Protestants increased when the king gave orders for the little Duke de Thouars to be brought to court, so that he might be educated with the *dauphin*.

This was a great blow to Madame de la Trémoille; the child was only five years old, and she had just lost her daughter Elizabeth. To part with the boy now, was to lose him forever. He would be severed alike from every domestic tie, as entirely as he would be estranged from Protestantism. She would sooner see him laid in his coffin than this. Monsieur du Plessis bestirred himself to resist the project. He represented to the king that its carrying out would create a real grievance for the Protestants. Already the Prince de Condé had been taken from them, and was it worthwhile, for the mere sake of having the boy about the court, to irritate the Huguenots further?

Henri yielded the point, and the child was allowed to remain at Thouars, under his mother's care. At the end of her first year of widowhood, however, Madame de la Trémoille, in obedience to the repeated commands of the king, repaired to Paris, leaving her children at Thouars.

The mother's heart was doubtless not a little cheered during this enforced separation by the letters which reached her from her little daughter, who was now about six years old. Her biographer says:—

> In the midst of grave family documents relating to the family of de la Trémoille—side by side with parchments filled with

pompous titles, or lengthy enumerations of estates and *seignorial* rights—one feels a curious stirring of the heart at sight of the big round-hand characters, written on ruled paper, which commemorate the first attempts of a child destined to do great deeds.

Here is one of the letters:—

> *Madame*,—Since you have been gone, I have become very good, God be thanked. You will also find that I know a great deal. I know seventeen Psalms, all Pibrac's quatrains, and the verses of Zamariel: and more than that, I can talk Latin. My little brother, (the Count de Laval), is so pretty, that he could not be more so; and when people see him, they are able to talk of nothing else but of him. It seems a long time since we had the honour of seeing you. Madame, I pray you to love me. Monsieur de Saint Christophe tells me that you are well, for which I have thanked God. I pray heartily to God for you. I humbly kiss the hands of my good aunt, and of my little cousins.
>
> I am, *Madame*, your very humble and very obedient and good daughter,
>
> Charlotte de la Trémoille.

In learning the Psalms by heart, Charlotte was taught to follow the custom of all Protestant families of the time. For her Latin attainments she had doubtless to thank the still older custom of teaching the language to quite young children, in order that they should be able to follow the celebration of the Mass and the other services of the Roman Church; and though for young Huguenots the knowledge for this purpose was not necessary, Latin was still regarded as indispensable to the polite education of both sexes.

The children of Madame de la Trémoille occasionally accompanied her in her frequent absences from Thouars at this time, but generally they remained at home when she resided at Court or visited her relations in Holland. Yet, although separated from them, she took care to be informed of all their doings, so that she knew about their faults as well as the progress they made; for when she is at the Hague, in 1609, her daughter, then no more than eight years old, writes to her as follows:—

> *Madame*,—I am exceedingly sorry to have disobeyed you; but I hope henceforth you will not have occasion to complain of

me, although hitherto I have not been too good: but I hope in future to be so very much so, that you will have reason to be satisfied, and that my Grandmama and my uncles will not find me ungrateful any more, as I hope to be obedient, and mindful of them. They have shown me their great kindness in having given me some beautiful New Year's presents: that is to say, *Madame* (the Princess of Orange) has given me a carcanet of diamonds and rubies; the Princess of Orange, a pair of earrings; His Excellency, three dozen pearl and ruby buttons. My uncle has given me a gown of cloth of silver. Monsieur Suart has done what you wished him to do.

I beg you to love me always, and I shall all my life remain, *Madame*, your very humble and very obedient daughter and servant,
Charlotte de la Trémoille.

In 1609 Charlotte and her mother were together again, without being separated for any length of time for the next ten years. During this period, all the letters extant are written to the Duke de la Trémoille, her brother, who was generally absent from his family.

The young duke was not such a good correspondent as his sister; and to the great annoyance of his mother, frequently delegated the writing of his letters home to some good-natured friend. He married his cousin, Marie de la Tour d'Auvergne, the daughter of the Duke de Bouillon and of Elizabeth of Nassau. In the young wife Charlotte found a true sister, and their mutual affection lasted through life.

Charlotte remained with her brother and sister-in-law at Thouars, and Monsieur du Plessis paid them occasional visits from his *château* of Forêt-sur-Sèvres. Although by nature and from circumstance a reserved and somewhat stern-mannered man, he seems to have been regarded with affection as well as with reverence by the family of his old friend.

Charlotte, when about nineteen years old, does not appear to have been strong in health. Her spirit, even in girlhood as throughout her life, was stronger than the flesh. It is unfortunate that her zeal as a correspondent frequently outruns her calligraphic powers, since her voluminous letters to her mother are full of interesting gossip; so much of them, that is to say, as are decipherable. The paper however, is no longer ruled, and the writing is not, as heretofore, done under the eyes of "*Ma Mie*," the careful governess. Equally without heed to writing and spelling, she pours forth details of neighbouring doings, tells who comes to and from the *château*, and of what Monsieur du Plessis has said.

Always a very woman, the liking for dress occupies a prominent place in her mind—if its expression on paper does not belie her. Madame de la Trémoille's mind's eye is treated with word-pictures, infinite in detail and variety, of her daughter's gowns "of cloth of silver, trimmed with gold fringe." *Mademoiselle's* jeweller and *mantua*-maker are important members of the household at sumptuous Thouars; and the young Duke de la Trémoille is no whit behind his sister in his taste for magnificence.

A portrait by Rubens of Charlotte, painted at the time of her marriage, shows us a bright, graceful girl. She wears a bodice of scarlet satin, and her hat is adorned with white plumes; she is looking over her shoulder with an arch smile.

The letters to her mother, though written in terms of the formal respect which the times exacted, are full of gaiety and lively sallies, and show that she enjoyed existence, sweetened as it was by close intercourse with her brother's wife, who still, when the sea divided them, and the clouds of Charlotte de la Trémoille's stormy life grew dense and almost without a ray of hope, remained the recipient of her confidences, till death severed the sisterly tie.

CHAPTER 2

A Marriage of Convenience

In 1626 Charlotte de la Trémoille was present with her mother at the Hague, the court, at that time, of Prince Fréderic-Henri of Nassau, her great-uncle.

In the only letter preserved at this time, Charlotte expresses a great dislike to Holland. She finds the Court very "triste," and already the conviction that "the world is a very troublesome place to live in" forces itself upon her.

Meanwhile, negotiations for her marriage were being speedily concluded, and in the month of July of the same year (1626) Charlotte de la Trémoille was married at the Hague to James Stanley, Lord Strange, eldest son of the Earl of Derby and Elizabeth de Vere, daughter of the Earl of Oxford.

The Earl of Derby, the representative of one of the most illustrious families of the English nobility, was lord paramount of the counties of Cheshire and Lancashire, and hereditary sovereign of the Isle of Man.

His eldest son, who took the title of Lord Strange, was only twenty years of age at the time of his marriage. Handsome, high-minded, brave, intellectual, he was worthy of the wife who shared so faithfully in the fortunes of his troubled existence. A marriage less of choice than of convenience, it was to prove a union that could put to shame many a love match; but the passing of the years was to test its value.

At first, the separation from the home and the scenes of her childhood and girlhood was very grievously felt by the young wife. The civil dissensions in France, scotched only, not destroyed, were beginning to regain their old virulence; and travelling, apart from its ordinary difficulties and perils at that period, was rendered almost impossible for women. In England a similar state of things was rapidly developing; and so, it came about that Charlotte, now Lady Strange, never again set foot in her native country, or beheld the loved face of her more than sister, the Duchess de Thouars.

After the conclusion of the wedding festivities, Madame de la Trémoille accompanied her daughter to England, to see her duly installed in her new home.

For a very short time Lady Strange now appeared at court, in the capacity of lady-of-honour to Queen Henrietta Maria, sister of the French king, herself but the wife of a year to King Charles I. Twelve months later, in the month of August, Lord and Lady Strange were established at Lathom House.

Lathom House was situated in Lancashire, about three miles northeast of Ormskirk, and eight from the sea-coast. The ground on which it stood, as well as its outlying territories and neighbourhood, had been in the possession of the Earls of Derby, and of the de Lathoms and Ferrars (from whom the Stanleys had descended) before them, from Saxon times. Orm, the Saxon lord of Halton, which is one of the thirty-eight manors mentioned in Domesday Book, married Alice, the daughter of a Norman nobleman; obtaining, thereby, large estates in the county.

Orm appears to have founded the church which was co-existent with the name of Ormskirk in the reign of Richard I., when Robert, son of Henry de Tarbosh and Lathom—who is supposed to be a descendant of Orm—founded the priory, (Baines), which was for long the burial-place of the Earls of Derby. The mansion, which was very ancient, moated and walled, and built for the defiance and self-defence which those turbulent and unsettled feudal days demanded, came into possession of the Stanleys by the marriage of Isabella de Lathom with Sir James Stanley in the reign of Henry IV.

The Earl of Derby of the earlier years of Charles's reign presented Lathom House to his eldest son and heir, James, Lord Strange, the earl himself making his home at Chester. Concerning her father-in-law, Lady Strange writes to her mother in the following terms after premising that her epistle is merely the replica of one previously written, but which had gone astray in transit; a matter of far from infrequent occurrence in those days, when postal facilities were only in the first throes of being:—

> I informed you *Madame*, that I had been to see my father-in-law at Chester, the capital city of Cheshire, where he has always lived, in preference to any of his other residences, for these

three or four years past. He speaks French; and conversed with me in very agreeable terms, calling me lady and mistress of the house; that he wished to have no other woman but myself (*sic*, for daughter-in-law?), and that I was to have full authority. We were well received by the townspeople, although our visit was not expected. Many came out to conduct us. I also told you, *Madame*, how greatly I found Lathom House to my liking; and that I have to thank God and you for placing me so excellently. I do not question *Madame*, that you will do all in your power about my money. I am waiting to hear from you regarding it. Truly *Madame*, necessity constrains me to be more importunate than I ought; but your kindness gives me courage. Indeed, my happiness a little depends upon it, in order to shut the mouths of certain persons who do not love foreigners; although, thank God, the best among them wish me no harm. Your son (in law) is well, I am thankful to say, and feels no return of his disorder. He almost lives out of doors, finding the air very good for him.

At this point however, Lord Strange must have come indoors; for the postscript is in his handwriting, which is of a sort preferable to his wife's, both in penmanship and spelling, this *post-scriptum* runs:—

Madame,—I cannot let my wife's letter go without myself thanking you for the honour you do me. If I were able to speak with you, I should rejoice in constantly assuring you that I can never be other, *Madame*, than your very humble and obedient son and servant—J. Strange.

In the autumn of this year, the first child of Lady Strange was born. The home was complete; but domestic peace and content were destined to be lost like a beautiful dream, in the gloom of the times. Charles had not reigned twelve months before the first signs of the coming struggle took form and shape; if even already, in marrying the Roman Catholic Henrietta Maria, he had not hopelessly offended his subjects. Marriage with French princesses has almost invariably brought disaster on our English kings, and violent death in some form; the union of Henry V. with the Princess Catherine of France being one of the exceptions proving the rule.

Even in his domestic affections the evil destiny of the Stuarts thus attended Charles; and truly his fate was an ill one indeed which placed him at the head of a kingdom at such an epoch in its history. The times were out of joint; and the vacillating, arbitrary Charles was not the man to set them right at this crisis, when the very strength of the divinity hedging a king was being questioned and tested by that sense of the rights of individual and collective humanity which was beginning to quicken on every side.

The state of England however, on Charles's accession, was but the effect of causes which had been at work for many a generation past. Looking back no farther than to the Wars of the Roses, we see the resistance of a proud and jealous nobility to supreme kingly power, and its subjection by the ruthless Henry VIII., who suffered no mortal to live, from loftiest to lowliest, who attempted to cross his path or to thwart his will. Henry's despotism, inherent in Queen Mary, and carefully nourished by her bigoted husband, Philip of Spain, was in Elizabeth softened by the chastening experiences of early life, and throughout her long reign kept in check by prudent counsellors.

During the time that she was on the throne moreover, the new religion was on its probation. In its form of "Church of England, as by law established," it had still to approve itself to the nation. But long before her successor James I. took her place, Episcopalianism had been accepted by the English people from Tyne to Thames. By Roman Catholics it might be regarded as a hollow pretence, and by nonconformists as a popishly tainted compromise; but by the bulk of the community it was recognised as an ark of safety, spiritual and temporal, whose bulwarks warded off the shafts of Rome as effectually as her course ran clear of the shoals and whirlpools of the sectaries.

The Church of England, risen purified from the ashes of Romanism, was, or at least was accepted as, the reproduction of the church of the early Christians. It contained the ideal scheme of a, perfect law of liberty—religious, social, and political; and allowed a range of thought and of speculation not to be found in any other formulated expression of Christian belief whatever. Only of papistry the Church of England was intolerant. Pains and penalties, in countless instances not one degree less cruel than "Bloody Mary" inflicted on the Protestant martyrs, did "good Queen Bess" and her successor, "gentle King Jamie," inflict on the confessors of the older creed. To all other Christians, the Church of England extended sympathy.

While her sanctuaries, retaining much of the pomp and ceremonial of Roman ritual, were served by consecrated bishop, priest, and deacon, the crypts beneath them afforded places for the simple and austere public worship of refugee Huguenots and Calvinists. Singing boys still chanted psalm and antiphon; and in the private chapel of

Elizabeth, the "morning star of the Reformation," the retention of the lighted candles on the altar betokened the belief in the reality of Christ's presence in the sacramental bread and wine.

The transubstantiation of Romanism—the consubstantiation of Lutheranism—the spiritual presence only of Christ in the elements of Calvinism—the unchanged condition of the bread and wine in the Lord's Supper of Nonconformity and of Dissent generally, were alike set aside by the Established Church. The answer quoted by Elizabeth when questioned as to her conception of the manner of the divine presence in the Sacrament of the Lord's Supper:—

Christ's was the Word that spake it;
He took the bread, and brake it.
And what that Word doth make it,
That I believe, and take it—

—was signally characteristic of the teaching of the Church of England, which claimed primitive Catholicity and unbroken Apostolical succession. The assertion was at once pious and safe, and eminently illustrates the temper of the communion which has embraced within its fold such children as Jeremy Taylor, Burnet, Nicholas Ferrar and his ascetic following, Sherlock, Laud, Stanley, Pusey, the Wilberforces; and whose rebuke to a Sacheverell was administered mainly on the score of good breeding, and, if it lost a Wesley, is not careful to cry *mea culpa*.

For a generation or two the interest attaching to the new-old teaching of the Church of England, and its general adopting, pretty well absorbed the attention of all classes, more especially of the upper and middle ranks; but the more the doctrines were assimilated, the more they nourished a sense of the need of temporal freedom, and roused speculation in thoughtful minds as to what was most needed and wholesome for the social well-being of the State. The old dogma of kingly supremacy had become, to say the least, unpalatable since the days of the despotic Henry VIII.

The English nation had no mind to endure tyranny from the new dynasty; and many had looked with suspicion upon James Stuart, not forgetful that the blood of the papist and haughty Guises ran in his veins, and that he held with marvellous tenacity to the dogma, if in his case one might not call it the hobby, of kingly supremacy. Fond of scribbling, and endowed in his own estimation with surpassing argumentative and theological faculties, he sustained and comforted his bodily and mental timidity by pompous assertion and spiritual aphorism concerning the right of kingly control over everything the sun shone upon within his realm. The dogma of the infallibility of the Pope, James I. matched by his postulate that the king could not; merely do no wrong, but that everything he did arid willed was to be applauded and obeyed.

The difficulty was to impose this view upon a sufficient number of his influential subjects to make it work satisfactorily; those wise and moderate counsellors of Elizabeth's reign, who survived into James' time, kept him in check, and their experience of feminine weaknesses and short-comings in Elizabeth's vigorous mind was further widened by an acquaintance with the depths of folly and of childish self-conceit into which an anointed king could fall. Such men as Lord Chancellor Cecil and John Hampden had troublesome conviction of this; and King James I., whom Sully dubbed the wisest fool that ever lived, and Henri IV. relegated to the grades of "Captain of Arts and Bachelor of Arms," however strong himself in the comfortable doctrines of the divine right of kings, failed in arresting the growth of the life of political liberty.

With much pompous declaration however, and long-winded argument, James did his best. Warfare of words was better suited to the man who, it is said, was apt to swoon at sight of a naked sword; and when all other argument and precept failed to produce the desired impression, he took refuge in citing the example of his brother monarchs of France and of Spain. James, by the mouth of his ministers to the Commons, said:—

The King of England cannot appear of meaner importance than his equals.

And in this creed he caused his son to be reared. An early death took the elder and promising Prince Henry from the coming troubles, and the sensitive, proud, obstinate, vacillating Charles was left to struggle with the coil of cruel circumstance already so rapidly beginning to tangle up.

As if to strengthen the effect of this mental sustenance with which Charles had been fed as regularly as he had partaken of daily material food, James sent the young prince or at least allowed him to go to Spain with the gay, extravagant, thoughtless Duke of Buckingham. "Baby Charles" and "Steenie," as the king called the two, travelled *incognito* upon this romantic pilgrimage, stopping by the way in Paris, to sow the seeds of future mischief at the Court of Louis XIII. in the duke's thinly veiled admiration for Anne of Austria. The journey to Madrid however, which was originated for the end of marrying Charles to the *Infanta*, defeated its own object; but Charles returned to England perfected by what he had seen in his travels—in his lesson of kingcraft. Endowed with a graceful presence, and, despite a certain coldness and reserve, with winning manners, he had a scholarly and thoughtful mind; but both nature and rearing had made him a man only of his day, or, more truly, of the time preceding it.

He had no gifts of penetration or of prescience. He could not look into the future, any more than he was able to read the existing signs of the times. He had been to Spain. His eyes had been dazzled by the glitter of spoil from the New World, the splendour and pomp and punctilio of the Court of Madrid, and the magnificence of the Spanish *grandees*. He had seen with his own eyes the success of Loyola's scheme of religious and political orthodoxy, and its supreme power of snuffing out obnoxious speculation, theological and scientific; but he could not discern beneath the rich embroidery of the veil its rotten foundation, which in two or three generations was to crumble like the cerements of the grave in the pure light of day, and disclose the corruption and festering beneath.

He had witnessed the brilliancy of the afterglow which the memory of the adored soldier Henri Quatre had left, and it was small wonder if his mind's eye failed to reach across the gulf of coming years to that time when *lettres de cachet* would make fuel for burning the Bastille, and the yellow *sanbenitos* of heretics should be changed for *bonnets rouges* and *carmagnoles*. The guillotine was to reek with the blood, not alone of aristocrats, but of the sons and daughters themselves, of Liberty, Equality, and Fraternity. "The Revolution," said one of its noblest victims, "is devouring its own children"; and the contagion of hatred against kings and queens and all their tribe spread over Europe till confusion grew worse confounded.

Looking back to those early days of Charles's reign, the question hardly fails to suggest itself, how far the troubles of the time would have been even aggravated had he married the *Infanta* of Spain instead of the French princess. Protestantism in Spain had been stifled at the birth; but in France it still had healthy breathing-room, tempering the atmosphere of Romanist belief, and influencing even the most devoted and uncompromising of Rome's adherents. Neighboured by Switzerland, Holland, and Germany, the philosophy of Erasmus, the humanitarianism of Arminius, the teaching of Luther and of Calvin, all mingled with the stream of orthodox theological speculation, till, overflowing into fresh channels, it verged so closely and so frequently on theories of Catholic reform, that Pope Urban made a vigorous attempt to stem the tide by his Bull Unigenitus, ostensibly directed against the Jansenists only.

Thus, in France, thought and religious speculation were kept not merely from stagnating, but in active ferment; while in Spain, the repressive Jesuit system froze and fossilised religion. Outside passive obedience to dogma, said the disciples of Loyola, could be no salvation; but in France, such cast-iron ruling was gone for ever in Church and State. The white plume in the cap of the Huguenot-reared hero of Ivry brought loyal subjects rallying round him, as entirely as the little leaden images of Our Lady and the saints, with which the bigoted Louis XI. decorated his hat-brims, had repelled his people.

The growing Puritanic spirit in England however, which had but scanty affection for Episcopalianism itself, was not likely to draw fine distinctions. In the popular acceptation of the term, "Catholic" was identical with papist and Romanist; for, with a singular indifference, the papists had been permitted to appropriate the term. The young queen was a Roman Catholic, greatly attached to the forms and ceremonial of her Church; bringing with her from France a train of Romanist priests and followers. Charles himself was the grandson of the woman who had died kissing the crucifix with her last breath. None of these considerations were lost sight of when the king began to ask subsidies of his faithful Commons, and showed generally a disposition to rule with a high hand.

He met with a strong resistance; and fearing the influence of Buckingham over him, the flame of accusations which had long smouldered, was fanned against the duke, until his removal was brought about. Thus, the Commons triumphed; but Parliament was dissolved.

These events took place a year after Charles's accession; and about that time Lady Strange arriving in England, entered upon her post of lady-of-honour to the queen. The coveted position has, before and since that time, been found to have its drawbacks, as rosebuds have their crumpled leaves; and Lady Strange seems to have relinquished her part in the court pageantry as soon as might be, retiring to the home which one day she was so bravely to defend—Lathom House, in Lancashire.

CHAPTER 3

Gathering Clouds

Established at Lathom, Lady Strange sent intelligence to her mother of the hope that ere long a child would be born to her; adding:—

The length of our sojourn here is not decided upon, but if the twenty thousand crowns do not come, it will not be easy to leave the place. Your son-in-law is well, thank God, and joins frequently in the chase. On Monday, a great number of people were here, and for several days my husband has had to entertain many gentlemen. He shows me great affection; and God bestows upon us the blessing of living in great contentment and tranquillity of mind. We have some trouble with the Isle of Man; and if Château-Neuf were here, we should have offered him the charge of it. The appointment is worth a thousand *francs*; and that in a place where one can live for next to nothing.

Pecuniary cares, which harassed Lady Strange all the rest of her life, were setting in. With the adoption of the Romanist faith by Henri IV., the prospects of the Huguenots darkened. The League took possession of the towns and castles belonging to the Duke de la Trémoille; the agricultural prosperity of France was again blighted by renewed civil warfare, and the tenant-farmers were in arrears with their rents and payments. The duke was not able to sell his acres of arable and pasture land, and consequently could not send his sister the money which was hers by right. The Earl of Derby was likewise impoverished by the loss of certain moneys which, hitherto appertaining to the male heirs of his family, had now become alienated and divided: yet upon these reduced incomings the earl was expected still to maintain all the old state and magnificence of the house of Stanley.

The Isle of Man was, moreover, a possession of exceedingly doubtful value to its *suzerain* lords. The people were turbulent, and difficult to rule and to please. As a separate and independent kingdom, they claimed certain rights and privileges, and it required an Act of Parliament to settle their differences. Lady Strange's dower would have been incalculably useful towards the settlement of all these troubles, and about the close of the year 1627 she writes:—

> I am not without anxiety on many accounts; but God of His goodness will provide.

She goes on to say that her husband is much pressed for money, and how great her satisfaction would be if she were able to help him with her own dower.

> I am assured *Madame*, that you will understand better than I do myself the need for this; and also what a happiness it will be to me to afford consolation and help to those to whom I have been hitherto but a burden."

Still, however, no money came, and Charlotte writes later on:—

> I should be glad to know that my fortune existed not only in words, but in fact. It causes me great grief and anxiety.

A letter, written to Madame de la Trémoille by Lady Strange on the eve of her accouchement, is strikingly characteristic of the brave and spirited, but wholly tender and womanly nature of the Lady of Lathom. Expressing constantly a deep longing to see peace established between England and France, and greatly desiring the general welfare of both her native and adopted country, feminine and domestic interests chiefly occupy her mind. Far from her own people, Lady Strange had hoped to have her mother with her during her hour of trial; but the coming of the duchess was found to be impracticable, and Charlotte thus writes to her sister-in-law in the December of 1627:—

> For the journey of *Madame* (the dowager-duchess), I see, dear heart, the same objections to it as you do; and though I have passionately desired her coming, I dread the discomfort and dangers to which she would be exposed; and for myself, I trust in God that He will not forsake me, although I am alone and inexperienced. But there, my dear one, I will think no more about it, trusting in God. I know, dear heart (*mon coeur*), that you remember me in your prayers, and how rejoiced you are for me in thinking of the hopes I cherish. Also, you are assured

that the blessing which Heaven may bestow upon us will be always at your service.

At the end of January 1628, Lord Strange informs the duchess of the birth of a son; and again, a month later, Lady Strange, writing in more detail of the important event, is critical upon the English mode of baby treatment, she says:—

> I forgot to tell you that he (baby) is dark. I wish you could see the manner in which children are swaddled in this country. It is deplorable."

Since the time of Lady Strange, custom in such matters must have considerably changed, for in these days it is the tight swathing and impeding garments of Continental babies which challenges the compassion of English mothers for the small, cramped-up bodies. Lady Strange continues:—

> My husband would have written to you, but he does not express himself in any language but his own. He is none the less your very humble servant.

On the 17th April she again writes:—

> I have informed *Madame* of the baptism of your nephew, whom God thus graciously received on Sunday, 30th March. (Old style. The Gregorian calendar was not used in England.) He was carried by my sister-in-law, and attended by the ladies of four gentlemen of rank of this country. I had him dressed in white, after the French fashion, for here they dress them in colours, which I do not like. The Bishop of Chester baptised him in our private chapel, and, as you know, by the king's name only. Afterwards, sweetmeats were served; and at supper, the roast joints were brought to table by gentlemen of this neighbourhood, as also upon several preceding and succeeding days.
> The king has presented him with two gold mugs, which is his custom with those upon whom he bestows the honour of his Christian name. In addition to this however, he has sent me a very beautiful present which cost two thousand crowns; the diamonds ornamenting it are very fine, and all faceted. I did not expect to receive it. The Duchess of Richmond, his godmother, has given him a large bowl and a gilded enamel knife, such as is used to remove the rolls and pieces of bread with from the

table before the fruit is brought in; and to me she has given a turquoise bracelet.

Previous to the birth of his eldest son, the young father, who was only twenty-two, was called to take his seat in the House of Lords, under the title of Baron Strange. This arose out of error. The fact had been overlooked that the barony of Strange formed one of the titles fallen into disheritage at the death of Ferdinand, Earl of Derby. The error led to the creation of a new peerage, which went to the house of Athol, and for several years Lord Strange sat in the Upper House, during the lifetime of his father, the Earl of Derby.

A new Parliament was now summoned; and Sir Robert Cotton, the mildest and most temperate among the prominent men of the popular party, was called to the king's counsel table. He spoke there with wisdom and frankness, setting forth the just grievances of the nation; and in order to win its due support, impressing the necessity for redress. Sir Robert recalled those words of Lord Burleigh to Queen Elizabeth:—

Win their hearts, and their purses and their arms will be yours.

Concerning her husband's summons to town, Lady Strange writes on 18th May 1628:—

I write under much anxiety; for I believe my husband goes the day after tomorrow to London. This is the more grievous, as the air there does not suit him; but God of His goodness will preserve him. As for our little one, he is very well, Heaven be thanked. I have already in two of my letters asked you for frocks for him, for he is very big for his age; and they are needed the more that in this country children are short-clothed at a month or six weeks old. I am considered out of my senses that he is not yet short-coated. I also asked you to send hoods. I hope that all may arrive together.

God grant that all that Parliament decides be for His glory, and for the good of the king and of the nation.

Lord Strange did not however, go to London at this time. Lady Strange writes a little later:—

My husband has not been summoned to London (June 1628). There are great disturbances there. One day all is confusion, the next everything goes well.

It is small wonder that, to such a state of things, Lord Strange preferred the tranquillity and domestic happiness of his ancestral home.

CHAPTER 4

National Grievances

The family of Stanley takes its surname from the lordship of Stonleigh or Stanleigh in the moorlands of Staffordshire. The appertaining house and estates had originally belonged to the de Lathoms.

Robert Fitz-Henry appears to have been the first representative of the family of Lathom. In the reign of Richard I. this Robert founded the Priory of Burscough for Black Canons, whose scanty ruins, standing in a field near Ormskirk, still tell of the great nobility and beauty of the original structure.

Burscough Priory was for a long time the burial-place of the Earls of Derby; but at a later period, many of the coffins were removed to the vault of the Stanleys in Ormskirk church, which was built by the sumptuous-minded third Earl of Derby. In the reign of Edward I. the grandson of Robert Fitz-Henry married Amicia, the sister and co-heir of the lord and baron of Alfreton and Norton. Sir Rupert, their son, married Katherine, daughter and heiress of Sir Robert de Knowsley, that magnificent estate being thus brought into the family.

Edmondson (1785, Mowbray Herald Extraordinary) writes:—

Of this ancient and noble family of the Stanleys, are the Stanleys of Hooton in Cheshire, from whom descended Sir John Stanley, who, in the reign of Henry IV., obtained in 1406 a grant in fee of the Isle of Man, and from that time till February 1736 (except during the civil wars), the Earls of Derby have had an absolute jurisdiction over the people and soil.... The grandson of Sir John Stanley, named Thomas, was summoned to Parliament in 1456 as Lord Stanley; which Thomas married for his second wife Margaret, daughter and heir to John Beaufort, Duke of Somerset, and mother of Henry VII. For his services to Henry he was created, 1485, Earl of Derby. From the eldest son, Thomas, born to him by his first marriage, descended the Earls of Derby.

The crest of the Stanleys is an eagle surmounting a child: and concerning it, tradition hands down the legend that the Sir Thomas Stanley who was the father of Isabel, his only legitimate offspring, had a son by a gentlewoman named Mary Osketell. Sir Thomas, who at the time of the boy's birth appears to have been well on in years—since his wife is described as an aged lady—artfully contrived that the infant should be carried by a confidential servant to a certain spot in the park, and there laid at the foot of a tree, whose branches were the favourite haunt of an eagle. Presently, in the course of their walk, came by Sir Thomas and his wife, and there they beheld the huge bird hovering with outspread wings above the infant.

The crafty Sir Thomas, who loved the little creature well, feigned to his lady that he believed that the eagle had borne it hither in its talons, and launched into enthusiastic praise of the providence which had thus so miraculously preserved the babe, and placed it in their tender care. The gentle-hearted, unsuspecting lady placed implicit faith in Sir Thomas's representations, and

Their content was such, to see the hap
That the ancient lady hugs yt in her lap,
Smoths' yt with kisses, bathes yt in her tears,
And into Lathom House the babe she bears.

The child was christened Osketell. When however, the knight felt death not very far off, his conscience began to reproach him for the deception which he had played upon his wife, and he bequeathed the bulk of his fortune and estates to his legitimate child Isabel, who was now married to Sir John Stanley. To the poor "love child," whom the king had knighted, he left only the Manor of Irlam and Urmston near Manchester, and some possessions in Cheshire. Here Osketell settled, and became the founder of the family of Lathom of Ashbury.

This story would seem purely legendary: at all events, so far as it connects itself with Sir Thomas; since, in the Harleian MSS., there stands an account of some painted windows in Ashbury Church, near Congleton, on which is represented a figure with sword and spurs, habited in a white tabard, hands clasped. Over its head, a shield set anglewise under a helmet and mantle, emblazoned *or,* on a chief indented *az.*, three tyrants; over all a bandlet *gules.* Crest, an eaglet standing on an empty cradle, with wings displayed regardant *or*, with this inscription:—

Orate pro anima Philippi fil. Roberti Lathom militis.

This Philip of Lathom was uncle of Sir Thomas. Still thrown back to an earlier date, the tradition would equally hold good, and it is not beyond the bounds of possibility that some ancestor of Sir Thomas was really answerable for the crest of the Stanleys which carries with it the motto, "*Sans changer.*"

Lathom House was built at a very early period, when the mansions of great families were castellated and fortified to withstand the attacks of the foemen, native or foreign. It stood upon flat, marshy ground in the midst of low, gradual acclivities, its situation being best described by comparison with the hollow in the middle of the palm of the hand. Its sturdy environing walls were six feet thick, strengthened with bastions surmounted by nine towers, which commanded each other. In the centre, facing the gatehouse, which was flanked by two strong towers, was the lofty Eagle Keep tower.

Externally, a moat surrounded the walls: this was twenty-four feet wide and six feet deep, full of water; and between it and the walls ran a stout palisading. The gatehouse opened into the first court; the dwelling part of the mansion was in the Eagle Tower. South and southwestward of the house was "a rising ground, so near as to overlook the top of it, from which it falls so quick that nothing planted against it on the other side can touch it farther than the front wall; and on the north and east sides there is another rising ground, even to the edge of the moat."

The Rev. Mr Rutter, his lordship's chaplain writes:—

Thus, it will be seen, that over and above these artificial defences, there is something picturesque and noteworthy in the situation of the house, as if nature hereby had destined it for a place of refuge and safety.

It could not be taken by assault of battery, since the cannon placed at the top of the high surrounding hills could not damage the walls so as to effect a breach in them.

Old Lathom House bristled with towers. Eighteen in all rose from its walls. Thomas, second Earl of Derby, writing in the time of Henry VIII., thus apostrophises his ancestral home:—

Farewell, Lathom! that bright bower;

Nine towers thou bearest on hye,
And other nine thou bearest in the outer walls,
Within ther may be lodged kings three.

From the time of its foundation, Lathom was associated with royal memories and noble deeds. Among its heroes was Sir Thomas Stanley, Chief Governor of Ireland, the father of the first Earl of Derby, Sir Edward Stanley—

There is Sir Edward Stanley stout,
For martial skill clear without make;
Of Lathom House by line came out,
Whose blood will never turn their back—Harl. MSS.

—and of Sir William Stanley, the brother of the first earl. Those days of endless Yorkist and Lancastrian fighting for the crown, causing such bitterness and division between father and son, brother and brother, brought about the death upon the scaffold of Sir William Stanley. He was executed for his brave adherence to the cause of Perkin Warbeck, whom he, with so many more, believed to be the Duke of York, said to have been murdered in the Tower by Richard of Gloucester. Sir William met his fate February 1495; and in the summer following, King Henry VII. made a royal progress northward, to spend a few days with his mother, the Countess of Derby, at Lathom.

After showing his house to his royal guest, the earl conducted him on to the leads for a prospect of the country which the roof commanded. The earl's fool was among the company in attendance, and observing the king draw very near the edge, which had no parapet or defence of any kind, Master Yorick stepped up to the earl, and, pointing to the perilous verge, said: "Tom, remember Will." The king not only caught the words, but their meaning; the chronicler concludes:—

And made all haste downstairs and out of the house; and the fool, for long after, seemed mightily concerned that his lord had not had the courage to take the opportunity of avenging himself for the death of his brother, (Burke.)

Thus exemplifying the vast difference that exists between a fool and a wise man.

The jester was an important personage at Lathom, as in all great families of the time. The homes of the nobility were each in themselves royal courts in miniature, and the quips and cranks of these "strange caperers" must have been, not merely acceptable and welcome, but in a manner indispensable to the many—from my lord himself to the kitchen scullion—when books were rare, even for those who possessed the accomplishment of reading them. The wise saws and modern instances too often wrapped up in the quips of a clever fool must have kept awake many a brave gentleman when he had laid aside baldrick and hunting horn, and the falcon slept upon his perch.

 Moreover, as extremes so frequently do meet, in justice to all concerned the fact should never be lost sight of that the fool so called was often furnished with a very superior if fantastic headpiece beneath his cap and bells, and in many instances was a poet of a high order. To wit, one such a "fool" as Master John Heywood, King Henry VIII's jester, would be nowadays as acceptable as half a score of *savants*.

In a catalogue, or, as it is called, a "Checkrowle of my Lord of Darby's householde," drawn up in 1587, "Henry ye ffoole" is enumerated last indeed, but obviously as a very distinctive member of the establishment. At this time the steward of Lathom had three servants, the controller three, and the receiver-general three. Seven gentlemen waiters had each a servant, and the chaplain, Sir Gilbert Townley, had one. Then came nineteen yeomen ushers, six grooms of the chamber, two sub-grooms, thirteen yeomen waiters, two trumpeters, and inferior servants: making the total number to feed, one hundred and eighteen persons.

As will be seen, a spiritual teacher figures in this list, in the person of Sir Gilbert Townley; but neither physician nor surgeon, nor, for that matter, a barber. Possibly, these indispensable members of a large household are both included in the person of "a conjurer," kept in his lordship's service, "who cast out devils and healed diseases."

The weekly consumption of food at Lathom in the sixteenth century was an ox and twenty sheep; and in the way of liquor, fifteen hogsheads of beer, and a fair round dozen tuns of wine, yearly. In addition to the above enumerated comestibles were consumed large quantities of deer from the park, game from the woods, and fish from the ponds. For magnificence and hospitality, Lathom House in the time of the Stanleys surpassed all the residences of the north; and its possessors were regarded with such veneration and esteem, that the harmless inversion, "God save the Earl of Derby and the King," was as familiar as household words.

And if in the days of Henry VIII. and Elizabeth this was held no treason, still less was it so in the days of Charles I. in the time of the Lord and Lady of Lathom whom peril and death itself could not render disloyal to their king, or a mockery to their motto, "*Sans changer.*"

This was the home in which Lady Strange spent the best part of the years of her married life, happily enough in the domestic relations of wife and mother, but hampered by the public and political complications in France, which were for ever hindering the payment of the money supplies belonging to her by inheritance, and troubled by yearly increasing anxiety for the disturbed condition of her adopted country.

Charles, from the beginning of his reign, had given great offence to the nation by the taxations which he strove to impose upon it for the carrying on of his foreign wars. This discontent was aggravated by the favour which he showed to the Duke of Buckingham. The duke had not merely a voice in every question of State affairs, for which privilege he did his royal master the doubtful service of defending him against the Parliamentary attacks which daily gathered in angry strength, but he crowned all by aspiring to and obtaining the command set on foot for the assistance of the Huguenots against the forces of Richelieu, which were beleaguering the city of la Rochelle.

Buckingham's religious convictions were however considerably less strong than his anger against the cardinal, to whom his behaviour had begun to give offence ever since the day when he first set foot in the French Court and had cast amorous eyes upon Anne of Austria, the beautiful wife of Louis XIII. Buckingham took his fleet to Rochelle, having persuaded Charles that the expedition would be regarded with special favour by the English nation, since it was to contend for Protestantism and Protestants against the proud Romanist arch-priest.

This might in a measure have proved to be the case had the undertaking been successful; and, since there is nothing that succeeds like success, it might have turned the whole course of subsequent events for Charles. But George Villiers was not of the stuff to measure arms with Armand de Richelieu, whose axiom was that there was "no such word as fail"—and the expedition was a total fiasco. Buckingham returned to England to organise a second attempt; but while waiting at Portsmouth for this purpose, he died by the hand of the assassin Felton.

Charles was now left to bear alone the bitter complaints of his people, who had been taxed for the expenses of the fleet, the ill-success of which had cast ridicule not only on England, but on the Protestant cause, and simply enhanced the growing triumphs of the Catholics in

France. The king furthermore, was giving great offence to Protestants of all denominations by the toleration which he granted the papists.

From the Independents, the growing party of the Puritans, and almost without exception from the Episcopalians, the Roman Catholics of the country met with no quarter. Many patriotic and loyal English men and women had remained faithful to the old creed, keeping spiritual and political conviction absolutely apart; but upon these, baleful reflections were cast by the foreign Jesuit party, and suspicion fell on the most unbigoted and inoffensive.

Charles's leniency towards his Roman Catholic subjects was far less the effect of any sympathy with their doctrines than that of a mistaken policy. His idea in coming to any sort of *entente cordiale* with them was to make terms for dispensations from the severity of the penal laws existing against them. He wanted the benevolences of them, and forced loans, for the purpose of carrying on his war against Spain, since he could not obtain the needful supplies from Parliament; and the nation objected on the double score of the illegality of such a measure, and the inadvisability of keeping up warfare with the Continent at all.

These offences on the king's part crowned the grievances he had caused by his levy of tonnage and poundage, and the new Parliament which was now summoned inaugurated proceedings by an inquiry into the "national grievances." In 1628 all this resulted in the bill known as the Petition of Rights, which, after some demur in the Upper House, was finally passed by the lords, and received the royal assent. This bill required the consent of both Houses to the furnishing by anyone of tax, loan, or benevolences. It claimed for the people exemption from enforced quartering upon them of soldiers and seamen. Martial law was to be abolished, and no person to be arbitrarily imprisoned.

Matters might now have improved; but Charles sprang a new mine by the tenacity with which he clung to the disputed right of tonnage and poundage. The Commons, unfaithful to their promise to look into the justice of the claim, arrived at the decision that anyone paying it should be held a traitor to his country. The offended king, calling the members of the Commons all "vipers," once more dissolved Parliament, made peace with France and Spain, and proceeded to act upon his declaration that he would govern without the aid of Parliament.

The blame of all these disputes was laid to the Duke of Buckingham. The sanction given by the king to the Bill of Rights did little to appease the storm of discontent. Five months after the prorogation of Parliament (23rd August 1628) Buckingham was assassinated by one of his disbanded officers. Lady Strange writes to her sister-in-law a month later:—

> I expect that before this reaches you, you will have heard of the death of the Duke of Buckingham, who was killed by one Felton, the lieutenant of a company to whom the duke had refused it after the death of its chaplain.
>
> He might have been saved, but a wish to die, and a melancholy disposition contributed to his end.
>
> His wife, (Lady Catherine Manners, daughter of the Earl of Rutland), whom he loved greatly, and who is very amiable and modest, is much to be pitied. The king has shown great displeasure at the deed, and for a whole day would see no one, nor eat till ten o'clock at night. He received the news at morning service, at which he remained, and on the Sunday, following was present at the sermon. He has sent word to the duchess that he will befriend her to the utmost. You may judge what a change all this will make at court. God grant that it may be to His glory, and for peace.

The subsidies voted by Parliament were however levied. Lady Strange writes to her mother:—

> The greatest people contribute to these subsidies, and each according to his possessions. My husband's great-grandfather was taxed at four thousand *francs*. He possesses, however, quite three times as much money as we have, and yet we gave as much. All this is greatly to the disadvantage of the wealthy; but the people are satisfied; and since the king has not power to raise these subsidies but when Parliament permits, it will not happen every year, but only on special occasions.

Lady Strange prefaces with these observations a new request for the payment of her marriage portion.

> If Château-Neuf has the honour of seeing you, he will be able to tell you *Madame*, how it injures my repute and that of my family that I have not yet had this sum of twenty thousand crowns. If my husband were not as good as he is, he would begin to grow suspicious, which, thank God, he does not. What most distresses me is that I find myself one of this household

only to increase its debts and expenses; and that also several of his friends from whom he borrowed money for his journey (to Holland, on the occasion of his marriage) were pressed to ask him to pay it back, and that he could not do so is a great trouble to him, as it is to me also; for there is nothing that he hates more than not keeping his word.

Chapter 5

A Chapter of Correspondence

About this time a fresh trouble arose for Lady Strange, and for her mother and sister-in-law, in the defection of the Duke de la Trémoille from Protestantism. He went to Rochelle; not, however, to take part in the defence of the Huguenots against Richelieu's attacks, but to join the besiegers. Being received into the Church of Rome by the Cardinal himself, he was at once nominated to the command of the light cavalry. Lady Strange writes to her mother:—

> I cannot get over my astonishment at my brother's change of religion. There has been a report of it for this long time past; and even the queen was told that it was quite certain; but she, finding that you *Madame*, were included in the defection, said she believed nothing at all about it. That led me also to doubt about my brother; but God has thought fit to send this affliction upon you *Madame*, and upon our house. It distresses me greatly, and even more than I could have believed. The letter from him which you have been pleased to send me shows his thoughts; but I cannot believe in what he says, that 'a worldly mind would have done differently.' The Catholics always talk so.

In writing to her sister-in-law, who had just given birth to a little girl, she adds:—

> I honour and love you with all my heart; and that makes me doubly disturbed at the change in your husband. It has marvellously astonished me; and I can hardly credit it, but I trust in the goodness of God to change his heart. Certainly, scarcely anyone will believe that it is out of anything but a mere human consideration: and truly, when one regards only that, it does lead one

> to lose no time in abandoning one's religious profession.
> I pity very much the pain you will suffer in not following his example; but nevertheless, dear heart, I doubt not that you will resist. God give you strength above your own, and we shall see you doubly serving the advancement of His glory, since you have now no help—I am told that if my brother could, he would have asked for my fortune: but that the law of the country did not permit it—I must confess to you *Madame*, that save from respect to you, I do not know what I should be driven to, by the contempt with which he treats us.

She concludes by imploring her mother's forgiveness of her second brother, the Count de Laval, who had taken refuge in Holland after some escapades in France.

During the sitting of Parliament, Lord and Lady Strange were in London, where she gave birth to a daughter, who died very soon after, suffocated in the nurse's bed. For a time, this accident greatly troubled her; the child, however, was a very young infant when it happened. The little boy was well and flourishing, and the mother appears to have found consolation before very long. Towards the close of the year 1629 she returned to Lathom, and no further correspondence is to be found of hers until October 1631. Then she writes in profound grief, for her mother had died, at Château Nonard, in the preceding August:—

> Dear Sister—It would have been a consolation in my extreme affliction to have been honoured by letters from you, and above all, to know that I continue to live in your friendship, which is one of the things I most desire in this world to be honoured by; and I am sure that you will always keep it for me—not that I deserve it, but for the sake of the love of her whom we mourn, since you did not doubt of the affection she bore for me; and as I have always loved you best after her, at this time, when God has taken her from us, I put you in her place, to give you all the respect, duty, and friendship which I entertained for her. God has taken her for our punishment, and to render her happy. I never liked this residence of *Château* Nonard, because it was so far from all her children; but Heaven decreed that should be so, in order to detach her from earthly things.
> As for me, I confess that I have no longer any pleasure in them. Touching what you bid me tell you of the feelings of my broth-

er de Laval, I did not see him until three days after the news arrived, and I saw him shed a few tears; but soon after, he was as merry as before. For me, I own that were I in his place, I should never have any happiness again; but I cannot say whether he conceals grief beneath. At all events, he shows no sorrow for the past. He only comes to see me now and again, and displays great impatience in my company, and a desire to be going again. He is so diversely spoken of, that I do not know what to believe of it all.

This letter is dated from Chelsea, where she had been staying for some time.

At this place she gave birth to a daughter, who was baptised Henrietta Maria, the queen probably being its godmother. About the same time, a second daughter was born to Madame de la Trémoille—Marie Charlotte.

In the month of March 1632, Lady Strange arrived in London, on her way to the Hague—probably with the object of settling the affairs of Charlotte of Nassau's inheritance. Differences were now beginning to arise between the Duke de la Trémoille and the Count de Laval, which gave their sister great concern. She writes:—

I hope that your husband will acquiesce in the last wish of her who brought us into the world. For you dear sister, I do not doubt that your goodness and generosity will override all other considerations.

The generosity and indulgence of the Duchess de la Trémoille was to be put more than once to the test by the Count de Laval.

A certain Englishwoman, Miss Orpe, with whom he had entangled himself, pretended that she was married to him, and took the name of Countess de Laval. Lady Strange was greatly disturbed at this; but her chief anxiety was always the money from France, which either did not come at all, or arrived much diminished in transit. The rents of Christmas were not paid by midsummer. She writes on the 2nd October 1638:—

I beg your forgiveness, dear sister, if I speak to you so freely, but I know you to be so reasonable and so just, that you cannot approve of what is not so. I have no doubt that your son has arrived safely in Holland. He will not have found it so prosperous there as usual. Pray God that he may have found the Prince of

Orange in good health.

Here the correspondence ceases for eight years—with the exception of one letter written in 1640, on the occasion of the death of Mademoiselle de la Trémoille. Letters in those troublous days frequently got lost upon the road, and those for a long time preserved in the family archives finally suffered many rude vicissitudes. These years were the most momentous ones in the life of Charlotte de la Trémoille. In those letters she made few allusions to the events which have rendered her name illustrious. She saw nothing extraordinary in what she did; simply doing the duty which came next. The duty accomplished; all her thoughts reverted to the past.

Fortunately, this grand life of a modest, noble-minded woman here takes its place in history; and the documents of the time enable us to supplement the silence of Lady Strange, now very soon to be Countess of Derby.

Chapter 6

Cavaliers and Roundheads

A few years before his death, the Earl of Derby retired to a country house which he had bought, on the banks of the Dee, near Chester. Weary of the cares of life, and of the ordering of his large estate, he made all his possessions over to his son, Lord Strange, reserving to himself a thousand pounds a year for his own maintenance. In 1640 Lord Strange was appointed to share with his father in the office of Lord Chamberlain of Chester. Two years later the old earl died; and his son succeeding him, "Madame Strange," as her French and Dutch relatives called her, became Countess of Derby.

In the course of time, since the murder of the Duke of Buckingham, the affairs of the country had gone from bad to worse, and year by year the breach between Royalists and Parliamentarians widened. Outwardly the kingdom not only seemed to prosper, but was in a manner flourishing. Her possessions abroad were increased by new colonies, and her harbours were filled with merchant ships sailing from all parts of the world. Art and learning prospered exceedingly. In the midst of the turmoil of ribaldry and fanaticism of the extreme parties, and the smoke and luridness of battlefields, learning and civilisation were steadily advancing.

Like Archimedes, men of science, painters and scholars, worked on, some of them amid the din of battle; and, with a happier fate than his, lived on, for the most part into calmer days. Others, sheltered in the retirement of country homes, and recking little of papist or puritan shibboleths, wrote and thought, and to this day their work remembers them. Trade flourished, and diversions and junketings were in nowise neglected. Amid all the royal troubles, courtly state was not only well, but splendidly maintained.

A refinement and dignity prevailed in Charles's Court which fascinated his loyal subjects; and the beauty of the queen, and the gracious if always melancholy aspect of the king, won hearts, and intellects to boot, which had originally inclined to the side of his disaffected subjects. The French nature of Henrietta Maria delighted in masques and gaieties and music; and though etiquette and sobriety ruled the king's household, dullness found no part there. Often the people had the chance of looking on their sovereigns as their gilded barge rowed down the river from London to Hampton Court, to the music of lutes and viols, and sweet choiring voices mingling with the song of the birds, not yet driven hence by the smoke and screech of an overcrowded city.

From Westminster Stairs on one side, and Lambeth Palace on the other, the banks were still open, clothed with grass and foliage, and dotted here and there with gabled and timbered dwellings, whose gardens glowed with fragrant flowers and ripening fruit. Tothill Fields were rookeries then, as now; but the birds were of another feather. Battersea Fields on the south side still grew simples and herbs for the medicaments of London apothecaries—the "Physic Garden" of Sir Hans Sloane opposite being but a concentrated, double-distilled essence of these older sources.

Beyond and behind lay the Five Fields, soon to become notorious for infesting footpads and highwaymen; for the numbers of the gentlemen of the road increased with alarming speed, as the means of travelling improved and increasing opportunities made more and more thieves.

Leaving the immediate environing of London, the village of Chelsea reflected its stately mansions and terraces in the clear Thames reaches. And so, onward by the winding stream, till under the shadows of fair Richmond woods the royal beeches and elms of Hampton Court bent their boughs in the summer breeze to their majesties and the courtly train in greeting and in welcome to the palace associated with memories and traditions, not all of them too fair and consolatory, of "my good Lord Cardinal" and his tyrannical lord.

In reasonable pastime and amusements, the average subject of King Charles's day followed the suit of the court. A sour forbiddance and abhorrence of amusements had not yet come to be the order of the day.

If fasts were duly kept, festivals were in nowise forgotten. The "all work and no play making Jack a dull boy" observance was not yet rendered paramount by the prick-eared, aggressive spirit of Puritanism; for the master enjoyed a sober junketing and relaxation every whit as much as the 'prentice loved his turn at the quintain, or a merry round with the maid of his choice, or a stage play in an inn yard. As to the shameful "sport" of bear-baiting, to give the Puritan his due, he did excellent work indeed when he succeeded in stamping it out; though his consideration for the bear appears to have been somewhat circumscribed, if, as more than one account tells, generally the first proceeding was to kill the bear.

Anything less than sweeping reform and a *tabula rasa* savoured ill to Puritan nostrils; and while Praise-God-Barebones took away the bears, he forgot the abhorrence of nature—human nature notably—for a vacuum, and that in a few years the lack of all rational diversions, the pulling down of maypoles, the silencing of all music but psalm-singing, would drive man and woman to try and drown care in the pottle-pot. It was small wonder that the English people so soon came to regard the Commonwealth as a not utterly unmitigated blessing. The promised millennium grew to be unsatisfactory to all but the very elect; and outside that pale, the desire for the king to have his own again was to spread fast and wide.

The intrinsic worth of that king they were less concerned about; and if, after a few years' experience of the merry monarch's rule, they found it full of flaws, they endured as they might: not perhaps altogether forgetful that if the young prince had not been hounded from his country to herd with all sorts and conditions of swashbucklers and adventurers, finding no rest for the sole of his foot, no true and sober counsel in the very years that temptations are strongest upon all men—especially men of his temperament—their restored king's virtues might have outshone his shortcomings.

To the moderate-minded the typical Royalist and Puritanic extremes of the civil war days could only have been vexatious to a degree. It is curious to observe how many scholars and writers of the middle of the seventeenth century make no allusion to what was passing around them. Take only the one instance of Isaac Walton, who at least lived in the very thick of the fray, in that pargeted and latticed-casemented old house of his at the corner of Chancery Lane. Truly, in his lives of the worthies and divines of the time, he alludes frequently to the religious and political divisions of the country, as indeed his themes entailed; but in his immortal volume, whose secondary title is the significant one of "The Contemplative Man's Recreation," scarce a shadow of the gloom of the times darkens its equable, sunshiny humour.

Soberly, but with intense enjoyment, Master Isaac Walton takes his way from Fleet Street, and, stretching his legs over Tottenham Hill—no short stretch neither—he falls in with his hunter and falconer, gossips along the road to Ware, whither he is bound that "fine, fresh May morning"; and so the three trudge on together in genial discourse to the text that "good company makes the way to seem shorter." How thoroughly the wayfarers enjoy the freshness of the country and the green beauty of the "new livery'd year"! How they delight in the milkmaid's song, and luxuriate in the "honest alehouse with its cleanly room, lavender in the windows, and twenty ballads stuck about the wall"!

Last, not least, in the general intellectual and mental life of England in Charles's reign, comes the band of poets, a goodly train, Cavalier or Puritan, or not greatly concerned for either, but writing in

numbers,
Since the numbers came.

Milton, Cowley, Herrick, Lovelace, Herbert, Wither, Dekker, Webster, and many more, breathing forth sweet words and quaint aphorisms which mingle in our everyday talk, and are too familiar for us to pause to think whence or how they rise to the lips. Those dead poets of Charles's reign resting beneath the hoary old stones of Westminster, or the sod of peaceful village graveyards, or whose dust the venom of bigots and fanatics has scattered, left their country a heritage which cannot perish while the English tongue endures.

Only a comparison between the closing years of James I.'s reign, and the opening ones of Charles II., a period of thirty-five years at the utmost, can afford a true estimate of the improvements in the public and social conditions of the country. Among these was the establishment of regular inland postal communication in 1635. The proclamation "for settling of the letter-office of England and Scotland" sets forth that "there hath been no certain or constant intercourse between the kingdoms of England and Scotland," and commands:—

> Thomas Witherings, Esq., His Majesty's postmaster of England for foreign parts, to settle a running-post or two to run night and day between England and Scotland and the city of London, to go thither and come back in six days.

Ireland was included in these arrangements. The horses for conveyance of the letters were furnished by the postmasters at the rate of twopence-halfpenny a mile. In 1649 letters were forwarded once a week to all parts of the kingdom.

Another public benefit was the setting-up of hackney coaches. These predecessors of our four wheelers and hansoms were first started from Hackney—then a fair-sized village—to London, for those who had business or pleasure in the metropolis. Very soon the coaches began to ply in London streets, making their stands at the inns. There were twenty of them in 1625 under the superintendence of one Captain Bailey, an old sea-officer.

For its linen industries Ireland owes a deep debt of gratitude to the memory of the Earl of Strafford. While Governor of Ireland, he observed that the soil of the Green Isle was suited to the production of flax. He sent to Holland for the seed, and to France and the Netherlands for skilful workmen. To promote still further the undertaking, he advanced a considerable sum from his own private fortune, thus establishing Ireland's most important manufacture.

England was later in the field: for linen was not produced in this country to any degree of perfection until twoscore years later, when the French Protestant refugees sought shelter here at the revocation of the Edict of Nantes. Under their skilful instructions, the English manufacturers wrought immense improvement in the material. It is small wonder that housewives and betrothed maidens of the olden days set such store by the contents of their linen-presses and dowry-chests. The Queen of Henry VI. could boast only two linen shifts. The scarcity of this commodity when Lady Strange first arrived in England, doubtless accounts for her writing for so many articles of clothing for her young family to be sent from France.

From such a quickening of industrial activity through the length and breadth of the nation, quite independently of the improvements in printing, or rather of the dissemination of books, in engraving and in etching, it is obvious that time no longer necessarily hung heavy on the hands of country gentlemen. The wits of the domestic "ffoole" were no longer so indispensable now that the lord of the manor had material upon which to exercise his own. If, *faute de mieux*, he had hitherto bestowed all his time on his hawk and his hound, the pleasures of the table, and a vast amount of sleep, he was no longer forced to confine himself to these pastimes. Worthy Master Fuller says:—

> To divert at any time a troublesome fancy, run to thy books. They presently fix thee to them, and drive the other out of thy thoughts. They always receive thee with the same kindness.

With many other noblemen and gentlemen of that time, the Earl of Derby fell in with this sound advice. Walpole, (*Noble Authors*), says:—

> His life was one of virtue, accomplishments, and humanity.

Neither firebrand, busybody, nor time-server—too high of rank to desire to be higher—James, seventh Earl of Derby, nearing on to middle life at the time of his father's death, lived chiefly on his own estates, and these preferably at Lathom House. He appeared rarely at court, finding full occupation in the affairs of his own estate, of which the kingdom of Man formed an important and seemingly difficult part to manage. One of his biographers says:—

> But peaceful years and charitable acts fill few pages in history; and Lord Derby owes his place there, not to virtues arising from his own choice and goodwill, but to those which were struck from him by the blows of fortune, as fire is struck from flint stones.

Chapter 7

Breast Laws and Deemsters

Of the Isle of Man, one chronicler tells us that its early history is "more than ordinarily obscured in the mists of the past;" another, that "the Isle of Man is almost the only place where there is any chance of seeing a fairy;" a third, that "nowhere in the same area are there so many relics of an unknown past."

The fact that the island owns no ancient literature, its laws being unwritten, and that it maintained scarcely any intercourse with other nations, renders it impossible to disentangle from myth and tradition any authentic chronicle of the little dominion which at a later period was to come under the rule of the Stanleys.

To "begin at the beginning" of Manx history, the precise date of the reign of Mannanen Beg Mac-y-Leir—which, being interpreted, is Little Mannanen, the son of Leir, and who is the mythic hero of Man—is somewhat difficult to determine, seeing that he is said to have reigned any time between thirteen centuries before Christ and four centuries after. As another name for him was Angus Oge, "The Immortal," this Mannanen may have lived to a good old age; but seventeen centuries is a far cry.

His parentage is further variously attributed to Scottish and to Irish kings; and he was the first law-maker of the island. Also, besides being a warrior, navigator, and trader, he was a skilful forger of weapons, and a mighty necromancer and magician, having the power to hide his dominions in mist at the approach of the enemy.

If Mannanen was killed by St Patrick, and his subjects were driven by that apostle to the alternative of becoming Christians or of being exterminated—for, saith the chronicler, "of the seed of the conjurer, there were none but what the saint destroyed" the founder of Man necessarily is a comparatively modern personage of sixth-century days. Something like an air of reality is spread over this tradition of Mannanen and St Patrick by the traditions of St Maughold, whose name appears in the English, Scotch, and Irish calendars, and who gives his name to the headland near Ramsey.

This Maughold or Macguil appears to have been a wild Irish chieftain who designed to murder St Patrick. The saint however filled Maughold with awe by exercising a miracle, and restoring to life one of his band of ruffian followers. This deed, more marvellous than useful, converted Maughold on the spot to the Christian faith, and he offered to do any penance St Patrick thought fit to impose.

The saint having considered awhile, bade the penitent to repair to the seashore, and there, entering a little coracle, have his hands and feet bound, and then let himself drift over the trackless waters till they should bring him to land once more; and so he was brought to the foot of the rocks eastward of the Isle of Man. Here he was welcomed by the Christian missionaries whom St Patrick had left in charge of the island; and after a long life spent in pious prayers and deeds and many austerities, and, in his turn, miracles, he died, and was buried in the church which afterwards bore his canonised name and stood in the midst of the city which he had founded on that rock.

After all this, it is cruel to find that the most laborious and learned seekers into the lives of the saints and early apostles of Christianity can discover not the slightest evidence of this visit of St Patrick to the Isle of Man, nor of any episcopate left there by him. The monkish compilers of the *Chronicles of Man* give their summing-up of this tradition to the same effect, in the fourteenth century:—

> Suffice it to say we are entirely ignorant who or what bishops existed before the time of Goddard Crovan, Captain of William I., because we have not found it written, nor have we learned it by certain report of the elders.

King Arthur is said to have conquered Man, and then, restoring it to its vanquished possessor, enrolled him among the knights of his Round Table. From its situation, the island was little likely to be left long in the undisputed possession of the latest warrior who might have conceived a desire of annexing it; and it undoubtedly changed hands many times between the Irish and Scots, not to speak of the Welsh and English. Finally, in the ninth century, the Scandinavians, who had made their power felt all over Europe, gained the upper hand in the island, and made it one of their central strongholds.

To balance the discredit thrown on the early Christian traditions of Man, stands the fact that monumental vestiges of each race recorded to have inhabited it have been found in it. Prehistoric remains, *kist-vaens*, burial-places, earthenware urns, flint arrow-heads, not unfrequently are dug up; also, circular huts of unhewn stone of the locality. A few Roman relics have been found at Castletown. Mediaeval remains are at Peel, Castletown, and Kirk Maughold, and many Runic and Scandinavian monuments in various parts. Querns, the ancient handmills for grinding grain, are found now and again. Such relics of early times all prove that if originally a desert, the Isle of Man was peopled at a comparatively early period in the world's history.

In the sixteenth century came the renowned Manx hero, Orry, from his Icelandic home. The story tells that he landed on a starlight night, and when the Manx men asked him whence he came, he pointed to the Milky Way: and so it is that the people of Man to this day, (1905), call the Milky Way *Road Moar Ree Orree*—King Orry's highroad. To Orry is ascribed the establishment of a civil government, and its powers and privileges as a separate though feudatory kingdom. It was long designated "The Kingdom of Man and the Isles." Its representative assembly is the oldest in Europe, coeval with the English Parliament, and is styled the House of Keys. Its Tynwald Court is held on the 5th of July on the Tynwald Hill, and is a signing and proclamation of the Acts passed by the Imperial Government during the preceding year, being proclaimed in English and in Manx.

In former times this assembling of the legislators was attended by great pomp and ceremony. The second Earl of Derby relinquished the title of King of Man, being content with the appellative of Lord of the island; but Sir John Stanley was bidden as king to meet his officers of state, deemsters, and barons in his "royal array, as a king ought to do—and upon the Hill of Tynwald sitt in a chaire covered with a royall cloath and cushions and his visage unto the east"; and many more injunctions to the king, and rules for the conduct of the great annual ceremonial, follow.

Since 1765, the Duke of Athoel, the last lord of the island, transferred his right to the English Crown—notwithstanding, the laws of Imperial Parliament are not valid in Man unless they are in accordance with its ancient laws and liberties, and have been duly confirmed by the Tynwald Court and proclaimed on the Tynwald Hill.

One or two of these laws still differ in detail from those of England. A debtor for example, if suspected of designing to abscond in order to defraud his creditors, is open to arrest. Public penance was performed in Man long after that observance became obsolete in England. This fortunate isle is not burdened with income-tax, poor-laws, or turn pikes; neither are stamps required for receipts of property transfers. A man, for a nominal compensation, may enter on his neighbour's lands and take thence limestone or building stone for his own needs.

The "Breast Laws" are ascribed to King Orry, and were the laws of the island, unwritten and delivered orally by the leaders of one generation to the next. Sir John Stanley, in the reign of Henry IV., caused these to be written. The government of the Tynwald consists, like the English legislature, of three estates—the Governor (Lord or "King"), Council, and the House of Commons (House of Keys). In the Council, the two deemsters occupy an important position. They are the supreme judges, both for life and property.

The staple food of all ranks in the island was for many centuries its herrings. The deemster's oath, on his appointment to office, contains this clause:—

> I will execute the laws of this isle justly betwixt our Sovereign Lord the King, and his subjects within this isle—as indifferently as the herring backbone doth lie in the midst of the fish.

Godred, the son of Orry, founded Castle Rushen, around which so many traditional and historical associations cling.

Fairies are by no means the only mysterious sort of creatures one may see in Man; if in the classification the light-toed, little court of Oberon and Titania alone be included, the very air must be full of spirits yet, if the mists which so often envelop the island were indeed and originally the work of Angus Oge, the Immortal. As Manx grandsires and grandams still tell, those sea-mists rose at his bidding to shroud his dominions from his enemies when they were seen approaching. Hence the hero was venerated as demi-god, the Irish Neptune. Under the ground, tongue of mortal should be guarded when it speaks of the giants and terrible beings who dwell there.

The main road to their abodes lies through the sealed and gloomy chambers and dungeons of Castle Rushen; but the boldest spirit must quail at the bare thought of penetrating those pitch-dark subterranean passages. Often the experience of the one man who made the attempt is related; and though he did live to tell the tale, it was only by the skin of his teeth that he escaped, and the merest intervention of Providence which prompted him "to open one door instead of another at which had he sought admission, where he would have seen company enough, but could never have returned."

Not only about haunted Castle Rushen, with its wishing-stone in the chapel, but all over the island, traditions abound, and strange beings wander at will. At Peel Castle, until recently, as soon as candles were lighted came that gruesome dog, the "*Mauthe Dhoo*," as he is called—dog or devil as he may be; and by way of agreeable contrast, the "harmless necessary" and exceedingly tangible cat is to be seen by the most incredulous and unimpressionable of mortals. The creature's deficiencies in the matter of tail only bear out the distinctive character marking all things Manx.

Whether in prehistoric times the Mauth Dog in a fit of canine prejudice, bit it off, or why otherwise the Manx cat boasts nothing of a tail worth mentioning, does not seem to have been ever satisfactorily explained. Only the fact the stump of a tail remains. In all other respects the Isle of Man cat can hold its own with other Grimalkins of the domestic feline tribe, and indeed its fur is somewhat exceptionally fine and thick.

The old heraldic Arms of Man were a "ship in her ruff"—a ship with furled sails—and were adopted by Hacon, King of Man, in the tenth century. With Goddard Crovan, son of the Icelandic Harold the Black, a new dynasty began. He slew Fingal, and allied himself with William the Conqueror. From this time the Irish, Manx and English royal families intermarried. The King of Man, in the reign of King John, paid the Pope of Rome homage for his crown. Soon after, Man fell into possession of the Kings of Scotland, but their oppressive rule drove the Manxmen to seek the protection of Edward I., who granted the little kingdom to Walter de Huntercomb. This knight presented it once again to John Baliol, King of Scotland and Edward's vassal.

The strange device of the "Three Legs" was then substituted for the old ship in her ruff as the armorial bearings of the kingdom. The most probable explanation of the device seems to be that the Three Legs represent the three kingdoms of England, Ireland, and Scotland, to which countries severally the island has in times past belonged, as now collectively it still appertains.

Piers Gaveston, the minion favourite of Edward II., was King of Man in his flourishing days. Later, for about fifty years, the Montacutes, Earls of Salisbury, ruled it.

In 1393, Sir William Scroop, who was afterwards beheaded, bought it of the Earl of Salisbury. Henry IV. gave it to Percy, Earl of Northumberland. On his forfeiture of it in 1405, it was given to Sir John Stanley, treasurer of the household of Henry IV.; and for three centuries the Isle of Man has remained under the Stanleys' rule. The feudal service required of them for its tenure was the presentation of two falcons at the king's coronation. Sir John Stanley transferred a great deal of ecclesiastical power into the hands of the deemsters, and established other wise regulations.

Thus, the Isle of Man became the brightest jewel in the possessions of the Earls of Derby; and now, in the opening year of the English Revolution, James, the seventh Earl, became Lord of Man. Of all that befell there under his not altogether wise, if always well intentioned and beneficent rule, will be seen later.

CHAPTER 8

No More Peaceful Days at Lathom

Charles was invariably unfortunate in his selection of advisers. When he lost Buckingham, he took into his place Sir Thomas Wentworth. This choice, on the face of it, would have appeared eminently wise, since at the beginning of his public career Wentworth was a favourite with the people and the Commons, chiefly on account of the Petition of Rights being practically his work. His temperament however, was not made for liberal partisanship. He was scholarly by rearing, proud, energetic, full of ambition, and, once on the side of the Crown, he made his power felt. In general demeanour he was a striking contrast to the amiable, courtly Buckingham, doing his work skilfully, with a grave ceremony.

Unlike Buckingham too, who was before all things a royal favourite, Wentworth was first a statesman; and while standing high indeed in the king's esteem, his usefulness was the quality which Charles more appreciated. Desirous of employing his powerful abilities to the greatest advantage, Charles rapidly advanced him in titles and dignities, until in 1631 Thomas, now Viscount Wentworth, was appointed Lord-Deputy of Ireland.

The deep-rooted attachment of Charles for the Anglican Church drew him into bonds of close sympathy with Wentworth's friend, Laud, who about the same time, was raised to the Archbishopric of Canterbury. Laud was a man honest of conviction, pure in intention, but unconciliatory of speech, and narrow in his theological views. His intolerance of dissent from the Church of England was rigid, whether in the direction of Puritanism or of Romanism. This fixity of purpose was little understood in his own day, either by Papist or by Puritan, and perhaps not even by his greatest admirers; so little comprehended by the Romanists, that the Pope was deluded into offering him a cardinal's hat.

Laud established his theory of canonical guidance and of church rule solely upon the Prayer Book, carrying out its directions in the spirit and the rubric, and finding in these neither ambiguity nor elasticity; and he imposed upon all his clergy a rigorous adherence to the ritual and ceremonial of the Anglican Church, as he understood it. Many refused this, and were punished as contumacious, being deprived of their cures; and when the people crowded to hear the preaching of these "confessors"—for as such they were regarded—to Gospel truth in its purity, all expounding or preaching was forbidden them. While Laud denounced the excess, as he regarded it, of ecclesiastical ceremony conducted in the private chapel of the queen, he offended the greater part of his own flock, clergy and lay alike, by the pomp and ceremonial which he introduced into the public services of the Church of England.

Possibly no servant of the Anglican Church ever grasped more entirely than Laud the real spirit and tendency of Anglican doctrine; and, had he lived in a later time, his sphere and mission would have been widely acknowledged. As it was, though the few regarded his death as a martyrdom, the multitude rejoiced at the removal of such a stumbling-block in the path of the true spiritual seeker. Music and vesture and change of posture in the Lord's house were choking husks, to be cast into the fire, and the advocates of these "mummeries" to be as summarily disposed of as might be.

The mistake of Laud was in imposing outward observations of religion upon persons who had long discarded the keif-denials and practices of the early Christians. Laud might and did closely abide by such rules himself, but they were less easily accepted by the general herd of professing churchmen, who had no mind for too much self-discipline: and hence the charge of pharisaism and needless austerities against the ritualist Laud and his disciples. The accusation of his papistical leanings holds good no further than that Laud, in common with many upright and charitably thinking Christians of all sects and nations, regretted the divisions among the followers of Christ, and strove to mould his teaching by a spirit which might one day develop a stronger desire for the unity of Christendom.

Laud's nature had in it, however, no temporising spark; and, though taxed with Jesuitry, he, at all events, did not understand that primary motive power of the Jesuits—of being all things to all men, or of gradual achievement. Charles, profoundly influenced by Laud, acted upon his counsel, and turned a cold eye upon the Protestants of the Continent, going the length of forbidding his ambassador in Paris to attend divine service in the Protestant chapel there; and, truly, the religious reform of France and Geneva wore a widely different aspect from that of England. No *via media* was offered by Huguenot and Calvinist. All was rigidly simple and austere in their public worship.

The Psalms, sermons, and long prayers composing it were read, or, at the best, given forth in nasal sing-song, which allowed no exercise to the senses or to the intellect of the congregation. All was, or was intended to be, exclusively spiritual. And to men and women of education and of intellect such limitations were irksome and unedifying. Hence, when the Reformed members of the upper classes came to pitch their tents in England, many of them quickly conceived a liking for the Church of England, and, as in the case of the Huguenot Charlotte de la Trémoille, fell naturally in with its teaching and ritual, and so, as by second nature, mostly became ardent Royalists.

In order to retain foreign sympathy and support, Charles was often prodigal in his gifts to and recognitions of his Continental friends. This, considering the poverty of his exchequer and the needs of the country, was reprehensible to a degree. Abuses increased. Taxation became unendurable, and the people resisted, their remonstrances often being couched in terms of respect and of loyal feeling which are singularly pathetic. Every day the agitation and discontent increased; until at last, the king, fearful of the spread of its contagion in the country, issued commands that all country gentlemen should remain upon their own estates.

Force had now to be employed to repress the popular discontent. Four of the champions of the people were whipped, mutilated, and put in the pillory; but instead of the portion of stones, filth, and rotten eggs, ordinarily allotted to the occupiers of that unenviable eminence, they received an ovation of sympathy and applause for their endurance and patriotic courage.

The time had now arrived however, when the popular cause was to be taken up by the wealthy and powerful. John Hampden, a Buckinghamshire gentleman, refused to pay the tax of ship-money. He was not the first by many who had murmured against its levying, as an illegal act, because unsanctioned by Parliament; but he was the first to contest the question in open court.

The Crown lawyers, on the other side, proved that the impost was of ancient origin, reaching as far back as the days when the Danes ravaged the English coasts in their dragon-prowed warships, and the people had contributed to the fitting-up and manning of vessels to keep them at bay. From time to time, as occasion had demanded in the interval of centuries, the tax had been revived, and dropped again when the requirement no longer existed. That this did now actively exist, the king's party maintained; since the navy in James's time had been criminally neglected, and the protection against foreign invasion was inadequate. The victory was to the king. Hampden was condemned, and suffered.

But the victory was a losing one. Hampden was hailed as the champion of the people, and the greatest patriot of the time. Henceforth all was contention between the royal party and the popular party. No action on the part of Charles and his advisers went uncanvassed and uncontested. The spirit of religious and political freedom waxed fierce; Laud's high churchmanship in England, Strafford's high-handed government in Ireland, the king's endeavour to propagate Protestantism in Ireland, and his attempt to force Episcopacy on Scotland, heaped fuel on fuel.

The king's accusation of high treason against the five members, with his command for their arrest, kindled the blaze of war. Mutual open defiance between the king and his subjects first reared its ugly head at Nottingham. Royalist and Roundhead fought a drawn battle at Edgehill, and henceforth bloodshed and strife ruled the country. Many moderate-minded men, before events reached this point, had withdrawn from the Parliamentary party. They foresaw with apprehension the lengths to which the "Reformers" were rushing; and, as it were, pausing to consider, remained to rally round the king, his truest, ablest advisers.

Among these were Hyde, Lord Clarendon, who became Chancellor of the Exchequer; and Lucius Cary, Lord Falkland, the hero, as he has been called, of the great chancellor's epic. (Walpole). And it is at this crisis that Lord Strange, not as yet Earl of Derby, first steps into prominence in the tragic scenes enacting in the drama, which only finds its parallel in the chronicles of modern times, in France, nearly a century and a half later.

Hitherto, since his marriage, Lord Strange had spent his time almost entirely upon his estates, devoting himself to the welfare of his own people and tenantry, and enjoying the pleasures of a country life and the interchange of stately though simple hospitalities. Of Lady Strange, little is recorded during these years. The old axiom says:—

Happy are the people who have no history.

The daily events in the life of this great lady, in whom discreetness and simplicity are such leading characteristics, were as the ripples upon a calm ocean, upon whose horizon for a long time little clouds scarce bigger than a man's hand threatened. Suddenly, after fifteen years of this comparative peace and tranquillity, the clouds gathered thick, lowering till the storm broke upon the Buckinghamshire plains.

The Parliamentarians were commanded by Lord Essex. Southwards lay the vale of the Red Horse, the famous charger cut into the red rock in memory of that ancestral kinsman of Lord Strange, who killed his horse, vowing to share the perils of the meanest of his soldiers. The Puritans called this figure "the Red Horse of the Lord, which He caused to ride about furiously to the ruin of the enemy."

Above the village of Radway, the king's tent was pitched in the midst of his redcoats. The royal standard, borne by Sir Edmund Verney, floated in the morning breeze. The position of the Royal Army was very strong, and, had it remained to await the attack of the enemy, complete victory for the king could hardly have been doubtful; but in spite of brave old Lord Lindsay's counsel, the king consented to the pushing forward of his impatient soldiers, and met the attack half way.

The king rode along in front of his troops, clad as Vandyck has presented him, a stately figure in full armour, with the ribbon of the Garter across his breastplate, and its star on his mantle of black velvet. In his tent he addressed his principal officers:—

> If this day shine prosperous for us, we shall all be happy in a glorious victory. Your king is both your cause, your quarrel, and your captain. The foe is in sight. The best encouragement I can give you is this: that come life or death, your king will bear you company, and ever keep this field, this place, and this day's service in his grateful remembrance.

Major-General Sir Jacob Astley's prayer is as memorable:—

> O Lord, Thou knowest how busy I must be this day. If I forget Thee, do not Thou forget me march on, boys.

That some spirits no stress of circumstances can attune to war, the case of William Harvey, the discoverer of the circulation of the blood, will attest. Sir Edward Hyde and Harvey had charge of the two young princes, Charles and James, during the battle. In the heat of the thunder of cannon, and the rain of shot, Harvey was found seated comfortably under a hedge, reading Virgil; though he consented, when urged, to retire into a place of greater safety. The result of that day is well known. Both sides claimed the victory; but the advantage, in absolute fact, was to the Royalists.

The ghosts of the slain in that day's fight are still said to haunt the old scene of battle; and some three months after the event, "apparitions and sundry noyses of war and battels" are recorded to have been seen and heard on Edgehill. The faces of Sir Edmund Verney, the king's standard-bearer, and of many of the other "incorporeal substances," destroyed in the flesh, were recognised.

CHAPTER 9

More Ardour Than Discretion

Charles, from the first day of his reign, had never known real peace of mind or enjoyed a sense of security. The words put into the mouth of his predecessor by Shakespeare,

Uneasy lies the head that wears a crown,"

—were ever, from first to last, realised by him to the full. Till that head lay severed from his body in its coffin at Whitehall, it found no rest. One by one he lost, by circumstances—generally the circumstance of violent death—the friendship and counsel of those dearest to him. Strafford and Laud had perished on the scaffold, and now he was called upon to part with the queen. In 1642, on the 10th of January, he left his palace of Whitehall, whose doors he never again entered but to step upon the scaffold. A little later he was at Windsor, and from thence it was arranged Her Majesty should repair to Holland, ostensibly for the purpose of taking over her daughter, Henrietta Maria—still but a child—to the Prince of Orange, who had married her six months previously.

The real object of the journey was however, to purchase arms and ammunition, and to seek the aid and support of the Continental Powers. The queen took with her the crown jewels to pawn or to sell, in order to raise money for the purchase of war supplies. After accompanying her to Dover, where she embarked for the Continent, Charles had gone northwards, and established himself at York, there to wait the issue of negotiations. That the issue of these could be doubtful, the most earnest desirers of peace could hardly hope. The breach, daily widening for so long, left no choice but to declare civil war; but both parties shrank from the blame of throwing down the gauntlet.

Finally, it was done by the Parliamentarians, in the person of Sir

John Hotham, who refused, as "governor to the Parliament," to open the gates of Hull. It is at this juncture that the Earl of Derby, in absolute fact still only Lord Strange, first came forth from his retirement to bear his loyal, unswerving part on the king's side of the contention. He was one of the first to present himself at the court at York, prepared in deed as by word to give his life's blood and the last penny in his purse for his royal master and the legitimate cause.

It was now proposed to form a royal guard at York from among the nobility of the neighbourhood. Fifty gentlemen refused to join his company, and at their head was Sir Thomas Fairfax, who further contrived, at great risk of being crushed by the feet of the king's horse, to fasten upon the pommel of Charles' saddle a widely-signed petition against war, and an entreaty that His Majesty would live in peace with his Parliament. On the 1st June the propositions for accommodation arrived at York from Westminster. They embodied demands for the complete abolition of royal prerogative, and exercise of supreme power for the Parliament. The king, in a burst of indignation, cried:—

> If I granted your demands, I should be nothing but an image the vain shadow of a king.

And he refused to listen further. The very terms rendered it obvious that the Parliamentarians expected no other response, any more than they desired it. Forty members only of the Lower House voted against war, and one member, the Earl of Portland, in the Lords. An army of the Parliamentarian party was at once organised, over which Lord Essex was nominated commander-in-chief.

On the king's side, his faithful subjects rallied quickly round him; and Lord Strange appears in their foremost ranks with a contingent of three thousand well-accoutred and well-provisioned men, raised from among his own people. On finding however, that the king, isolated as it were at York, was destitute of all assistance, and knew not where to obtain weapons, Lord Strange placed at his disposal everything the arsenals of his mansions contained.

Such generosity and self-devotion on the part of so powerful a nobleman was hardly likely to go uncontested by the sycophants and timeservers who swarm in royal courts. The earl himself speaks of "the envy and malice against which he had to defend his honour." This jealousy found its opportunity when, the hasty preparations made, the question became in what county of the north the royal standard should be raised. His biographer relates:—

After listening with a grave and serene dignity, to the several suggestions and reasons for the uplifting of the standard in five or six of the more northern counties, Lord Strange begged the king to turn his considerations upon Lancashire. Its neighbouring counties were equally favourably disposed towards the royal cause. The people were robust, and well fitted for good soldiers.

For himself, Lord Strange added, he was but an unworthy lieutenant of His Majesty; but he would undertake to find, at his own expense, three thousand foot soldiers and five hundred horse. Further, he would use his best endeavour to enlist and enrol seven thousand men of the county, thus furnishing His Majesty out of Lancashire alone a force of ten thousand men. From thence, access was easy to the neighbouring counties. His Majesty would find himself at the head of a powerful army, and be able to march upon London before the rebels had had time for raising troops to resist."

The king determined to abide by this counsel. The standard was to be unfurled at Warrington in Lancashire; and Lord Strange was commissioned to levy forces and supplies, and to stir the population to the contest. He rallied the Royalists at three points at Preston, Ormskirk, and Bury. That done, he prepared to go southward with the same object, first to Cheshire, and then into North Wales, of which he was lieutenant. At this point, the malignant spirit of the so-called court party interfered; in every probability to their own downfall, as to the ruin of the royal cause.

Had the vacillating king remained true to himself and to this powerful supporter at the difficult crisis, the whole tide of affairs might have turned in the royal favour. Time, at least, would have been obtained, and the disaffected party would have been forced to reconsider its demands; but this was not to be. Hardly was Lord Strange gone on his arduous mission than the slanderers set to work to prejudice Charles against him. The old earl, said they, was dying; Lord Strange was ambitious, little favourable to the court or conforming to its views. What if all this levying of troops should be a cover for mischievous designs? Was not Lord Strange allied to the blood-royal?

The Stanleys had not been always faithful to the party they seemed to favour—to wit, that Stanley, his ancestor, who marched at Richard's side to Bosworth field, and remained to crown Henry of Richmond, his stepson, king. Had not Earl Ferdinand, this Lord Strange's uncle, openly declared his claims upon the throne? This man—this James

Stanley—had married a Frenchwoman, a Huguenot, reared in the pernicious doctrines of the Low Countries, one of the house of Nassau, which had stirred the United Provinces to revolt. In such hands His Majesty could not be safe.

These arguments touched the characteristic weakness of Charles's nature. Prone to look upon the less hopeful and more shadowy side of a question, he lent an ear to these representations of a jealous faction, and gave orders for the raising of the standard at Nottingham. Lord Strange was suddenly and unceremoniously deprived of his lieutenancy of Cheshire and of Wales.

When he heard of these decisions of the king, he was greatly disturbed for the moment. Then, "recovering himself with that greatness of soul which belonged to his fine character," he replied to the messenger of the news:—

> May my master prosper—my poor self is of no consequence. If this counsel be good for him, I shall not trouble myself more for what happens to me. My wife, my children, and my country are very dear to me; but if my prince and my religion are safe, I shall bless the enemies who work their good, though it be at the price of my ruin.

By the advice of the friends whom he was accustomed to consult in cases of perplexity, he despatched a messenger to the king with assurances of his fidelity, declaring that it was in vain that his enemies strove to hinder him in serving him to the best of his power; that he would never draw the sword against him; that he placed his lieutenancies of Cheshire and of Wales at His Majesty's disposal; and that he begged him also to take back that of the county of Lancashire, so that no one could accuse him more of pretentions against the king.

These frank assurances exercised their due effect upon Charles, who now recognised the true value of so loyal and powerful a servant; but the doubts thus cast upon Lord Strange had given great offence to his friends and adherents, and materially injured the royal cause in Cheshire and Lancashire. Many of the country gentlemen, who had been ready to risk life and money for their king, retired to their estates once more; others went over in large numbers to the Parliamentarian side.

This exodus was such a large and important one, that its leaders offered Lord Strange the command of their forces, or whatever other position he might prefer. The offer was indignantly refused, and

Lord Strange prepared to join the king, who had now written him a letter with his own hand, calling him to join; and the royal standard was raised at Nottingham on the 28th August 1642. Though things were no longer as they were, the ardour for the king having cooled on account of his suspicious treatment of the earl—for such he now was, his father having just died—Lord Derby did his utmost, and rallied around him from among his own tenantry and friends a goodly force of three regiments of infantry and three squadrons of horse. With these he was ordered to make an attack on Manchester, which was now in the hands of the rebels.

Scarcely had he arrived with his soldiers before the place over which he anticipated an easy victory, than the king summoned him to join his army at Shrewsbury, since the Parliamentarians were marching upon them under Lord Essex. Full of regret at being called off, Lord Derby obeyed this mandate, to find himself once more the object of mistrust and of jealousy. Directly he arrived his command was taken from him, the king telling him that he was now wanted in Lancashire to keep watch there upon the rebels.

"Worms will turn." The earl was a man, though one of very equable temperament; but he was proud. For a moment he remained silent, in an effort to restrain his indignation. Then he said to the king:—

> Sire, had I merited this indignity, I should have also justly deserved hanging; but my honour and my rank bid me claim your justice against those who are thus insolent to Your Majesty, as they are to me. And if there be a man living (Your Majesty excepted) who dares accuse me of the least action to your disadvantage, I desire your permission to go and seek this calumny upon his lips, at my sword's point.

The king was troubled. He sought to calm the earl, he said:—

> My affairs are in such a bad state, my lord, the rebels are marching against me; and this is not the moment for us to quarrel among ourselves. Have a little patience, and I will show you justice.

The earl was silent, swallowing his anger; but once more his soldiers and friends, getting wind of the treatment to which he had been subjected, waxed indignant, and refused their service. The earl however, succeeded in allaying their discontent; and on quitting Shrewsbury to return to Lathom House, he left his troops loyal and determined as himself in the king's service.

The Parliamentarians of Lancashire soon learned of the earl's treatment by the Royalists, and once more took advantage of it to try and tempt him over to their side. They said:—

> The Earl of Derby ought to resent the outrages which he had suffered at court from the king's bad advisers. His enemies were the enemies also of the nation. They attacked the religion of all decent people; leaving His Majesty none but papists, or those inclined to popery.

The message which Lord Derby received went on:—

> The intention of Parliament was to remove from about the royal person such dark and dangerous designers, in order to ensure the true Protestant religion. His lordship should receive a command worthy of his greatness, and of that of his ancestors, if he would engage in the good cause.

Lord Derby did not even give himself the trouble to pen a reply to this message. He said to the colonel charged with its bringing:—

> Say, I beg you, to these Manchester gentlemen, and let them acquaint those in London, that when they have heard I have turned traitor I will listen to their proposals; but until then, if I receive any more papers of this kind, it will be at the peril of him who brings them.

Prince Rupert, the king's nephew, who arrived at this time to assist the Royalists, and was placed by his uncle at the head of the cavalry, was one of the hot-headed, ardent folk, who are apt to encumber with their assistance. Brave, and audacious to a degree, accustomed to rough German warfare, he did much damage to the royal cause by his wild raids over the country, pillaging and ravaging wherever he went, but was of not overmuch service in the day of battle. This was the state of things between the Royalists and "the Rebels" when the two opposing armies met, and fought out, on 23rd October 1642, that drawn Battle of Edgehill.

Chapter 10

Back at Lathom

More than once in the early days of the civil war which had now fairly broken out in the country, the king seemed to miss that tide in his affairs which, if taken at the flood, promised to lead on to an issue very different from that one which he did ultimately reach. After the Battle of Edgehill, though the Royalists suffered many reverses, their star was undoubtedly in the ascendant. There were several reasons for this, chief among them possibly, that the country at heart had not the desire to fight, father against son, brother against brother. Differences of political and religious creed might be sharply defined, but for such trials by ordeal of bloodshed a large majority of men on either side was not willing.

General sympathy consequently belonged to the Royalists, who were regarded as on the defensive. In a sense the Royalists were the popular party. They had rallied round their king in his hour of need, and sentiment was with them, as it is still, and as it is likely to remain till the end of time—or at least until that day when the name of king is wiped out from speech. Reason and prudence and much more that is desirable might weigh heavily in the Parliamentary balance, but chivalry and brightness of spirit and loyal daring had their fascinations. The sombre Puritan belief was setting in more and more darkly over the land, and the youthful English nobility and yeomanry had no mind for it. By education and rearing, they revolted against its limitations.

They were not, on this account, all such reckless, daredevil, licentious fighters, any more than the men of the opposite party were all prick-eared, pragmatical pretenders to holiness; but that the strength of the Royalists lay in an element which the Parliamentarians did not possess, Cromwell, now rapidly coming to the front, was not slow to recognise.

Discussing this question one day with Hampden, the astute lieutenant who was to eclipse the lustre of all the members of his party, replied to Hampden's speculative remarks upon the weakness of their own cavalry men, and the strength of the king's—"What can you expect? Our cavaliers are old menials or pot-house lads; theirs are sons of gentlemen, younger members of families of high rank. We ought to have men animated by a spirit which is able to make them go as far as gentlemen may go; otherwise I am certain that you will always be beaten."

"That is true," said Hampden. "But what can be done?"

"I can do something," replied Cromwell. "I will bring up men who have the fear of God before their eyes, and who will put some conscience into what they do. I will answer for it that they will not be beaten."

Then he went to work and beat up recruits from among the tenantry of the Eastern counties—men who engaged in the contest for conscience sake, fiery fanatics, who spent in prayer the time they did not give to fighting. Thus, came into the world Cromwell's Ironsides.

Another very material encouragement was experienced by the Royalists in the return of the queen with a convoy of troops and ammunition. Burlington, where she landed, was bombarded, and the bullets fell into the room she occupied. She was forced to take flight into the open country, where she remained hidden under a bank. Lord Newcastle came to her rescue, and conducted her to York, where the Roman Catholics of the North rallied in great strength about her.

She now sought to negotiate terms with several of the Parliamentarian leaders, who were already tiring of their cause; but the king's final conditions, upon which he consented to an arrangement, gave such offence to Parliament, that the deputies were recalled by a message so peremptory that they had not time to wait for their coaches, and started back to London on horseback. In the meantime, the Earl of Derby had been successfully fighting for the royal cause in the North. He took Lancaster and Preston from the Parliamentarians. There is little doubt that he would have followed up these triumphs by the subjection of Manchester, though it held out with great determination; but again, he was thwarted by demands for his men to be drafted elsewhere.

Despite the rudeness and insults of this course, the earl strove to endure them in an unmurmuring spirit. He was forced to see, without contesting, an attack on the little town of Wigan, which he had garrisoned under the Scotch General Blair. The town was taken and pillaged. The sacramental vessels were even stolen from the church, and, in accordance with the fanatical spirit of the time, which was beginning to know no bounds, one of the Puritan bigots hung them round his neck as idolatrous trophies. When his people and soldiers vented their indignation at the treatment to which their beloved and honoured chief was subjected by the Court, and at the hands of the master whom he was striving with all his might, and at such sacrifices, to serve, he quoted the noble passage from Tacitus: "*Pravis dictio factisque ex posteritate et fama metus*" ("It belongs to fame and posterity to strike bad actions and bad words with fear.")

Nothing now remained for the earl to do under such an enforced inactivity but to return to Lathom House, in order to superintend the work begun there of fortifying and victualling it, to ensure the safety of his wife and children, who resided in it during his long absences.

The loyal, single-minded earl was not likely to be a favourite with the ruck of the court party. For the butterfly courtiers he was too austere, and for the place-seekers too honest, for them to be desirous of his presence near the king, who was at Oxford, or the queen, who was at York. The uttermost confines of the kingdom were not too far to banish him, in the opinion of many; and accordingly, under sufficiently specious pretexts, thither he was sent, although the Parliamentarians were rapidly gaining ground in the North; but, as the earl writes in his memoirs:—

The old saying is verified, 'Misfortunes never come single-handed.'

He goes on to say, writing to his son, Lord Strange:—

I received letters from the Isle of Man, indicating threatenings of a great revolt.

Many there, following the example of England, began to murmur against the government—thanks to a few malicious and seditious spirits. They had learned the same lesson as the Londoners, coming tumultuously to court to demand new laws, and modification of old ones; saying that they would have no bishops, and would not pay tithes to the clergy. They despised authority, and set free several persons whom the government had arrested for their insolence. He continues:—

I had also learned that an armed ship which I kept there for the defence of the island had been seized by the Parliament ships—which turned out to be true. His Majesty, therefore, had those about him, such as Lord Goring, Lord Digby, Lord Jermyn, Sir Edward Bering and several others, who advised me to repair immediately to the island, in order to prevent mischief in time to be of service to His Majesty, and for the preservation of my heritage.

But in this again the earl might have coupled with his quoted axiom of the arrival of evils in battalions, the fable of the old man and the ass; for while he pleased the king and his lords, his enemies set his departure to the Isle of Man to a desire to be out of the general struggle. The earl treats these calumnies with the contempt they merited. It suffices that his son knows and understands him. He writes:—

As to the others, it matters little to me whether they understand or not.

Lord Derby delayed only long enough to return to Lathom, where he mustered all the men, and got together all the money and ammunition possible "to defend and protect my wife and children against the insolence of the enemy." Then he embarked for the Isle of Man.

The earl concluded:—

I left my house and my children, and all my affairs in England in charge of my wife, a person of virtue and of honour, worthy of her high birth and rank, who thus found herself alone, a stranger in the land, and (so it was thought) destitute of friends, provisions, or arms for defence. It was imagined that Lathom House would be an easy conquest, and a commission from Parliament was procured to subdue it by treaty or by force.

Chapter 11

Queen of Her Home

For more than half a score of years following the earliest years of her married life, records concerning Lady Strange are scanty. It is only a short time before she becomes Countess of Derby that she begins to live in history. Till then, she passed the ordinary existence of a highborn lady of her time—those ladies notably who affected home life more than Court life. Her provincial rearing at Thouars, coupled with her simple Huguenot education, no doubt conduced to this preference. Another reason which made a country lady of Charlotte de la Trémoille was probably the remoteness of Lathom from the capital. No doubt she occasionally appeared at court; but a journey then from the North to London, for women at all events, called for serious consideration before its undertaking.

The choice of locomotion lay between a pillion-ride on horseback, in fair weather or foul, as it might be, and a clumsy springless wooden coach occupying a good week upon the road, provided all went well, and that the huge wheels did not wedge themselves into the ruts or the mire of the king's highway, or the Flanders mares did not stumble or cast a shoe five miles from a smithy. For such were some of the mishaps which befell travellers in the good old times, not to speak of the attacks of highwaymen. Just however, as the blessings of penny post have their shadows, conversely the lack of facilities for travelling had its brighter side. Gentlefolks were apt to be more quiet-minded in those days.

The imperative necessity for constant "change" had not come to be recognised. If ladies were troubled with the migraine or the spleen, or ailments of the sort, they had to seek their remedies from the local apothecary, supposing he lived anywhere within hail; or, better, select some mint tea or tansy drink or other herbal concoction out of their own stillrooms; or, better than all, shake off the distemper in a goodly game of "Hoodman Blind," or "Hunt-the-slipper." The home of the good wife in any rank was her kingdom, and her daughters were reared in her own creed of domesticity, although it is a heresy to imagine that the women of those times were mere household drudges.

Allowing for the scarcity of books, the average of educated matrons and maids stood high. A knowledge of the classics and of the dead languages can be by no means claimed as a monopoly by Girton and Newnham and kindred modern shrines of female erudition. Again and again in the abstracts and chronicles of the time we come upon references to Mistress this and Dame the other, who read and wrote both Greek and Latin, and could quote you a passage from Virgil, or explain you the form of elegiac verse, and above all found real enjoyment in such pursuits; yet, judging from their correspondence, there was little or no pedantry mixed up with their classical knowledge. Such Gorgons of learning as Margaret Duchess of Newcastle do not come into this or any category; they are simply warnings and terrible examples of the "weaker sex."

There is small question that many of these gentlewomen were indebted for their attainments in classical literature to the chaplains, who continued to be regarded as indispensable part and parcel of the households of the nobility and wealthier gentlemen of the kingdom. Generally speaking, the post was almost a sinecure. The lay members of the Anglican Establishment were not unduly eager to take advantage of the privileges permitted by their spiritual mother, of making confession, or of seeking direction from their clergy; and when my lord's chaplain had put in an appearance to read morning, and possibly also evening, prayers, and to give thanks at meal-times, he had done pretty well all that was required of him; and indeed was not unfrequently given to understand that his withdrawal from table when the sweets and cakes were placed upon it would not be hindered.

His salary might not be princely, but his duties were certainly light; and to a studious-minded man, who did not set undue value on worldly considerations, the house chaplain might enjoy a comfortable learned leisure in the seldom-invaded library of his patron's mansion. If sons and daughters were included in the domestic circle, he probably was called upon to complete his round of service by giving them instruction; but in those times of hawk and hound and bowling-greens and tennis, average youths were apt to throw learning to the dogs as soon as they dared, and it was the maidens who mostly profited by his instructions.

Hence such women as "Sidney's sister," Lady Russel, the Countess of Pembroke—who erected a monument to her sometime tutor, Samuel Daniel, the poetic historian—and many more who could at once ply the needle exquisitely, understood brewing and baking and the mysteries of the still-room, and were well-informed "*gentlewomen*" in the most pronounced acceptance of the term. The style of the correspondence even of those who followed up their classical acquirements less closely, reveals unconsciously as it were, an intimacy with the ground-work, so that through quaintnesses and archaic expressions the educated mind shines distinctly; and beside those old letters and pieces of composition the scrawl of many a latter-day college and school miss who owns a smattering of half a dozen ologies, would make a sorry figure, with its misbegotten face.

This is the case with the letters of the Countess of Derby. In her there was not the slightest trace of *précieuse* taint; her mode of expression is as clear as it is elegant and eloquent. To be sure, after twenty years' residence in England, we find her spelling Lancashire *Lenguicher*, for which she deserves no quarter; but this appalling exception only proves the rule of her graceful diction.

That Charlotte de la Trémoille however, while possessing such command of her pen, was pre-eminently a woman of ready wit and of prompt action, the great crisis in her stormy life amply testified. Lord Derby had scarcely set foot in the Isle of Man when a message reached the countess at Lathom House from Lord Holland, the Parliamentary governor of Manchester, requiring her to accede to the conditions which he offered her, or to surrender Lathom House. Her reply was given without loss of time. It did not become her, she said, to give up her house, nor to purchase repose at the price of honour. That was the answer which Lord Holland's deputy took back.

The countess, nevertheless, was conscious of her weakness. The supply of provisions and of ammunition within the walls of the house was utterly inadequate for withstanding a siege. More than all, it was not sufficiently garrisoned. Lady Derby therefore, offered no defiance; she sought only leave to defend herself and her household, by retaining a company of her own men of the Royalist party for protection against the molestation of the Parliamentary soldiery; but leaving the estate and the surrounding park at their mercy. Consent to this request was grudgingly accorded. Her biographer says:—

Thus she remained through eight months, a prisoner in her own domain, rarely leaving the house for fear of meeting some affront, deprived of her revenues, blamed alike by friends and foes; by these, for not having defended possessions and liberty; by those, for not yielding up the house as she had the surrounding estate; but she waited with patience for the moment when she might openly resist, working unceasingly and secretly at collecting provisions and ammunition; one by one getting in the men and barrels of powder under cover of the night, repressing the zeal of her garrison, which burned to revenge the insults she daily received, and in all ways silently preparing for the siege which she anticipated.

A noble patience which, in such a high heart as Lady Derby's, called for more courage than even that which she exercised in the midst of the fray itself; the courage of a woman and of a general, which knew how to endure all, while waiting to see how to dare all.

So the still waters ran deep, so under the white ash the fiery coal smouldered and glowed, and despite the keen vigilance of the Parliamentary Colonel Rigby, who was in command of the troops stationed in the neighbourhood, the countess succeeded in mustering a garrison of three hundred men within those old towered and moated walls, and sufficient provision to sustain it under a lengthy siege. Ammunition was less plentiful, and would have to be husbanded; but throughout defence, not defiance, was the watchword.

The countess took the command-in-chief; but her want of military experience was supplied by Captain Farmer, a Scottish gentleman, whom she nominated major at the head of six lieutenants chosen from among the neighbouring gentlemen who came to offer their services.

Of all these preparations the rebel party had not the vaguest conception. Matters might have continued for some time longer in this condition, had it not been for a sudden small encounter which took place between the soldiers of the opposing sides. Colonel Rigby then resolved to annihilate this "nest of delinquents" without further delay; and orders were given to march. Whither, the majority of the men were far from being certain. The attachment of the Northerners of Derby, Cheshire, and Lancashire was very strong for the ancient race of Stanley.

To go against an Earl of Derby was hardly less than actual laying of rough hands on their anointed king, and to that pass only the fiercest malignants had as yet desired; thus for a while the soldiers were permitted to suppose that they were bound for Westmoreland. On Sunday however, when a halt was made at Wigan, and a large contingent of the soldiers attended service in the church, the preacher took for his text the 14th verse of the 50th chapter of Jeremiah:—

> Put yourselves in array against Babylon round about; all ye that bend the bow, shoot at her, spare no arrows; for she hath aimed against the Lord.

Then in the course of the sermon which followed, the preacher compared the Countess of Derby to the great city of Babylon; and finally this messenger of the Gospel of Peace announced that he reserved the verse which followed—"Shout against her round about; she hath given her hand; her foundations are fallen, her walls are thrown down,"—for the text of the sermon which was to celebrate the victory over Lathom.

The next day all lingering doubts came to an end; for the order to halt was given within two miles of Lathom House, and on the 28th February Captain Markland arrived to demand an audience of the countess. He brought with him a letter from Sir Thomas Fairfax, and a Parliamentary decree promising pardon to the Earl of Derby if he would make his submission. Sir Thomas, promising to abide faithfully by his part of the contract, further required the countess to deliver Lathom House into his hands. The letter was couched in courteous terms.

The countess responded in the same spirit of outward calmness and moderation. She expressed herself greatly astonished at being called upon to render up her husband's house, without her having given the Parliament any offence; but that, in a matter of such importance, and one which at the same time touched on her religion and this present life, concerning moreover her sovereign, her husband and lord, and all her posterity, she asked a week for reflection, to settle her doubt of conscience, and to take counsel on the questions of right and of honour which it involved.

The countess thus replied for the purpose of gaining a little longer time. Each day was showing more and more a splendid promise of the courage and fidelity of her garrison; but they needed more experience and instruction from their skilful leaders. Sir Thomas Fairfax refused the concession thus demanded, and sent her a summons to repair at once in her coach to New Park, a house belonging to the earl not far from Lathom, for the purpose of an interview with him there, in order to discuss the whole affair at length.

The pride of the highborn lady now rose beside the courage of the heroic woman, her answer to this message was:—

> Say to Sir Thomas Fairfax, that notwithstanding my present condition, I remember my lord's honour as I remember my birth, and that it appears to me more fitting that he should come to me than that I should go to him.

After two days spent in messages and replies, the general demanded a free and safe entry into Lathom House for two of his colonels, and the countess promised to let them come and depart again in safety.

In due course the two colonels arrived. The sight which met their gaze as they neared Lathom House must have caused them some astonishment. The old house bristled with arms. The Parliamentarian assumption that an easy victory was about to be obtained over a houseful of women, children, a few men-at-arms and old servants, was dispersed to the four winds by the sight of these towers and walls manned with soldiers, and the batteries and ordnance facing at all points. Whether the countess desired to inspire the ambassadors with respect and awe, or whether she feared a sudden attack, she was there to meet the Parliamentarian deputies in formidable battle array. They were conducted to the mistress of the mansion between lines of armed men drawn up on each side, from the gates of the outer court to her presence in the Great Hall, each company ranged under its lieutenant.

At the upper end of the hall, her two little daughters at each side, and her women round her, stood the countess. With a majestic air she bade the officers be seated, and waited to hear them unfold what their general, Sir Thomas Fairfax, had to propose. The brush of the painter who should succeed in depicting that scene would have to be skilful indeed. Words might bring to the mind's eye the ancient hall, bright with the hues of the women's attire, the *cuirassed* buff coats tied with their fringed silken scarves, the gleaming arms of the Royalist soldiery—and in their midst the plainly clad Parliamentarian officers in their linen bands, close-cropped hair, and the tightfitting head-gear which has earned the enemies of Charles I. their eternal sobriquet of Roundhead.

All this and much similar detail of that scene in the old presence chamber of Lathom House rises to the imagination like a brilliant and stately dream of pageantry; but it would be another matter to picture faithfully the repression of varying and contrasting mental agitation working in that assemblage—the courage and the dauntless bearing of the stately lady, the inquiring gaze of her young daughters, the eager, attent gaze of her women amid the rugged and resolute soldiers of their own side, and the endeavours of the emissaries to maintain an unruffled and undiscomfited aspect in the face of the surprise they were experiencing.

Their astonishment could only have been of a very complete kind, and the countess owed no small debt of gratitude at this crisis and later on, to her chaplain, the Rev. Mr Rutter. "*All is fair in love and war,*" says the old adage, and this faithful and astute ecclesiastic contrived to hoodwink an officer of the Parliamentarians who was among the besiegers. This person was an old friend of Mr Rutter's from early childhood, and the clergyman had given him to understand that Lathom House was in no way prepared for sustaining a prolonged siege. Possibly at the time Mr Rutter confided to his gossip this particular bit of information it was true to the letter, but "*tempora mutantur*," and during those stirring days at Lathom the times changed very quickly indeed.

The conditions brought by the emissaries of Sir Thomas Fairfax were as follows:

1st. All the arms and ammunition at Lathom should be delivered over to Sir Thomas Fairfax.

2nd. The Countess of Derby and all living in Lathom House should be at liberty to retire with their belongings to Chester or to any other town occupied by the enemy. If they thought proper to submit to Parliament, they might retire to their own homes.

3rd. The countess, with all her servants, could reside at Knowsley House, and maintain there twenty men-at-arms for her defence, or she would be permitted to rejoin her husband in the Isle of Man.

4th. For the present, and until Parliament should further inquire into the matter, the countess should receive for her maintenance the revenues of the estates and land of the earl, her husband, in the hundred of Derby; and Parliament would be called upon to preserve this revenue to her.

The countess rejected these proposals. She found them neither honourable nor certain. She said, with a lofty sarcasm:—

Since Parliament has not given its pronouncement on these points, you are not in a position to carry out your own propositions, gentlemen. It would be more prudent for you first to ascertain its good pleasure. As to myself, my good gentlemen, I will not embarrass you by petitioning for me. I should regard it as a far greater favour if you will leave me in my humble condition.

The two colonels did not press their points. They were in no mood for doing so. Colonel Rigby burned to wipe off the score of some insult which he fancied he had once received from the earl, and both the deputies saw from the first strong determination in the eyes of the countess. All the same, they did not care to allow themselves to be conquered by a woman, and both sought to represent to her the error of her ways, and to reproach her with the evils visited on the country by her party, and by her own friends and adherents. The countess gravely replied:—

I know how to take heed to my ways, and to those of my people. You will do well to do as much for your ministers and your religious helpers, who go about sowing discord and trouble in families, and whose ill-conditioned tongues do not even always spare the sacred person of His Majesty.

Henry Martin had said to Parliament, "It is certain that the ruin of one family is better than that of many families," and when he was asked of whom he spoke, he replied without hesitation, "Of the king, and of his children."

The lieutenants of Fairfax, "the two solemn personages," disappointed, baffled, and browbeaten, were forced to go back, with what comfort they might, to the camp of the Parliamentarians.

Sunday was a day of rest for the besiegers, as for the besieged. While they were being preached against in the camp of Fairfax, probably with equal sincerity the Countess of Derby assisted with her children, and the greater part of her garrison, at divine service in the chapel of her mansion, where four times a day during the siege she caused prayers to be read by her chaplain, always herself attending, and gathering fresh strength for her heavy task at the feet of Him who has willed Himself to be called The Lord of Battles. (De Witt.)

On Monday Colonel Rigby again arrived at Lathom, to receive and to carry back to his general the proposed conditions of Lady Derby. There were four in the articles of their summing up, and ran thus:—

> I demand to remain another month in peace at Lathom. The duties confided to me here are of a double nature. I owe my fidelity and my loyalty to my husband; my allegiance and my service to my sovereign. Since I have not obtained their consent, I cannot render up this house without manifestly wanting in my duty towards both. If they consent, I will peaceably yield up this house, asking only a free egress for myself and my children, with my friends, my soldiers, my retainers, my belongings, my ammunition, and my artillery, in order to go to the Isle of Man. I shall maintain a garrison in my house for my defence.
>
> 2ndly. I promise, during my residence in this county, and when I shall be in the Isle of Man, that my arms shall not be employed against Parliament.
>
> 3rdly. While I remain in this county, no Parliamentarian soldier must be quartered in the lordship of Lathom. After my departure no garrison is to be put into Lathom, nor at Knowsley House,
>
> 4thly. None of my tenants, neighbours, or friends, now in the house with me, shall be molested, nor suffer in their person or their property, after my departure, for having come to my aid.

Fairfax was not deceived by these conditions. He read between the lines of clause 2, and knew perfectly well that *his* Parliament and Lady Derby's Parliament were very different things. His Parliament might be what it might, and at Westminster; the countess's was composed as heretofore, of three estates, king, lords, and Commons, then assembled at Oxford; and his counter-propositions went back for the last time to the Lady of Lathom. She would be permitted all the time she wished, with liberty to transport her arms and possessions to the Isle of Man, with exception of the cannon, which must remain for defending the place. Further, tomorrow morning Lady Derby would have disbanded all her soldiers excepting her own servants, and she would receive a Parliamentarian officer and forty Parliamentarian soldiers to serve her as guards.

Lady Derby said to the messenger, this time a fresh man, one Morgan, a Welshman:—

> I refuse utterly, a little man, short and peremptory, who met with a great staidness to cool his heat, and he had the honour to carry back this last answer; for her ladyship could screw them to no more delays.
>
> Though a woman, and a foreigner, far from my friends, and despoiled of my property, I am prepared to endure all your utmost violence, trusting in God, both for protection and deliverance.

All temporising being at an end, the Parliamentarians, in a council of war, decided to open the siege. Some were for attempting the place by assault, and bringing the matter to rapid conclusion; but perhaps the sight beheld by those two colonels within the walls of Lathom deterred the general from this course, and led him to adopt *festina lente* for his watchword. Here the tactics of the Rev. Mr Rutter served the Royalists to good purpose.

The worthy parson's Parliamentarian crony now came forward advising for the siege, and assigning his good and sufficient reason therefor. He had, he said, been in conversation with his old friend the chaplain of Lathom House, and that veracious clergyman had allowed him clearly to understand that the supplies within the house were very small, and not sufficient to feed the garrison for a fortnight. Upon this valuable and authoritative information the siege was determined on; and the enemy began to dig trenches, to aid in which work the people of the neighbouring villages were compelled to give their services.

CHAPTER 12

A Sad Massacre

That Lord Fairfax was reluctant to attack Lathom House is very certain, whatever his reasons may have been. By some these are attributed to shame at employing force against a woman; by others they are set to the wholesome remembrance of what his deputies had beheld within the precincts of the old mansion on that February morning.

Meantime the weeks fled on, the trenches were nearly completed. Close on three months had passed, and the garrison, far from showing signs of being starved, made their evidences of strength and activity very conspicuous and troublesome by shooting at the trench-makers, and harassing them in every possible way, so that the work proceeded very slowly. It was only towards the end of April that the circle of ditchwork began to meet.

About this time, one more attempt to dissuade Lady Derby from holding out any longer was made; ostensibly by six of her neighbours, gentlemen of rank and distinction. When they asked an interview with her, she received them with gracious courtesy, and, still more, credited them with intentions of real goodwill towards herself. Notwithstanding, she saw with her usual clearness of perception, that they were but the puppets worked by the strings in the hands of the Parliamentarians, and had been made to see the matter in their light. These worthy delegates conjured her ladyship:—

> By love of their country, not to expose herself to great personal dangers, or the whole land to destruction, which she could easily avoid, by relaxing the rigour of her resolutions, and by lending an ear to their propositions."

The countess evinced none of the haughty contempt to these gentlemen which she had shown the Parliamentarian officers. She vouchsafed a reasonable explanation of the course which she had adopted, and then added that they would do better to expostulate with the men who pillaged and ravaged the country, rather than with her, who "asked as the one favour that she might be left in peace in her own house."

The little band retired, shouting as they went, "Long live the king, and the Earl of Derby!" and the Parliamentarians knew that they had taken another false step.

Still holding back, Sir Thomas Fairfax made one more forlorn attempt to bring the indomitable lady to reason; and now, in the person of Colonel Ashurst, substituted gentleness and some courtesy. He was bidden to tell the countess that, cancelling all the former conditions, she and all those with her in the house might depart whither they would, with their arms and baggage, artillery included, giving the house into the hands of Sir Thomas Fairfax. This was on condition that the arms should not be employed against the Parliament; and that "everyone in the house should depart immediately, excepting one hundred persons who should go at the end of ten days."

To this proposal the countess's answer was:—

Tell your general that I have not yet lost my veneration for the Church of England, my allegiance to my king, and my fidelity to my husband; I cannot therefore render up this house until I have lost that respect and fidelity, or given my life in their defence. Do not reckon, then, that Lathom will be yours.

The siege was now determined on. The trenches encircled the house. The blockade commenced.

The leaders had the courage to starve a woman; but not to fight with her. (Halsall.)

Yet once more Sir Thomas Fairfax stayed his hand, seemingly with little regret. A letter reached him from Lord Derby. The earl wrote from the Isle of Man, demanding the right for his wife and children to have perfect freedom to leave Lathom, and thus to spare their weakness the horrors of a siege. He feared the brutality of the besiegers, and believed that the house could be but scantily supplied with provisions. When the countess heard of this letter to Sir Thomas Fairfax, it had only the effect of adding fuel to the flame of her courage. She said to the messenger, a preacher in the employment of Captain Rigby:—

Tell Sir Thomas Fairfax that I thank him for his courtesy. I shall always obey the commands of my lord, and the general can treat with him; but until I am certain of his good pleasure, I shall not give up his house, and I will not forsake it; I await the issue of these events, as God may will it to be.

Meantime, Lord Derby had returned from the Isle of Man, and the countess contrived to send him a dispatch, which found him at Chester, occupied in an endeavour to muster troops to march to her assistance; but as yet the earl had a mere handful of men only, 'and three thousand soldiers surrounded Lathom.

Notwithstanding, the sorties from the house continued; cannon commenced to fire upon the walls, but thanks to the configuration of the ground, very ineffectually. The garrison was interested in watching the manipulation of a mortar which was planted on a little mound at the distance of half a musket range from the house. The first *grenadoes* from it passed over the roof of the house, to the great joy of the besieged, whom the countess had supplied with the skins of the beasts slaughtered for the daily food of the soldiers, in order that they might extinguish the flames with these if the house should catch fire.

Four days of prayer and pious exercises interrupted the operations of the besiegers, four days of "sleep," says the Royalist chronicler, profoundly incredulous in the matter of Colonel Rigby's piety. At the expiration of this time the garrison determined to waken the besiegers by an angry sortie; they spiked several of their cannon, and took a number of men prisoners. The countess, proud of having left hardly any of her own men in the hands of the enemy, would have surrendered these in exchange; and she offered to render up all the prisoners she had made, if the Parliamentarians would release some of the king's friends detained at Manchester, Preston, and Lancaster. This Colonel Rigby promised to do; but he was wanting to his promise. The narrator of the siege of Lathom says:—

"It was part of their religion, to observe faith neither with God nor men; and there ensued a sad massacre of the prisoners at Lathom, whom the countess could neither keep or release." (Halsall.)

She was always engaged with her two daughters, Mary and Catherine, superintending everything, providing for the nourishment of the soldiers, seeing to the distribution of powder, tending the wounded, frequently upon the ramparts, always in chapel at prayer time, and smiling disdainfully when a bullet happened to fall into her sleeping-chamber. She did not even deign to change her apartment until she had received such a visit three or four times. "I will hold this house while there is a bit of wall to shelter me, and a corner of roof to cover my head," she said, when she installed herself in the Eagle Tower in the middle of the building. A bomb had fallen and burst in the dining-hall during dinner, breaking all the casement panes, and smashing the furniture, but not wounding anyone. The children were beside their mother, but they had not stirred; scarcely had they changed colour. The countess bestowed a glance of approval on them. That was all, and the repast was proceeded with.

Sir Thomas Fairfax, who from the beginning had never been heartily with his task, discovered towards the end of April that his presence was indispensable at York; and he delegated the command of the siege of Lathom House to Colonel Rigby. With the departure of Fairfax, the entire face of matters was changed. Lady Derby had no longer to do with:—

> A gentleman, a sincere patriot, but a well-reared man, with a noble heart, and of pure hands. Her chief assailant now was an old attorney, a wretched lawyer, a pilferer, a thief, a hypocrite, determined not to be beaten by a woman.

He so little understood his new trade, that he allowed his plentiful supply of powder to be so flung about and wasted, that the besieged were able to renew their supplies of it from the trenches. (De Witt.)

There was no letting "I dare not wait upon I would" with this Roundhead warrior; and no sooner had he assumed the command than he announced his intention of attacking the house with mortar and cannon. The countess was however, permitted the alternative of "giving up her house, garrison, arms and ammunition next day before two o'clock in the afternoon." She was in the courtyard when the drummer who brought the summons presented himself at the gates. She took the letter, and, having glanced at it, said to the Parliamentarian:—

> You deserve to hang at these gates. But you are only the foolish tool of a traitor's vanity. Therefore, convey this answer to Rigby, (and she tore the paper in two.) Tell this insolent rebel that he will have neither our persons, goods, nor house. When our resources are exhausted, we shall find a fire more supportable than Rigby's. If God's providence does not come to the rescue, my house and my possessions shall burn before his eyes; and I, my children and my soldiers, sooner than fall into his hands,

will seal our religion and our loyalty in the flames.

She spoke in a loud, firm, and resonant voice. Her soldiers pressed round her. "We will die for His Majesty, and for our honour!" shouted they with one accord. The drummer departed from Lathom to cries of "Long live the King!" The mortar to which the Parliamentarians pinned their faith was indeed a terrible engine of destruction. It was a monster which vomited forth flame and bombs with somewhat impartial energy to both besieged and besiegers. It was invaluable, of course, to the Parliamentarians; but it refused to be humoured, and while serving their turn upon their enemies, had done themselves no small damage. It might be, and was, the terror of the garrison; but it was a dangerous friend to those whom it served. It was capable of throwing stones thirteen inches in diameter and of eighty pounds' weight, and also *grenadoes*, balls of iron filled with powder and lighted by fuses.

On Easter Monday it lodged a twenty-four pounder in the countess's chamber in the Eagle Tower, where she was having breakfast with her two daughters.

The chronicler says:—

The little ladies had stomach to digest cannon; but the strongest soldiers had no hearts for *grenadoes*, and might not they at once free themselves from the continual expectation of death?

At all events they determined to try; and at four o'clock next morning a small contingent of twenty-four soldiers stole noiselessly forth, creeping under the shadow of the cannon until they reached the little fort which commanded the mansion. At the same time Captain Fox, issuing by another door, was in possession of the earthworks which guarded the mortar. To reach this point, a deep ditch and a high rampart had to be scaled. The first care of the two captains was to mount the ditch, while the soldiers were prepared to defend themselves against the enemy, if it should try to regain the position.

All the household of the countess sallied forth and crowded round the mortar, eager to give a hand to the ropes which were now passed about it to drag it within the walls.

Captain Ogle, with a detachment of soldiers, protected the men who pulled the ropes, and very soon, amidst the joyful shouts of the whole garrison, and to the consternation of the besiegers, the savage monster went rolling into the courtyard to the feet of the countess, who forthwith summoned Chaplain Rutter, and, in company with all her people, rendered thanks to Heaven in the chapel.

The soldiers wanted to take the artillery as well, but the pieces were too heavy, and they contented themselves with spiking them, as they had vainly striven many times to do with the mortar.

This action cost the Lathom men two soldiers; the loss of the enemy was more considerable." (Halsall.)

All the time it was going on, the gunners on the walls never ceased peppering the Parliamentarians, and did great havoc among those who were near the fort and the trenches. The ditch was levelled in this sally.

The joy at the capture of the mortar knew no bounds in the house. The monster whose flames had so often threatened to burn the older parts of the house, which were constructed mainly of wood, now lay in the courtyard silent and impotent. The soldiers indulged their feelings by bestowing on it a kick when they passed it, for all the terror it had caused in its time. Everybody was the more delighted from the fact coming to their knowledge that Captain Rigby had invited his friends and neighbours that same day to assemble to witness either the ceding or the burning of Lathom House. They were invited to be there at two o'clock.

And they punctually arrived in time to console Rigby, who was sick with shame and rage at finding himself beaten by a woman and a handful of soldiers. (Halsall.)

The besiegers now began to lose heart. Captains and men deserted the camp; the rain, which fell incessantly that spring, destroyed their trenches, and the undertaking throughout had brought them little credit. On the 23rd May the countess was once more required, in insolent terms, to capitulate, "and to submit to the mercy of Parliament." Lady Derby replied with a bitter smile, "You mistake. You mean the cruelties, not the mercies."

"No, madam," replied the puzzled delegate, "the mercies of Parliament."

"The mercies of the wicked are cruel," quickly responded she. Then she added that it was not Parliament, but its corrupt agents with whom she refused to treat. "Let them make terms with my lord," she went on; "failing that, they will have neither me nor my friends while there is life in us." When the deputy persisted, she said:—

This insolent rebel shall make no more proposals. If he does, his messenger shall hang at my gates.

For the last time the ambassador retired. Nothing daunted the countess. She paid no heed to all the gloomy rumours which reached her of the Royalist reverses. Prince Rupert, on the other hand, had vanquished the rebels at Newark, and was now marching to the assistance of Lord Newcastle, who was at York, menaced on all sides. The Earl of Derby implored the prince to take his way by Lancashire, and relieve Lathom House and his wife and children. He promised the troops £3,000, which he had borrowed on the jewels of his wife, she having contrived to find a way of conveying them to him during the siege.

A few hours after the departure of the discomfited Parliamentarian delegate late at night, one of Lady Derby's couriers arrived at Lathom House. To obtain his entrance he had killed the enemy's sentinel. The news which he brought the countess was that Prince Rupert was on the way to the relief of Lathom House, and that my Lord Derby accompanied him.

Deep thankfulness pervaded all hearts in Lathom House. The countess however, annexing a leaf from the enemy's book of axioms, trusted in God, "but kept her powder dry." While rendering heartfelt thanks to Heaven, she abated not one tittle of her unceasing vigilance.

In silence now the Parliamentarians guarded their trenches. The sound of their mocking rhymes and songs was heard no more. The prowess and successes of Cromwell and of Fairfax were no longer vaunted. No more was said about taking the king in a mouse-trap. On the evening of the 26th May the guard was so carelessly mounted, that Lady Derby resolved on a grand sally next day, beginning at three o'clock in the morning.

But Prince Rupert was at hand—Prince Rupert, the terror of his foes, if not also, like that Parliamentarian mortar, the terror of some of his friends—and at one o'clock the Parliamentarian soldiers took up their arms, folded their tents, and silently departed from Lathom, after a four months' fruitless siege, the loss of five hundred men, against the loss of six of the besieged, and the expending of one hundred barrels of gunpowder. Like a wise man, economical of his blood, Rigby stood no longer upon much order of going, but went at once.

Still foresight and prudence detained the prince and the earl to punish the enemy upon the way, and to destroy chances of any speedy or sudden return to the attack; but it was not long before the victorious Lady of Lathom stood at her gates to receive her husband, and to bid him welcome to the home which she had so gallantly defended.

Sir Richard Crane attended the Earl, laden with twenty-two trophies taken by her kinsman Prince Rupert at Bolton and Liverpool, to present in homage to his "fair relative and companion in arms." These banners, after floating proudly in the breeze on the towers of Lathom, Lady Derby hung in the chapel in reverent "gratitude to the God in whom she had put her trust, and in memory of the deliverance which He had sent to her." (De Witt.)

Captain Roshern and Captain Chisenhall were raised by Prince Rupert, at Lady Derby's request, to the rank of colonel. The first was made governor of Lathom House, the other followed the prince's fortunes.

The occasion ended, Charlotte de la Trémoille was now once more but a gracious gentlewoman, a loving wife and mother. No word in her correspondence makes the slightest allusion to her brave actions and heroic endurance. Home and her children once more engrossed her thoughts. Prince Rupert, ere he bid his hostess farewell said:—

Take good care of them, the children of such a father and such a mother will one day do their king such service as their parents have done theirs.

And indeed "Faithful unto death" would have been the only motto for that seventh Earl of Derby and his wife, Charlotte de la Trémoille, had they ever needed to replace the one graved on their unsullied shield of "*Sans changer.*"

Chapter 13

A Lull in the Storm

On the conclusion of the siege of Lathom House, the Countess of Derby went with her children to the Isle of Man. This appears to have been done by the advice of Prince Rupert, who well knew, not only the animosity of the Parliamentarians against the earl, and therefore against his family, but also the jealousy entertained against him by the king's party.

In the old castles of Rushen and of Peel, Lady Derby spent the ensuing years of King Charles Ist's stormy reign, for the most part in peace, compared with the turmoil and anxiety of the previous months.

As for the brave old mansion, it remained for some time in the charge of the garrison left in it. Finally, by the desire of the king, whose fortunes were now too low to come to its assistance when again it was attacked by the Roundheads, it yielded, but with honours for all it contained, and the garrison marched forth with their arms and baggage. Neither were they called upon to take the oath to Parliament.

Whether it would even have yielded when it did is more than questionable, had it not been for an Irish soldier:—

> The one traitor the garrison contained, who swam the moat and informed the enemy of the deplorable condition of the besieged—at the end of their food and ammunition.

The matter was now easy to compass—brute strength against weakness. The doors were burst open, the house sacked, its towers thrown down, and its walls levelled with the ground. Three little pieces of the battlements alone remained to tell of the long, brave defence it had made. Cromwell's sequestrators sold its doors, its floors, and all else of it, and the receipts of sale are still to be found in the Ormskirk parish records. (Seacome.) Finally, the peasants of West Derby were invited to take away the stones and timbers without any charge. (Heywood) A later chronicler says:—

Nothing remained of the old place, along whose banks knights and ladies have a thousand times made resort, harking to stories as varied as those of Boccaccio. The Maudlin Well, where the pilgrim and the lazar devoutly cooled their parched lips the brewing-house the training round all now are changed, and a modern mansion and a new possessor fill their places.

The new mansion which a later earl raised upon the honoured ashes of the old is a splendid house; but with it our story has not to do. The noble presence of Charlotte de la Trémoille never graced its Ionic colonnades and spacious chambers; and it is to her once more that we will turn, in her old feudal stronghold in the Kingdom of Man.

Yet one more word, before biding *adieu* to Lathom, as to the Maudlin Well mentioned. A question arises which suggests itself for antiquarian solving. In later times a "Lathom Spaw" came into some repute in that neighbourhood. Was this "Spaw" the old Maudlin Well of the Stanleys' famous home?

For the first time after several years, Charlotte de la Trémoille's correspondence recommences. Probably from time to time, during the siege of Lathom, and the first year or two of her sojourn in the Isle of Man, she wrote to her relatives in France, but these letters have been lost or stolen. It is only in the month of August 1646 that she writes from the Isle of Man in no small anxiety. Her eldest son, Lord Strange, had secretly left the island to go, no one knew whither. "We are told that he is in Ireland," she writes to her sister-in-law," but the letters he left behind with us say that he was going to you." She adds that if this be the case, and the duchess receives him graciously, forgiveness from both parents for his escapade will not be long withheld from him.

Lord Strange had, in fact, made his way to Paris, where the Duchess de la Trémoille, his aunt, had received him kindly, and treated him with maternal solicitude. On learning this gratifying intelligence, it is Lord Derby who writes to thank Madame de la Trémoille in terms of almost enthusiastic courtesy for her obligations, he writes:—

No service which I could humbly render you, *madame*, would be too difficult for me, so that I might prove to you with what devotion I am, *madame*, your very humble and very obedient brother and servant, Derby.

The earl was probably glad that the youthful heir of his home was out of the country; for the royalist cause was growing desperate. It was death now to anyone who should have to do with the king. The Parliament sent proposing an amnesty. Its terms were: his acceptance of the Scottish Covenant, the abolition of the Anglican Church, and the entire relinquishment of power into the hands of Parliament. Thirty-six persons were excluded from this amnesty, and a price set upon the heads of seven of them. Third on the list, after Prince Rupert and Prince Maurice, stood the name of Lord Derby; and in the next letter of the countess she speaks of a proposed journey to London to intercede for the earl:—

> After a journey from the Isle of Man, which lasted forty-eight hours, upon a dangerous sea, in a wretched boat; but if God blesses my efforts, as I have prayed Him to do, I can bear anything.

She further speaks hopefully of obtaining her husband's pardon, she writes:—

> The Lords will, I think, easily grant it.

From the Commons she looks for more obduracy:—

> But God will give me wisdom and prudence. The king continues to refuse to do what Parliament desires, and declines to listen to the preaching of its ministers.

There are natures which can meet martyrdom; but flinch at slow torture, and spiritual discourses in those days were nothing if they did not stretch to a good hour at the least. The sword of the Spirit was a long one. On the 25th March the king had been sold by the Scotch to the Parliament. He was now at Holmby House in Northamptonshire, only to go thence upon the road which terminated on the scaffold of Whitehall.

In addition to all these grave cares Lady Derby was burdened with the settlement of her brother's affairs. He had recently died, and his title and estates were claimed by Miss Orpe, who asserted that she had been privately married to him. Lady Derby complains bitterly of the part which the queen took in this matter. She openly gave countenance to Miss Orpe's pretensions. Notwithstanding, Lady Derby and the Duke de la Trémoille gained their suit; and his estate was shared between them.

From this time, it was that the opponents of the king became divided against themselves. The Independents and the Presbyterians had little in common sympathy. The Independents formed the majority in the army, and the Presbyterians, jealous of their power, were now anxious to disband the army. In this difference the Independents, gaining the day, formed a military Parliament, and took possession of the king; but the hope that this raised in the minds of the Royalists, and among them the hopes of the Earl and Countess of Derby, was doomed to be disappointed. The king in the hands of the Independents was merely a puppet to play off against the Presbyterians.

The Earl of Derby was all this time being treated with comparative leniency, considering that his loyalty to his party amounted to a passion which no terrors or threats could ever quench. Total inaction was imposed upon him; and policy prompted him to compliance. "*Reculer pour mieux sauter*" was the watchword now for the ardent-spirited earl. To attempt to do anything for his royal master's defence at this time was but to hurry him the faster to his doom; though there was a gleam of hope in the treatment which the king was now receiving. During some months which he spent at Hampton Court, the semblance of kingly state and of loyal respect surrounded him.

It was the calm and deceptive tranquillity which precedes the tempest. Like the old *trève de Dieu* of mediaeval days—the oasis which travellers come upon in the desert, and perforce must leave again—those few little months at Hampton Court, with his children once more about him, must have been very blessed to the king. Despite the gloom on all sides of the horizon, sunshine was overhead, sweetness was in the air.

Lord Derby during his enforced inactivity took up his pen, and began his *History and Antiquities of the Isle of Man*. He wrote it for the instruction of his son, and its title *in extenso* explains his intentions in writing it:—

> With an account of his own proceedings, and losses in the Civil War; interspersed with sundry advices to his son.

The advice is excellent. After some details concerning the early history of the island, its noble chronicler writes:—

> Sir John Stanley, who was the first of our family to possess it, took out in letters-patent the name of the King of Man. His successors did the same until the time of Thomas, second Earl of Derby, who, for good and wise reasons, decided to relinquish

this title."

I know no subject who owns a dominion as important as this.

And then the earl adds that, lest it may be found to be too important, his son will do well to observe this rule, which will enable him to keep the kingdom uncontested: "Fear God, and honour the king."

Further on, the earl takes blame to himself for not having seen how he might have added to the prosperity of the Manx folks by turning the island to more profitable account, "for he who is not careful of what he has, is not worthy to possess it." He advises that manufactories and more trade be established in Man.

Then the sea will be covered with ships, and the land with inhabitants, to the great advantage of the whole country.

He further gives excellent advice as to the selection of a bishop for the island. He must be one, he says, who is a pious and worthy person, seeing that the clergy do, their duty, and therefore one who must reside in the island, and have no benefice elsewhere. Further, the earl would have a university, which, from the great natural advantages of the island, might be maintained at moderate cost and be serviceable to many:—

Finishing by putting something into the purse of its *suzerain* lord. But of this I will talk with you more, if it please God that I see you again, and have a quiet mind.

He adds more good counsel for personal conduct, and for the general business of life. This work was never finished, as the earl intended it, but is published as he left it in Peck's *Desiderata Curiosa*, vol. ii.

In September of 1647 Parliament at last definitely made allowance for the maintenance of the earl's children. It was one-fifth of his revenue, the same as they meted to the rest of the "delinquents." The allowance was made upon Knowsley, and thither two of the earl's three daughters, Catherine and Mary, were at once sent. Lord Fairfax issued orders that Major Jackson, who had established himself with his family in the mansion, should clear out, and the guardians were further enjoined to see "that the said Major Jackson" did no damage to house or park before he went. Lady Derby writes from London, 14th March 1648:—

I am advised to go to Lancashire, and live there on the little which has been allowed to my children; for I receive nothing;

and I hope that I may be able to make it go further if I am on the spot. One must live economically, and make the best of what one has.

There seems to have been no false sentiment about Lady Derby's nature. And if the theories of Lavater are in any way correct, it is easiest to recall her living personality through the portrait of Vandyke, who, mighty portrayer that he was, gives Charlotte de la Trémoille on his canvas the frank and happy face of a good wife and a good mother, if not as specially beautiful or striking, as Scott has depicted the widowed Countess of Derby and "Queen in Man" in his *Peveril of the Peak*. Scott claims his rights as a romancer to give us the famous Countess of Derby as it suited his great novel to depict her.

The Wizard has indeed drawn a curiously different personality from the real wife of James Stanley. On the other hand, her wifehood was almost past before Julian Peveril of the Peak was born. It is the woman advancing in years, with the memory of dead joys and loves and countless bitter wrongs heavy upon her, whom Scott characterises. When Charles II. was king, Charlotte de la Trémoille must have been greatly changed; but it is in having changed her creed that Scott misses the strong individuality in which he might have clothed her, without overleaping fact by a hair's-breadth.

No one comprehended better than he the play of light and shadow upon every act and word of man, woman, or even child, which is cast by religious conviction or the lack of it. Scott, while apologising for the dereliction, has transformed the born Huguenot, the staunch Anglican of two-score years' profession, into an ardent, even fanatical Roman Catholic. How completely she stood between the Scylla and Charybdis of Rome and the Sectaries, the extract from the following letter illustrates with striking emphasis:—

> For my husband and myself, in the matter of religion, it is, thank God, so deeply graven in our hearts, that nothing by His grace can take it from us; and if Parliament really held the interests of religion and the glory of God, which you think they entertain, they would not have the cruelty and injustice which signalise all their actions. And for religion, they have misled the people of this nation, until now they see their error, and groan under the burden of tyranny. Those even, who are most attached to their party, deplore their own misery and ours, and would find it difficult to tell you what their belief is, there being as many

religions as there are families.

The *Test* is publicly maintained; books are printed denying the existence of the Holy Spirit. Those who do this are not punished for it. God's commandments are scorned—even the Creed itself. Sunday worship is neglected, and not constrained to be celebrated anywhere. The sacraments are administered according to each person's fancy; the ministry is neglected. Anyone who considers himself capable of preaching, may do so without any licence or examination; even women may do it. Baptism is neglected, and not given to children; and there are other things still worse, which make those who have any religion left in them shudder to see such abuses.

For our ill-wishers, we have them, but not more than the Lords in Parliament have them, it being the desire of the Commons to have no Lords, but to make all equal. That is understood by the Lords, but not the remedy for it. If you could hear the prevailing discontent, you would hardly be able to credit it. I speak of those who have ventured all for Parliament, and are enemies of the king's party.

This has reached such a point, that if the Scotch come, as we are led to think they may, there are not many who would not join them. This has of late led to changing all the leaders who were most affected to Parliament; replacing them by men who only regard their own faction; and though it was decreed in Parliament that if the army did not approve of this, it was to be changed, one day undoes what the other has done.

This is not credible, excepting to those who see it all; and while I was away, they had a difficulty in persuading me that it was true. If I had the honour of seeing you, and speaking with you for a little while, I know you would soon be convinced of the truth, and would regret to see the Protestant religion suffering, and the Papists turning it to their advantage.

National affairs were now in a state of hopeless entanglement—Presbyterian against Independent, and both against the king and all who had held by him through fortune good and ill. There could be no quarter for the Royalists. "There is no doubt," writes the countess in March of 1648, "that affairs will settle themselves." She wrote prophetically when she added:—

There is such discontent prevailing, that those who are in authority say—*in confidence*—that things cannot remain long without a change.

On the next 30th January King Charles I. made his "good exchange" upon the scaffold at Whitehall; penalties of high treason were declared against all who acknowledged Charles Stuart as king; the House of Peers was abolished; and Cromwell was at the head of public affairs.

CHAPTER 14

Lord Derby Taken Prisoner

No letters of either Lord Derby or his wife now exist written during the passing of that sad time. If any were written by them, they were lost, or not preserved.

In July following the king's execution, Lord Derby, now in the Isle of Man, wrote his memorable letter to Ireton, who offered him tempting bait, no less than the free restoration of all his other estates and lost power, if he would deliver up the island to Parliament:—

> I received your letter with indignation, and with scorn return you this answer: that I cannot but wonder whence you should gather any hopes that I should prove like you, treacherous to my sovereign; since you cannot be ignorant of my former actings in His Late Majesty's service, from which principles of loyalty I am no whit departed. I scorn your proffers; I disdain your favour; I abhor your treason; and am so far from delivering up this island to your advantage, that I shall keep it to the utmost of my power to your destruction. Take this for your final answer, and forbear any further solicitations: for if you trouble me with any more messages of this nature, I will burn the paper and hang up the bearer. This is the immutable resolution, and will be the undoubted practice of him who accounts it his chiefest glory to be His Majesty's most loyal and obedient subject,
>
> Derby.
>
> From Castle-town, this
> 12th of July, 1649.

Lord Derby further promulgated an announcement to similar effect, "inviting all his allies, friends, and acquaintance, all his tenantry in Lancashire, and Cheshire, and other places, as well as all His Majesty's faithful and loyal subjects," to repair to the Isle of Man, as a refuge and a rallying-place. No menaces or dangers, added the earl in the proclamation, could trouble him, nor dangers deter him. A letter written by Lady Derby, the year of the king's death, bitterly complains of the duplicity of Parliament dealings in respect of the disposal of their property:—

> As to the sects, their numbers daily increase, and their tenets are enough to make the hair stand on end.

She has been very ill for weeks past, and would be more than content to die and be at rest, but for the loved ones she would leave behind. Once more she descants upon the aberrations of the hydra-headed fanaticism which made such rampant strides in the last half of the seventeenth century, and once more, on the other hand, is amazed at the freedom which Roman Catholics are permitted. Only for the Church of England breathing space is not allowed; but her husband, she assures the Duchess de la Trémoille, who appears to entertain fears lest Lord Derby might waver, is more "Protestant" than ever.

In the midst of all these real trials, she discusses with great interest a point of Court etiquette: the mighty question of the *tabouret*; and it is with as intense gratification that the countess hears finally that the *tabouret* has been accorded to her niece on her marriage, as it had once been given to herself.

Another domestic incident of a disagreeable nature took place about this time, in the marriage of the heir of the Stanleys, Edward Lord Strange, with a Mademoiselle de Rupa, a German lady of neither position nor fortune. His parents never forgave this offence, and, to crown all, Lord Strange entertained some dreams of compounding with Parliament, fearing that hope for the Royalists was utterly gone, and that they would all be left at last to starve.

Truly trouble was heavy on the friends of the murdered king's son, who was now wandering in Scotland, after the execution of Montrose. Bradshaw's hatred against the Earl of Derby was intense, and, with the ingenuity bred of spite and cruelty, he attacked him in the part most sensitive in such a man, through his children. For two years the two daughters, Catherine and Amelia, had been left in peace at Knowsley. Lady Derby, 8th June 1650, writes:—

> Now, one Birch, governor of a little town called Liverpool, has taken them prisoners, and carried them there, where they are under guard.

The countess attributes this treatment to the pressure Parliament intends putting upon the earl, she concludes:—

> That is all, dear sister, which I can tell you of this pitiable story. I pray God to protect them, and do not fear that He will do so. It is said that they endure bravely. I am less troubled for the elder, but my child Amelia is delicate and timid, and was under treatment from M. de Mayerne (a doctor in whom Lady Derby placed great confidence). The place where they are is very ugly, and has bad air, and they are very wretchedly lodged.
>
> But these barbarians think of nothing but pursuing their damnable plans; one might think that if all the demons of hell had devised them, they could not have been worse.

The sufferings of these two innocent girls increased. They had not bread enough to eat, and must have starved but for the charity of the poor Royalists and the fidelity of their attendants, who went begging for them from house to house. They complained at last to Fairfax, who wrote thereupon to the earl:—

> If his lordship would place the Isle of Man at Parliament's good pleasure, his children should be liberated, and enjoy half of his revenues.

The earl replied that he was deeply afflicted at the sufferings of his children. It was not the custom of noble minds to punish innocent children for their parents' faults. He begged Sir Thomas Fairfax to give them back to him, or to let them pass free to France or to Holland; but if this were not possible, they must trust in the mercy of the Most High, for he could never deliver them by an act of treachery.

The contest between king and Parliament, or, more truly, between king and Cromwell, was raging in Scotland. Of that country Charles II. was now crowned king. He should be crowned King of England too, while a Royalist lived. That was the Royalist determination, and Cromwell's sudden illness favoured hope, in addition to the prevailing disaffection in the opposite camp; for betwixt Covenanter and Presbyterian and Independent, and all the myriad political and religious sectaries, little love was lost. Cromwell, however, recovered, and attacked Perth. Charles announced his intention of going to England. The Duke of Argyle sought to dissuade him from this, and withdrew his aid. Cromwell followed the king to Carlisle in pursuit. Charles immediately summoned Lord Derby, and the countess writes, 1st September 1651:—

> We are still here (Isle of Man), by the goodness of God, who has safely guided my husband to the king his sovereign I learn that the king has received him with great joy and proofs of affection, and I await special details with impatience; though I fear they cannot reach me quickly, because of the vessels of the enemy, which are all round our shores.

Charles informed Lord Derby, in a letter in his own hand, that the Presbyterians of Lancashire were ready to join under his leadership. This Lord Derby found to be true only *cum grano salis*, and that no small grain. He had brought with him three hundred gentlemen, for the most part Roman Catholics, from the Isle of Man; these, the Covenanting partisans of the king insisted, were to be sent back again, before they joined issue in the struggle. This equally Lord Derby refused. He demanded for these gentlemen the same latitude and liberty the Lancashire Presbyterians required for themselves; and if they could not accord it, though he despaired of success without their aid, he had no voice but to dispense with it; and, mounting his horse, the earl rode away with his little band of Royalists to encounter Colonel Robert Liburne, close by Wigan, a town which had always remained true to the royal cause.

A hand-to-hand struggle ensued. Two horses were killed beneath the earl, and were replaced at the peril of his own life by a faithful French servant. Finally, in the confusion Lord Derby escaped into the town, finding refuge in a poor woman's cottage. She drew the door bolts, and maintained such a stout defence of her little domain, that the earl had time to escape by the back of the house, and rejoined his friends; but he was fearfully wounded, and scarcely able to sit his horse for weakness.

As soon as he could stir, he made his way in disguise to Worcester, where the king's forces were mustered, and on 3rd September 1651, in the Battle of Worcester, which ended in the routing of the Royalists, Lord Derby, with Lord Cleveland and Colonel Wogan, protected their royal master, when all was over, through the enemy's ranks with their own swords and bodies, and then conducted him to Whiteladies, safe with the loyal Giffards and Pendrells. Thence, followed by some of his friends, he found his way to the coast, and escaped to France.

With Lord Lauderdale, Lord Derby took his way back to the North, his noble heart well-nigh broken, and his body weak and torn with wounds. At Wigan his course was stopped by a detachment of the victorious Parliamentarians, under Major Edge. The earl and his friends gave their names, and surrendered, under condition of receiving quarter. This was promised on condition of their yielding up arms, and considering themselves prisoners. Lord Lauderdale was conducted to another part of the country. Lord Derby was taken direct to Chester.

Arrived there, he wrote a long letter to his wife, which he obtained leave to be transmitted to her by Mr Bagalay, a prisoner of war in the city—a long letter, full of solicitude for his wife and family, and for all in any way dependent on him. He tells her that though a prisoner in body, his heart is free and at peace, having "no other sadness in it than the regret at knowing her suffering and sorrow, and that of his poor children." Colonel Duckenfield, he informs her, will proceed in the name of Parliament to take possession of the Isle of Man. Once more, not as from a prisoner, but as from one "whose soul is his own, as in his best days," he will give her his advice how to receive Duckenfield, but that he will transmit by word of mouth to his trusty messenger.

> Take care of yourself, my dearest heart, and of my dear Mall and Ned and Billy. As to those who are here, I will give them the best advice I can. My son, (Lord Strange, now arrived in England), with his wife, and my nephew Stanley have been to see me I will only say now that my son shows me much affection, and that he is gone to London with an ardent desire to serve me.

That he hopes little from this filial devotion is evident.

> The cold and the wind of the coming winter are more easy to be borne than the malicious attacks of a venomous serpent, or an obstinate and perfidious enemy . . . .May the Son of God, whose blood was shed for us, preserve our life, so that by God's mercy and goodness we may see each other once again on this earth, and then in the kingdom of Heaven, where we shall be safe from rapine, theft, and violence!—I remain ever your faithful Derby.

There could be but little quarter for the noble prisoner. With the son of Bradshaw, Colonel Birch, and Colonel Rigby, the vanquished hero of Lathom House, among his judges, his doom was virtually pronounced.

When brought before the tribunal of these men and of one or

two others, who from one cause or another were little inclined in his favour, and styling itself a court-martial, he was voted guilty of a breach of the Act passed 12th August 1651, which prohibited all correspondence with Charles Stuart or his party. Consequently, he had committed high treason and sentence of death was pronounced. When he heard himself called traitor, he cried: "I am no traitor—I—" "Silence, sir," said the President. "Your words are of no account. Hear the act of accusation to the end."

Neither books nor counsel were allowed him, and he defended himself. This he did with skill, pleading in the first place that quarter had been promised. A show of consideration was vouchsafed to what he said; but, with casuistry which would have done credit to the Sorbonne, his representations were overruled, and his execution fixed for the 15th October at Bolton.

On Monday, 13th October, Mr Bagalay was permitted to wait upon him.

> He discoursed his own commands to me. With many affectionate protestations of his honour and respect for my lady, both for her birth, and goodness as a wife, and much tenderness of his children.
> Then in came one Lieutenant Smith, a rude fellow, and with his hat on; he told my lord he came from Colonel Duckenfield, the governor, to tell his lordship he must be ready for his journey to Bolton. The earl replied, 'When would you have me to go?'
> 'Tomorrow about six in the morning,' was the man's answer. The earl desired to be commended to the governor, and for him to be informed by that time he would be ready.
> Then said Smith, 'Does your lordship know any friend or servant that would do the thing your lordship knows of? It would be well if you had a friend.'
> And the earl replied, 'What do you mean? Would you have me find one to cut off my head?'
> 'Yes, my lord,' said Smith. 'If you could have a friend—'
> 'Nay, sir,' interrupted the earl; 'if those men that would have my head will not find one to cut it off, let it stand where it is. I thank God my life has not been bad, that I should be instrumental to deprive myself of it... As for me and my servants, our ways have been to prosecute a just war by honourable and just means, and not by these ways of blood, which to you is a trade.'

When Smith was gone, the earl called for pen and ink, and wrote his farewell letters to his family; and while he wrote, Paul Morceau, his lordship's servant, went out and bought a number of rings, which they wrapped in parcels, and these were addressed as parting gifts to his children and servants.

The earl's letter to his wife began in these terms:—

My Dear Heart—Hitherto I have been able to send you some consolation in my letters, but alas! I have now none to offer you. There only remains for us our last and best refuge, the Almighty, to whose will we must submit; and when we see how it has pleased Him to dispose of this nation and of its government, there is nothing for us to do, but to put our finger on our lips, and bring ourselves to confess that our sins, with those of others, have drawn these misfortunes upon us, and with tears implore Him to have pity on us.

Having given up their beloved little last stronghold to Duckenfield, the earl advises the countess to retire to some peaceful spot:

Then, having leisure to think of your poor children, you will be able in some way to provide for their subsistence, and then prepare to rejoin your friends above in that happy place where peace reigns, far from differences of opinion.

I entreat you, dearest heart, by all the grace God has given you, to use your patience in this great and cruel trial. If any evil befall you, I should, as it were, be dead; but till then I live in you, who are truly myselfs better part. When I am no more, think of yourself and of my poor children. Have courage, and God will bless you.

I thank the great goodness of God, who gave me such a wife as you, the honour of my family, and for me the most excellent of companions, so pious and deserving, so entirely all the good that can be said, that it is impossible to say enough. I beg, with all my soul, God's forgiveness if I have not sufficiently recognised this great benefit, and with clasped hands I equally entreat you to pardon anything I may ever have done to offend you. I have no time to say more. I implore the Most High to bless you, as well as my dear Mall, Ned, and Billy. Amen! Lord Jesus!

Then followed the few touching lines to

My Dear Mall, My Ned, and My Billy—I remember how sad

you were to see me go away; but I fear that your grief will be redoubled when you learn that you will never see me more in this world. It is my advice to all of you to conquer down your grief. You are all of a nature for that to do you much harm. My desire and my prayer to God is that your life may be happy. Strive to lead it as purely as possible, and shun sin as much as is in your power.

I am able now to give you this advice, having such remembrances of the vanities of my own life that my soul is full of grief. . . . . Love the archdeacon well; he will give you good counsel. Obey your mother cheerfully, and do not be troublesome to her. She is your example, your guardian, your counsellor, your all after God. There never has been, and never will be, one to surpass her worth. I am called, and this is the last letter that I shall write you. May the Lord my God bless you, and keep you from all ill; that is what your father asks in a moment when his pain is so great at leaving Mall, Neddy, and Billy. Think of me.

Derby.

He spent the rest of that day with his two other daughters, and his son, Lord Strange, who had returned from his fruitless journey to London to obtain his father's pardon. It was refused by the members of the House leaving one by one, so that not enough were left to vote. In the morning before his execution they started for Bolton. When he came to the castle gate, four Royalist gentlemen, who were also condemned, came out of the dungeon (by the earl's request to the marshal) and kissed his hand, and wept on taking their leave.

Giving them his blessing, and a few brave farewell and comforting words, the earl passed on, not on his own horse, for it was feared the people might rescue him, but upon a little nag.

Mr Bagalay continues:—

After we were out of the town, people weeping, my lord, with an humble behaviour and noble courage, about half a mile off, took leave of them, then of my Lady Catherine and Amelia, and there prayed for them and saluted them, and so parted. This was the saddest hour I ever saw, so much tenderness and affection on both sides.

The earl, on that last night of lying down to rest on earth, said:—

Once, the thought of dying sword in hand in the fight would not have troubled me; it would something have startled me, tamely to submit to a blow on the scaffold; but now I can as willingly lay down my head upon a block, as ever I did upon a pillow.

The clean shirt he put on next morning, he gave orders was to be his winding-sheet. "I will be buried in it," he said to Morceau.

Then he called for Lord Strange to put on his order, telling him that he should receive it again, and so "return it to my gracious sovereign, ... and say I sent it in all humility and gratitude, as I received it spotless and free from any stain."

The scaffold—which by one of the delicate refinements of Puritanism was fashioned of the old wood from Lathom House—was not ready till three in the afternoon, for the people, with tears and protestations, refused to drive a nail into it.

At last, when it was ready, the earl ascended the ladder, and, standing at the east end, addressed the people. It was a long address, and full of noble and just and eloquent thoughts. Still, when he had done, the block was not ready.

The delay now began to fret him. At last the executioner seemed to be prepared, and, turning once more to the people, Lord Derby said:—

Good people, I thank you for your prayers and for your tears. I have heard the one, and seen the other, and our God sees and hears both. Now the God of Heaven bless you all. Amen.

"How must I lie?" he then asked. "Will anyone show me? I never yet saw any man's head cut off."

Then, after much delay and bungling on the headman's part, Lord Derby:—

Laid him down again, and blessing God's name, he gave the signal by raising his hands.
The executioner did his work; and no other manner of noise was then heard, but sighs and sobs.

CHAPTER 15

Peaceful Times at Knowsley

With the death of the earl perished the happiest and noblest part of Charlotte of Derby. For all its storms, their married life had been a true union. The alliance, which originally could not have been more than one of consent on the part of a marriageable young man and woman, had developed into a gracious, healthy life which sorrow and death itself had no power to destroy. The bud of *the mariage de convenance* had proved a more glorious flower than many a passionate love-match has culminated in. But now the noble heart of James Stanley beat no more with its patriotic devotion, and henceforth Lady Derby had to bear the burden of the endless contest alone.

That for good or for evil, life in its fullest sense was over for her, she tells her friend of years, the Duchess de la Trémoille, in a letter dated 25th March of 1652. The duchess's letters to her are, she says, so full of sympathy and kindness, that if her sorrows could be consoled, Madame de la Trémoille would console them.

> But alas! dear sister, I am no longer able to complain or to weep, since all my happiness is in the grave; and I am astonished at myself that I have been able to endure all my misfortunes, and be still in the world; but that has been the will of God, who has helped me so powerfully, that I do not know myself in having survived all my miseries. The last letters of that glorious martyr give me proof of his affection being beyond all that I deserved to hope; and his dying commands bid me live, and take care of his children...

The body of the Earl of Derby had already been laid by Lord Strange and Mr Bagalay to its rest in the tomb of his ancestors at Ormskirk before Lady Derby knew that the blow had really fallen;

and it is doubtful whether the first intelligence of it reached her by the mouth of friend or foe. When the earl was executed, the countess was busy fortifying the Castle of Rushen, to defend the last possession left them of all their broad territories.

Castle Rushen contained the insignia of the Stanley sovereignty over the Isle of Man—the leaden crown.

When Captain Young landed from the *President* frigate, and, presenting himself before her, commanded her to render up the island in the name of Parliament, she refused, saying, as she had ever done, that she waited her husband's orders.

The earl was dead.

Even after that, knowing the worst, she still refused. She held the island now for her king. Then treachery came to the help of the enemy. William Christian, the receiver-general of the earl, won over the garrison, and surrendered the island to the Parliamentarian fleet, which completely surrounded the coasts.

These Christians had long occupied high positions under the rulers of Man, being deemsters and controllers of special departments of public government. But already more than once the earl had had good grounds for displeasure and mistrust against them. He had some time before deprived Edward Christian of authority in favour of one Captain Greenhaigh; (though he had not withdrawn his countenance from the family of Christian), who, in the meantime, had died. When Lord Derby left Man to go to the assistance of Charles II. he confided the forces of the island to William Christian, this unfaithful Edward's son.

Never was confidence more misplaced. William Christian allowed himself to be corrupted; he admitted the Parliamentary troops into the island at dead of night, and daybreak found Lady Derby and her children prisoners in Castle Rushen. For two months she was detained prisoner in the island; then they let her go free, in a forlorn quest of justice from Cromwell.

"She who had brought to this country fifty thousand pounds sterling had not so much as a morsel of bread to eat, and was indebted for all to her friends, almost as unfortunate as herself."

This William Christian is a great hero with Manxmen. Iliam Dhône, or "Fair-haired William," is the subject of a long and doleful ballad, which is still popular in the island. Eleven years later, when the king had his own again, and the murdered earl's son Edward was once more the Lord of Man, a day of retribution came to William Dhône. He was tried for that day's work of giving up the Isle of Man to the Parliamentarians, and shot for a traitor on Hango Hill. The young earl met with great blame for his part in this act. There were extenuating circumstances for William Christian's actions. The trial was a mock proceeding. A tale goes that a pardon was sent him on the day before the one fixed for his execution, and that it was laid hands on, and intercepted by an enemy, being afterwards found in the foot of an old woman's stocking. The ballad runs:

Protect every mortal from enmity foul,
For thy fate, William Dhône, sickens our soul.

Audi alteram bartem. The Christians and those they represented of the Manx people had had grievances against certain high-handed doings of the late earl, but, the tale all told, sympathy for fair-haired William's fate is not easy to muster; and if it be true that the Countess of Derby had a share in hastening his end, it is not necessary to be blind to the fact that she would, if she could have compassed it, have visited similar lynch-law justice on those "courtmartial" judges who condemned her husband to the block. In her virtues and in her failings—sins, if so they were—there was nothing small about Charlotte of Derby when great crises hung over her.

These past, she was just again the ordinary *grande dame* of her time. The daily round and common task of existence pleased her well enough. Henceforth the remaining years of her life were devoted to two primary ends—the placing in life of her children, and the recovery of her money and lawful possessions. For this last, her fortunes ran side by side with those of the exiled king and of many another devoted Royalist family; but they were at their lowest ebb on the days succeeding Worcester fight. Steady, but so gradual as to be for long imperceptible, was the inflow of the tide; and only the passing years really marked the turn of national affairs.

Parliamentary differences, jealousies of political parties, sectarian bitterness, which it pleased them to call religious opinion, were all seething to the great issue. The powerful mind of Cromwell was not for ever to be proof against myriad influences. If he desired the Crown, he dared not accept it: as he dared not do many things which appealed to his own inclinations.

Having abolished the Anglican Church, he would have reinstated it. Anything was better than the wild fanaticism that was overrunning the land—Anabaptists, Quakers, Muggletonians, Fifth Monarchy Men, *et hoc genus omne*, who, all claiming the one divine spirit, seemed animated by a million devils of hatred, pride, and malice. Haunted by memories, saddened by domestic sorrows and bereavements, grown fearful of the pitfalls for his own death lying in his path, the existence of the Lord Protector was one he must have been well willing to break with.

Colonel Titus promulgating his views of "Killing no Murder" in his tract; Ralph Syndercombe plotting his bloody deed in the little Shepherd's Bush cottage; and how many more biding their time? But it was not so the end came to Oliver Cromwell.

When he had prayed for peace—the much needed peace—for the people and for himself, "Lord, pardon them all," he went on, "and whatever Thou mayst do with me, grant them Thy mercy, and me also. Give them peace." The dawn of 3rd September broke—the anniversaries of Dunbar and of Worcester, Cromwell's "lucky day." Parched with the thirst of his aguish fever, they put a cup of drink to his lips. "I will neither drink nor sleep," he said. "I am thinking only of making haste. I must depart." And so, he died.

And so, when Richard Cromwell had just tasted of the cup of dignities his father had left him, and but too gladly set it down again, and retired to his quiet country home in the lanes of Cheshunt, Charles II. was brought in triumph to Whitehall.

That home-coming is a tale told too often to tell again here even though Lady Derby has much to say about it in her graphic correspondence. Many details of how gracious His Majesty was to her, how handsome but for this or that his queen would be, are mixed up with those of her children's marriages. When those sons and daughters reached marriageable years, the worst of the Royalist troubles were past. There was no difficulty in their making suitable alliances. Amelia was married to the Earl of Athole. Catherine, less happy in her union, became Marchioness of Dorchester. Mary, "dear Mall," became Lady Strafford. Two of her sons died while still children.

Of absorbing interest to herself—as indeed they all might well be—the incidents of court life, and the doings of her children and friends, drag somewhat heavily for us, like the more commonplace though dazzling groupings in some stirring drama whose curtain is about to fall.

Her own little day of life was nearing its setting. She died at a fitting time. The son was not the father. The rebound from Puritanism and religious hypocrisy o'erleaped itself. The licence of Court life soon came to be a scandal and a grief to many of Charles II.'s most loyal servants, as assuredly it might have made the stately martyred king turn in his grave. To the Mistress Nellys and my Lady Castlemaynes nothing was sacred; and when these frail "beauties" had contrived to humble their queen in her own presence-chamber, or to secure a Clarendon's downfall, they were well pleased with their day's work.

With some prescience of this, the Countess of Derby, no longer compelled to remain in London, spent much of her time at Knowsley. Chancellor Clarendon, who had been negotiating arrangements for the restitution of her pension, had left England in disgust at the indifference of the court and the ingratitude of the king, who was prone to make a hand-clasp and a "God bless you, my old friend," do duty for more substantial repayments to impoverished Royalists.

On 6th February 1663 the countess was ill, and writes thus:—

If the winter is as bitter where you are as it is here, it is a miracle to think your health has improved. Mine has been very indifferent for more than a month; but God has preserved it for me. I pray Him to enable me to use it to better account than I have done in the past, and it is that which impels me to hasten to tell you that it has pleased His Royal Highness to give to your nephew Stanley the post of first and sole gentleman of the bedchamber, which is a very desirable one, and, what is of more importance, that it is the voluntary act of His Highness, to whom, and to the duchess, he owes all the obligation. His youngest brother has a cornetcy in the King's Guards. His Majesty has done him the honour to tell him that this is only a commencement. Therefore, I have hope . . . All that I have to add is that I pray God to give you many long and happy years, with all the content you can desire. Permit me to say also as much to my brother.

Here the Countess of Derby lays down her pen for ever. On the 31st March 1664 she died.

The chaplain of Knowsley, after inscribing her name in his death register, wrote after it: "*Post funera virtus*"; and her memory and her works will live on in the hearts of the English people.

This noble friend, true wife and mother, loyal subject, Charlotte de la Trémoille, was the embodiment of all the significance of the motto of her house,

Je maintiendrai.

The Lady of Lathom

Charlotte de la Trémoille, Countess of Derby

Contents

Preface	117
Parentage and Early Days	119
Marriage and First Years in England	128
The Beginning of Troubles	143
The Siege of Lathom House	154
Renewal of Correspondence	178
Letters After the King's Death	192
The Last Days of a Noble Life	205
Widowhood	227
The Year Before the Restoration	241
Life at Court	251
Last Letters	268

Preface

Why has Sir Walter Scott, that great painter of life and character, so completely failed in his portraiture of the Countess of Derby—the "Lady of Lathom" as she is still called in the neighbourhood—who plays such a prominent part in his romance of *Peveril of the Peak*? How is it that, in addition to all the liberties he has taken with historical facts, he has made of this noble lady, as simple as she was heroic, a mere queen of melodrama? It must be because he only knew her by her exploits, and not her personal self at all. Into the depths of her heart he had never penetrated. But, strange to say, we are now enabled to do this.

The veritable and original letters of Charlotte de la Trémoille, Countess of Derby, to her mother, Charlotte de Nassau, and her sister-in-law, Marie de la Tour d'Auvergne, have lately been discovered, by the descendant of these illustrious women, the present Duc de la Trémoille. The correspondence of ancient families has, in France, necessarily gone through strange vicissitudes: these precious papers were found hidden in a barrel at the bottom of a cellar. They are very numerous, and yellow with age and damp. Many of them are in cypher, but the care of the Duchesse de la Trémoille—to whom most of them were addressed—has, in all cases, added the key: so that they are quite intelligible.

The dates would have been difficult to guess at, but that the same sisterly hand has marked them at the back of almost every letter. The whole have been confided to me by M. le Duc de la Trémoille; and thus I have been enabled to study for my own pleasure, and, by his permission, to make public, the inner life of this remarkable woman,—as unfolded by herself to her dearest and nearest of kin, in this correspondence, which extends over forty years. With it I have interwoven a thread of necessary biography, and of the history of the period; in which I have largely made use of an old book, the *Genealogical History of the House of Stanley*; also, Captain Halsall's relation of the *Siege of Lathom House*, and the *State Trials*.

And, although the facts of the trial and execution of Lord Derby are sufficiently well known, I have preferred to give them at length—both because the denouement was indispensable to the drama, and because the portrait of the noble husband ought to stand beside that of the heroic wife. The publications of the Cheetham Society have also assisted me much.

With my thanks to my translators, who have so skilfully reproduced in English—and as yet it appears *only* in English—the story of one Frenchwoman told by another; and my acknowledgments to the Earl of Derby for having lent the portrait of his illustrious ancestress to be engraved here;—I entrust to the goodwill of the British public these curious remains—discovered two centuries after her death—of one of the most notable women in British history.

Guizot de Witt.

CHAPTER 1

Parentage and Early Days

Our lives have not been cast, nor were those of our fathers, in quiet times, and the future does not offer the prospect of more repose to our children; but when we revert to the history of past centuries we find its records darkened by so many political convulsions, so many social revolutions, such sudden and cruel changes in the fortunes of families, that we turn with something like relief to the age in which our lot has fallen, and learn to estimate at its true value the personal security which we enjoy. It is well sometimes to look back to the past, to reflect on its trials and its periods of violence and suffering, that we may refresh our souls by the example of the virtues displayed in those rude and cruel times.

Born in the midst of the religious wars of France, Charlotte de la Trémoille, Countess of Derby, experienced in England all the shocks of the Rebellion of 1640 and of the Protectorate of Cromwell, and died in 1664, only three years after the restoration of Charles II. There was, indeed, no calamity that she had not seen, no sorrow, public or private, that she had not suffered.

France was hardly beginning to breathe under the government of Henry IV., when, at the Château of Thouars, in 1601, Charlotte was born. (The Château of Thouars was situated in that part of ancient Poitou which now forms the department of Deux Sévres.) Her father, Claude de la Trémoille, then in his thirty-fifth year, had been a soldier from his earliest youth, having served in the royal armies against the Protestants. He afterwards embraced the Reformed religion, and, from his rank no less than his merit, soon became one of the foremost men of his party. He sided with the King of Navarre against the League, fought bravely at Coutras, was one of the chief Protestants who went to the succour of Henry III., at that time besieged in Tours by the Duc de Mayenne, and after their reconciliation accompanied the two kings to the siege of Paris.

Henry III. was assassinated just as the French Protestants began to look for the triumph of their faith and the realisation of their hopes. After his death Claude de la Trémoille fought at the side of Henry IV. at Ivry, and at the siege of Rouen. Henry's recantation suddenly extinguished the hopes of Protestantism, and, though its adherents remained faithful, their ardour was gone.

The king had paid dearly for the submission of the League, and had few favours left to bestow upon his faithful companions in arms, who had "carried him on their shoulders on this side the Loire, and who had spent in his service their blood and their substance." M. de Rosny alone was able to maintain his position at court—thanks to a friendship which dated from childhood, as well as to his own able and faithful services. His profoundly politic mind was little fettered by that severity of conscience which chained M. du Plessis-Mornay in his government of Saumur, far removed from the court and its splendours.

M. de la Trémoille did not concern himself with politics; the king had need of his sword—and in 1595, he fought so bravely at the Battle of Fontaine-Française that, as a reward, the property of Thouars was erected into a peerage.

The great Catholic nobles now reappeared at court, and there was no longer any room for the Protestants. Gradually they left Paris, and retired to their estates and *châteaux*, seeking and finding some occupation from time to time in a synod or general assembly of the deputies of the churches. It was at Châtellerault, in 1598, on the occasion of one of these gatherings, that the marriage contract was signed between Claude de la Trémoille, Duc de Thouars, Peer of France, Prince of Tarente and of Talmont, and the most high and *puissant* Lady Charlotte Brabantine de Nassau, daughter of William the Silent, Prince of Orange, and of his third wife, Charlotte de Bourbon Montpensier.

A great heritage was it, this blood of the glorious Nassau race; and the Countess of Derby was destined to transmit it untarnished.

The times were hard for the Reformers. In vain was the free exercise of their religion secured to them by the Edict of Nantes in 1598: the animosity of the court triumphed over the goodwill of the king, and ominous clouds of a mournful future were already gathering over their heads. Restless and undisciplined, the deputies of the churches refused to listen to the wise and loyal counsels of M. du Plessis-Mornay; the political tendencies of the party began to appear; the Duc de Bouillon, deeply compromised in the affairs of the Maréchal de Biron, had just quitted France, and the Duc de la Trémoille now never left his Château of Thouars. He had four children, two sons and two daughters, and he lived in great splendour on his estate, where he gave a magnificent reception to M. de Rosny, who had just entered upon the government of Poitou.

The Duc de Bouillon had been forced to relinquish all his towns and *châteaux*, with the exception of the fortress of Sedan, which belonged to him independently of his sovereign.

M. de Rosny did not conceal from M. de la Trémoille that his brother-in-law was in great danger, and that the king was very much irritated against him.

Henri de la Tour d'Auvergne had owed his marriage with Charlotte de la Marck, heiress of the Bouillons, to the favour of Henry IV. She died, leaving him in possession of all her wealth; and he took for his second wife Elizabeth of Nassau, daughter of William the Silent and of Louise de Coligny, his fourth wife: she was, consequently, the sister of Madame de la Trémoille, and the king's displeasure against the Duc de Bouillon troubled the peace which the family at Thouars had hitherto enjoyed.

M. de Rosny advised M. de la Trémoille to appear again at court. "The king intends to continue the war," he said; "and you must serve against Spain."

M. de la Trémoille was still young; for many years he had lived in idleness, annoyed at not being in active service; and he allowed something like a promise to escape him, which promise M. de Rosny, on his return to court, would not suffer him to forget.

The king was desirous of seeing about him those of his servants who were of the Reformed religion, not thinking it safe to leave them in their *châteaux*, where they might employ themselves in hatching plots.

M. de la Trémoille had resolved to start for the court, in spite of his wife's misgivings and those of M. du Plessis, who was on a visit at Thouars.

"I see no reason for your going, except the words which have escaped your lips," said the Governor of Saumur to him.

"But if I could get employment?" said M. de la Trémoille.

M. du Plessis shook his head.

He had scarcely returned to Bonmoy, near Saumur, when he heard from Madame de la Trémoille that her husband had been seized with gout in the arm, and, if he were not speedily better, she begged him to come to them. On the night of the third day she sent him word that, if he wished to see his friend alive, he must come quickly.

Arriving there he found M. de la Trémoille prostrated with fever, and almost constantly insensible. He recovered, however, from this state of torpor, and showed his joy on seeing M. du Plessis again by many expressions, which, though short and broken, displayed all his usual clearness. He was able to commend to this dear friend his wife and children, who were about to lose him so early, and in such troubled times.

But the cares of this present life were beginning to fade from his view. M. du Plessis spoke to him of his hope of salvation.

"No other matter concerns me now," said the dying man; and, disregarding everything else, he so collected his thoughts that, when anyone spoke to him of a future life, he always replied with some sentence which showed his readiness to die, the full assurance of his faith in Christ, and the clear-headedness for which he had been so remarkable when in health. (*Memoirs of Madame du Plessis-Mornay.*)

He was breathing his last when Madame de la Trémoille, who had never left her husband's pillow except to nurse her daughter Charlotte in smallpox, was told that the Princesse de Condé, sister of the Duc de la Trémoille, wished to see him. She was detained at some distance by an accident to her carriage, and she begged her sister-in-law to send for her.

The Princesse de Condé had been for a long time on bad terms with her brother. Evil reports had been circulated about her at the time of her husband's death. She had been accused of having poisoned him, and had had some trouble to establish the legitimacy of her son, who was born after the death of the prince. Moreover, since 1596, she had abjured the Reformed faith, and had given up the little Prince de Condé, her son, into the king's hands, that he might be brought up in the Catholic religion.

So many offences could not be atoned for by one tardy visit; nor was there even the hope of a reconciliation, for M. de la Trémoille never spoke again.

"I cannot see her," exclaimed the duchess. "She will be the death of her brother, and the sight of her would kill me. M. du Plessis, do not suffer her to come."

M. du Plessis hesitated; he did not feel this matter so keenly as the poor wife. Fully expecting his friend's death, he was unwilling to banish the sister from her brother's dying bed, which perhaps might arouse in her some salutary impressions.

But the Duchesse de la Trémoille, ordinarily so calm, was now beside herself with grief. M. du Plessis was forced to write to the *princesse* as respectful a letter as he could, begging her to put off her visit till another time. She continued her journey without going to Thouars; but she never forgave this affront, which she attributed to M. du Plessis, who had some difficulty in clearing himself with the king on this score.

Just as the Princesse de Condé received the letter of M. du Plessis, her brother died at the Château of Thouars, in his thirty-ninth year, leaving his wife and children to the protection of the Elector Palatine, Prince Maurice of Nassau, the Duc de Bouillon and M. du Plessis, the last of whom was the only one of the three who resided in France, and consequently the only one who could exercise any important influence over the education of the children entrusted to his care. The Duc de la Trémoille had, at his death, desired that his children might be brought up in the Reformed religion.

Great was the sorrow felt, not only at Thouars but throughout the whole Protestant party. The Duc de Bouillon an exile, and the Duc de la Trémoille in his grave,—those of the "Religion," as they were called, had no longer any leaders. M. du Plessis himself, dispirited and out of favour, had not returned to court since the fatal conference he had had at Fontainebleau in 1600, with the Bishop of Evreux, and every day some slight sign indicated but too plainly the coldness of the king. M. du Plessis was reproached for his friendship with M. de la Trémoille, who was the brother-in-law of the Duc de Bouillon, still a rebel. Wherefore, it was asked, did M. du Plessis associate with such malcontents?

Meanwhile the Reformers were uneasy concerning the king's supposed sentiments towards them; more especially when it was known that His Majesty desired to have the little Duc de la Trémoille, who, born in 1599, was only five years old at his father's death, entrusted to him to be educated with the Dauphin.

Madame de la Trémoille was overwhelmed by this news. She had just lost her second daughter, Elizabeth; if the king took her son from her the child would be estranged from the Protestant faith; separated from all his natural connections, he would no longer belong to his mother;—better that she saw him lying in his grave! M. du Plessis, though more guarded in speech than the poor mother, was also much alarmed, and caused it to be represented to the king that the Reformed party would be justly suspicious if all the children destined to be their future leaders were taken away from them; that they had already lost the Prince de Condé; and it concerned His Majesty not to irritate his faithful subjects for the sake of so trifling an advantage as the presence of a child at court.

The king yielded, and Henri de la Trémoille remained at Thouars during the first year of his mother's widowhood.

In 1605, she went alone to court, leaving her children at Thouars, as we learn from the letters she received from her daughter Charlotte.

Amongst the important papers of the Trémoille family, side by side with parchments weighted with pompous titles, or long enumerations of estates and seignorial rights, it is touching to see the ruled paper and the large writing which indicate those first letters written by the child who was destined to accomplish such great things.

Charlotte was about five or six years old when she wrote thus to her mother:—

> *Madame*,—Since you went away, I have become very good. Thank God, you will find me quite learned. I know seventeen Psalms, all the *quatrains* of Pibrac, all the *huitains* of Zamariel, and, above all, I can talk Latin. My little brother is so pretty! he could not be prettier; when visitors come, he is quite enough to entertain them. It seems, *Madame*, a very long time since we saw you. Pray love me, M. de St. Christophe says you are well, for which I have thanked God. I pray to God for you. I humbly kiss the hands of my good aunt and of my little cousins.
> I am, *Madame*,
> Your very humble and very obedient and good daughter,
> Charlotte de la Trémoille.

Most Protestant families have kept up the pious habit of learning the Psalms by heart; some people yet remember the *quatrains* of Pibrac; but who has ever heard of the *huitains* of Zamariel? The measure of the verse and the name of the poet have alike vanished from the memory of man.

It would seem that the Duchesse de la Trémoille was often absent from Thouars while the education of Charlotte was going on. Her children sometimes accompanied her, as we see by a letter of

Charlotte's from Paris, addressed to her brother the little Duc de la Trémoille; but they more often remained in the country while their mother resided at court or visited her Dutch relations. In her absence, however, Madame de la Trémoille kept up the direction of their education; and she was evidently well informed of their faults as well as of their progress, for her daughter writes thus to her at the Hague, in 1609:—

> *Madame*,—I am very sorry that I have been disobedient to you, but I hope you will never again have occasion to complain of me. Although I have not been very good, I hope to be so good for the future that you will have no cause of dissatisfaction; and that *Madame* my grandmamma, and *Messieurs* my uncles, will not find me ungrateful any more, but hoping to render them obedient and very humble service. (The Princess of Orange, Louise de Coligny, Maurice of Nassau, and Prince Frederic Henry, his brother.) This new year they have shown their kindness by giving me beautiful New Year's presents; *Madame* (the Princess of Orange), a carcanet of diamonds and rubies; Monsieur le Prince d'Orange, some earrings; His Excellency, three dozen of pearl and ruby buttons. *Monsieur* my uncle has given me a dress of silver tissue. M. Suart has done what you told him. Pray love me always; and I will remain all my life, *Madame*,
> Your very humble and very obedient
> daughter and servant,
> Charlotte de la Trémoille.

Amongst so many pearls and diamonds let us hope that poor little Charlotte had received from her mother one of those beautiful dolls, in the costume of a Frieslandic lady, with red cheeks, a lace cap, and a gold band on her brow, which must surely have delighted the hearts of little Dutch girls then, as they do still. Later in her life we detect in her a tenderness for dolls, which makes us believe that the associations of her childhood were not exclusively with earring drops and silver-tissue dresses.

Charlotte is again with her mother in 1609, and for ten years the only letters of hers we have are to her brother, the Duc de la Trémoille. Generally separated from his family, he is a very lazy correspondent, sometimes even, to his mother's indignation, employing the pen of a stranger. In 1619, he married his cousin, Marie de la Tour d'Auvergne, daughter of the Duc de Bouillon and of Elizabeth of Nassau; a union which entirely satisfied his mother, and gave to Charlotte a true sister, whose devotion and affection were to endure as long as her life. From the year 1620, we find her at Thouars, with the young Duchesse de la Trémoille. M. du Plessis, also, came to visit them from his Château de la Forêt sur Sèvres. Though sad and lonely, he had evidently considerable influence, and was of much importance in the family of his friend.

Charlotte was at this time nineteen years of age. She does not appear to have been very robust; she had had fever, and tells her mother that she was taken ill at a great dinner. Throughout her life, indeed, her mind was stronger than her body, and her letters often contain accounts of attacks of illness. Her correspondence with her mother, however, is not the less active on that account. She seizes every opportunity of sending her news of their country doings, of the comings and goings, the questions and the answers of M. du Plessis. But her writing, so legible on the ruled paper and under the eye of *"sa mie,"* degenerates sadly. She has no longer time to trouble herself about orthography; she writes in such defiance of rules and principles that it is often necessary to read the sentences aloud to gather her meaning.

Madame la Duchesse de la Trémoille, who used to compliment her on her writing, has no longer any cause for approbation. The silver-tissue dresses, and even the gold fringe, have again become prominent features in the details of her life. The numerous accounts preserved by the Duc de la Trémoille's steward testify to her large expenditure and very decided taste for dress; *Mademoiselle's* jeweller and tailor fill an important place in the family budget. One would like to believe in the truth of a portrait of Charlotte, painted by Rubens at the time of her marriage. It represents her in good health, bright and blooming. She wears a corsage of scarlet satin, and a hat with white feathers, and is looking over her shoulder, and smiling with an arch expression.

Indications of liveliness and animation appear in her letters even through the antiquated formalities of the period, and the profound respect with which her mother inspired her. She writes to her mother:

> I will not repeat the news of this place, M. du Plessis will tell it so much better than I can write it. The subject most spoken of just now is the building of a church.

And, after having consulted her mother to know if she ought to contribute to the undertaking, she adds:

> My brother has not shown us the letter you wrote him, and he has not shown that or any other to my sister-in-law, although

she shows him all hers. She often tells me that he does not take pains to be in as good temper as when you were here; and that she saw you were of the greatest use to him. It seems to me, however, that they get on very well together; although he is often so dull that one cannot coax a word out of him. With me he is always on the best possible terms, and often comes to look for me in my room.

The intimacy between the brother and sister was not to last; but the confidence between the sisters-in-law was destined to go on increasing, in spite of a separation of nearly forty years, and to end only with life.

CHAPTER 2

Marriage and First Years in England

Charlotte must have been again with her mother, who had taken her to Paris, when she writes to her sister-in-law, Madame de la Trémoille:

You will have learned from others how well the arrangement of our fortunes has turned, out, thank God! and how well *Madame* has treated my brother; how much better than he could have ventured to hope. For my part I am not surprised, when I think of her invariable goodness. What she reserves is less for her own benefit, than for that of others.

"*Madame*," as her children always called her, doubtless made her family arrangements with the view of entering on sonic treaty of marriage for her daughter, for at the beginning of 1626, we find them at the Hague, at the Court of Prince Frederic Henry of Nassau, her uncle, the brother of Prince Maurice, who had died the preceding year. The only letter of this period that we possess is addressed by Charlotte to her sister-in-law. According to the custom of the time, she makes no allusion in it to her coming marriage with Lord Strange. The negotiations for this alliance were nevertheless far advanced, as we may gather from the correspondence of the lawyers with the Duchess Dowager.

But Charlotte is out of spirits and not happy in Holland, she writes:

We are in a country where there is very little zeal, and it is entirely without reason that they are suspected of it: as for going to war in defence of religion, that is far from their thoughts.... The French must not look for aid in this country. Your brother, who governs things here as well as he can, is not amongst those who are most content. Indeed, scarcely anybody is content; here as elsewhere all the world complains of its leaders. In fact, I see that the world is a place in which it is very difficult to live; the longer I am in it the more clearly, I perceive this. May it please God to give me His guidance in it, and you, my heart! perfect content.

Can it be the near prospect of her marriage, or only the *ennui* of her life at the Hague, that suggests to Charlotte de la Trémoille these serious reflections? She mingles with them a description of a ballet danced at court before the Persian ambassador:

> He believes that women who dance are good for nothing, but he has been made to change this opinion. He has a good understanding, and is very polite. He thinks that His Excellency is emperor of this country, and cannot be persuaded that the States are above him.

A genuine daughter of the house of Nassau, Charlotte de la Trémoille nourished a little bitterness against the States, and thought this opinion of the ambassador very wise and sensible.

The struggle had already begun which was to terminate in the ruin of the Republican party and the bloody death of the brothers De Witt.

At the Hague, in July, 1626, Charlotte de la Trémoille was married to James Stanley, Lord Strange, son of the Earl of Derby (or "*d'Herbie*," as it was written in France), and Elizabeth de Vere, daughter of the Earl of Oxford. He was only twenty years old—handsome, brave, and cultivated, and descended from a family in itself one of the most illustrious in England, and which had also intermarried with the blood royal. He possessed considerable influence in the counties of Chester and Lancaster, and was heir to the Lordship of the Isle of Man.

Charlotte's great grief on her marriage was her separation from all whom she loved at a time when sea voyages were difficult, often even dangerous, when letters were always long on the road, and were not unfrequently lost. She was destined never to return to France, and, though to the last day of her life cherishing the hope of a re-union, she never again beheld that sister who was so dear—who remained to her so steadfastly faithful.

In conformity with the custom of her day, the Duchesse de la Trémoille accompanied her daughter to England to establish her in her new home. It was the month of August, 1626, more than a year after the accession of Charles I. to the throne of England, and rather less than a year after his marriage with Henrietta Maria, sister of Louis XIII., and daughter of Henry IV. and Marie de Medicis—a princess at once charming and frivolous, capricious and witty, with whom he was passionately in love.

Charles had scarcely begun his reign when serious disagreements arose between him and his people. The great political movement which had gradually changed all the monarchies of Europe into absolute sovereignties had begun to make itself felt in England also. No monarch had adopted the principles of absolutism with greater eagerness than the vain and feeble James I. He had brought up his son in the doctrines that he himself held, and in that romantic visit which Charles had made to Spain to secure the heart as well as the hand of the *Infanta*, the prince had seen royalty under its most majestic and sovereign aspect, rarely opposed, and always certain in the end to rise above all opposition by the force of its own will, obtaining from its followers and the people a respect and devotion almost religious.

> Charles's marriage with the *Infanta* did not take place, but Spanish royalty remained in his imagination the idealization of the regal condition, being in perfect harmony with the natural gravity of his own character, and with a certain dignity, heightened by a little timidity, which made him dread the efforts and the struggles of a liberal Government. (Guizot's *History of the English Revolution*.)

This liberal government, to which neither kings nor people on the continent ever gave a thought, possessed in England an element unknown elsewhere. The old aristocracy were subdued as in France, but a great middle class composed of country gentlemen and *bourgeois* had formed itself there earlier than in other countries, and was rapidly developing. The Reformation had given a great stimulus to the upgrowth of this class; the English people, called on to decide for themselves in matters which concerned their eternal welfare, assumed the right of judgment in political matters; and it was in vain that Charles, by convoking the Parliament, a few months after his accession to the throne, hoped to strengthen the bonds which united him to his people: "disunion was in reality complete, for both the one and the other thought as sovereigns." (Guizot's *History of the English Revolution*.)

The dissensions between the king and the people grew more and more serious, and the dissolution of the Parliament was not long in coming. For six months the king had tried to govern alone, but his growing embarrassments had obliged him to reassemble his Parliament. They had lately pretended to redress the public grievances. Now they accused the Duke of Buckingham, and demanded his banishment. He was the friend and counsellor of the king, as he had been of his father; all the faults of the Royal Government were attributed to him, and the accusations with which the public voice had charged him were now brought against him by the Commons. The duke refuted them, and for the most part with success. But it was his favour and influence with the king that was the point aimed at by the Parliament.

In the month of August, 1626, the young Lady Strange arrived in England, and, it is said, she was for a short time in London in attendance on the Queen Henrietta Maria; but of this I find no evidence in her correspondence.

In August, 1627, we find her at Lathom House, the mansion of her husband in the county of Lancaster, whence she announces to her mother her anticipation of her first-born, adding:—

> The time of our stay here is not yet determined, but if the twenty thousand crowns do not come it will be a hard matter to get away. Your son-in-law is quite well, thank God, and often goes out hunting. On Monday we are to have a great many people here, for it is our wedding-day, and my husband is going from home for several days with a number of gentlemen. He shows me the utmost affection, and God gives us grace to live in much happiness and peace of mind. We are in trouble about the Isle of Man, and if Chateauneuf had been here we should have offered him the charge of it. The appointment is worth a thousand *francs*, and in a place where one can live almost for nothing.

The twenty thousand crowns which Lady Strange expected did not come, and the family remained at Lathom. The Earl of Derby had relinquished this house to his soil, and he himself lived at Chester, where his daughter-in-law paid him a visit, as she writes to her mother towards the end of the year 1627. All her late letters had been lost, as was often the case; and she recapitulates the little events of her life:

> I wrote you word, *Madame*, that I had seen my father-in-law at Chester, where he always lives, never desiring to go to any of his other houses; he has been there now for three or four years. He spoke to me in French, and said very kind things to me,

calling me lady and mistress of the house, a position which he said he wished no other woman to hold; that I had the law in my own hands entirely. We were very well received in the town; though we were not expected many people came to meet us. I told you also, *Madame*, how much I liked Lathom House, and that I had every reason to thank God and you for having married me so happily.

I do not doubt, *Madame*, that you will do everything in your power with regard to my money; indeed I expect this from you, and *certes*, *Madame*, necessity constrains me to importune you in the matter more than I ought; your goodness emboldens me to do so, and truly, my happiness partly depends on it, that I may be able to shut the mouths of some people who do not love foreigners, though, thank God, the best of these wish me no harm. I am thankful to say that your son is now quite well, having had no return of his complaint. He is constantly out of doors, the air being very good for him.

Lord Strange must, however, have come in before his wife's letter was despatched, for the postscript is in his handwriting. Both handwriting and spelling are much better than Charlotte's.

Madame,—I cannot allow my wife to write without myself thanking you for the honour you have done me; if I could write with as much ease in your language as in my own, I would not fail to assure you on all occasions that I shall always be, *Madame*, your very humble and very obedient son and servant,

J. Strange.

The money difficulties which continued to weigh upon Charlotte all through her life were already beginning to trouble her. Her own family was illustrious, powerful, and possessed of great estates, but the late wars had burdened these estates with many debts. Towns and castles belonging to the Duc de la Trémoille had been seized by the League; amongst others the fortress of Rochefort, which M. du Plessis and the Maréchal d'Aumont had in vain attempted to recover. The farmers paid their rents irregularly, and the estates could not be sold; consequently, the Duc de la Trémoille was unable to send his sister's fortune to England.

The historian of the house of Stanley asserts that she received fifty thousand pounds sterling; but, even if so large a sum had been due to her by her brother after their mother's death, and when the heritage of their brother the Count of Laval fell in, I doubt if the house of Derby ever derived such great benefit from it.

The embarrassments of the family with which Charlotte had allied herself were also very great. Lord Derby, the father of Lord Strange, had succeeded his brother in the title; but a considerable portion of the estates was not entailed upon heirs male, but constituted dowries for the three daughters of Ferdinand, the fifth Earl. The division was settled only after numerous and expensive lawsuits; the possession of the Isle of Man especially being the subject of long disputes, which were at last terminated by an Act of Parliament.

William, sixth Earl of Derby, found himself obliged to support all the honour and magnificence of the House of Stanley with a fortune greatly inferior to that of his ancestors. His estates were burdened with debts, and Charlotte's fortune was necessary to clear them.

Since the month of November, 1626, she had received only one sum of twelve hundred pounds sterling, for which we find a receipt. She writes again towards the end of 1627:—

> I am not without anxiety about many things; but God of His goodness will provide for all. I forgot to tell you, *Madame*, that my husband is on the point of doing that which he is bound in honour to do, though I have never said a word to him about it; and he has even fixed the sum at two thousand pounds sterling (her jointure). Although I hope, please God, that I may never need it, yet I shall always feel deep obligation to him. I owe it entirely to his goodness, which makes me still more anxious that he should derive some benefit from my fortune, from which he has as yet received so little help. I am sure, *Madame*, that your goodness will see, even better than I do, what need we have of it, and also how happy it would make me to afford some relief to this house, upon which I have hitherto brought nothing but expense.

But it was in vain for Lady Strange to write, or for her mother to speak: the payment, not only of the capital, but even the interest, of her fortune was delayed; and this was a constant grief to her.

She writes:

> I should be very glad now to have it known that my fortune was not only a thing talked of, but a fact. This makes me very unhappy.

The civil war was now raging in France in all its horrors. Louis XIII. and Richelieu were besieging La Rochelle, while the Duc de Rohan, at the head of the Protestant Army, occupied the country in the southern provinces. His mother, the Duchess Dowager, was shut up in the fortress, within her own house, which, however, she had no wish to leave. "Do not be uneasy about me," she wrote to her son; and both by her words and her example she kept up the courage of the citizens of La Rochelle.

In England, much concern was felt for the dangerous position of the French Protestants; and the Duke of Buckingham resolved to turn this generous sympathy to the profit of his passions and his personal interests. He was in love with Queen Anne of Austria, and being kept at a distance from the French Court by the vigilance of Richelieu, he induced the king his master to declare war against France, proposing that he should himself take command of the fleet which was to attempt the deliverance of La Rochelle. Very little money could be obtained by means of a forced loan to fit out the expedition. The English people distrusted the sincerity of Buckingham's zeal; they might no less have doubted his ability.

On the 29th of October, 1627, the expedition which he led was stranded before La Rochelle, and this misfortune was universally attributed to the incapacity of the leader. Lady Strange expresses the feeling of the court rather than that of the country when she writes to her mother on the 29th of November:

> Here nothing is spoken of but the misfortune which has happened to the duke. He is not blamed for it, but the fault is laid on the delay of the intended succours.

And she adds:

> He has brought back with him M. de Soubise (brother of the Duc de Rohan); I am surprised that he was willing to return. They say that the former is to go out again soon with fresh forces. All this makes me despair of peace. If it were in my power to make any overtures in this direction, which it is not, my distance from Court would prevent my doing so. And, besides, the person who is allied to us takes no part in politics; not so much that he has no taste for them, but he is of a certain disposition unfitted for public life; and, also, he is not liked by the superior powers. (Does she speak here of her husband, of her father-in-law, or of M. de Soubise?) Besides, his power is

not what it once was, and I think it is diminishing. I believe also that peace will only come through those who have begun the war. As for the queen she interferes with nothing, and thinks only of how to kill time. The king and she live very happily together.

Lady Strange was scarcely older than the Queen Henrietta Maria, but she had other things to think of, than of "how to kill time." In the midst of her anxiety for the public welfare, and her desire to see peace re-established between France and England (she seems to have troubled herself very little about the fate of the Protestants of La Rochelle), there reappear continually her natural human interests in the character of wife and mother. Alone, and far away from her own people, she was expecting her hour of trial. She had hoped for the presence of her mother, but in December, 1627, she thus writes to her sister-in-law:—

> I feel very much as you do, my heart, about *Madame's* coming to me; though I longed passionately for it, yet the troubles and dangers which I know she must have encountered made me always dread what has happened. But I trust that God will not forsake me, though I am alone, and do not know much about such matters. May it please Him to give me the same happiness as Madame de Duras:—but, oh! my heart, I must not think about it anymore; I commit myself to God. I know well, my dear, that you remember me in your prayers, and that you rejoice with me in my hopes of motherhood. You may be sure, dear sister, that the child which God may be pleased to give me will be devoted to you.

We have no letter from Lady Strange herself informing her mother of her son's birth; but on the 26th of January, 1628, Lord Strange writes to the duchess:—

> *Madame*—Although we had resolved to send to you by express if possible, yet I have thought it my duty to inform you by letter of my wife's safe delivery of a son. I fear that if you should hear of it from others you might be anxious about her, whereas she is doing well, and the child also, thank God. I must leave it to Mademoiselle de Beaulieu (a midwife who had come from France) to tell you all the particulars. I will only add that we believe her to be now out of danger, this being her seventh day,

and that she will very soon write to you herself. Our joy would have been complete if we could have had the honour of your presence; but that will be when God pleases. That He may long preserve you is the earnest desire, *Madame*, of

> Your very humble and
> very obedient son and servant,
>
> Strange.

Madame, I have not written to your sons about the birth of your grandchild, feeling sure that you would do us the honour of acquainting them with it.

A month later, Lady Strange writes to her sister-in-law, informing her of her confinement, she says, speaking of her child:

> I forgot to tell you that he is dark. I wish you could see the manner in which they swaddle infants in this country, for it is lamentable. Three days after mine was born, he was found in the middle of the night sucking his thumb. Imagine the rest! My husband would have written to you; but he does not like to venture in a foreign language. He is, nevertheless, your humble servant.

And again, on the 17th of April:

> I have written to *Madame* an account of the baptism of your nephew, who, by the grace of God, was received into the Church on Sunday the 30th of March (old style). He was carried by my sister-in-law, and his train was borne by four ladies, the wives of knights of this county. (The Gregorian calendar had not yet been adopted in England; thus, we must always reckon ten days forward in these dates.)
>
> I had him dressed in white, after the French fashion; for here they dress children in colours, which I do not like. The Archbishop of Chester baptised him in the chapel of the castle, and the only name which he received was that of the king, which you know well. Afterwards, there was a collation; and, both on that day and for several days before and after, the dishes at supper were carried by gentlemen of the county.
>
> The king has given him two gilt cups, the usual gift with which he gratifies those on whom he confers the favour of giving his name; but to show us special honour, he has sent me a very pretty present, which is worth quite two thousand crowns: the

diamonds are very beautiful, and are all cut with facets. I did not expect this. The Duchess of Richmond (the godmother) gave him a large basin, and a silver-gilt knife, which is used when the loaves of bread have been removed from the table; and to me she gave a turquoise bracelet.

The young father (he was scarcely twenty-two) had the year before been called to the Upper House by the title of Baron Strange, in consequence of an error in the letters of convocation; it having been forgotten that the Barony of Strange was one of the titles that had fallen into abeyance at the death of Ferdinand, fifth Earl of Derby. This error led to the creation of a new peerage, which reverted in course of time to the House of Athol; and Lord Strange sat for several years in the House of Lords at the same time as his father, the Earl of Derby.

Early in 1628, the king called a new Parliament. Lady Strange said, on the 19th of May:

> I write this in much trouble, for I fear that my husband must go the day after tomorrow to London. This change is doubly vexatious to me, for the air does not agree with him; but I hope God will preserve him. Our little one is very well, thank God. I have already, in two of my letters, begged you to send me some long frocks, and now I must ask you the same thing again, for he is very strong, thank God, for his age; and in this country, where they put into robes infants of a month or six weeks old, I am thought out of my senses because I have not yet given him any. I also begged you for some child's caps.
>
> I hope these will all come together. It will be an amusement for me in the absence of my boy's father, which I dread greatly, for I have never been so far from him before; and in these times there is always something to fear. God grant that all that is resolved upon in this Parliament may be for His glory, and for the good of the king and the country. Here nothing is talked of but the victories of M. de Rohan. I wish I knew the truth about them.

Lord Strange did not go to London. His wife wrote in the month of June, 1628:

> My husband was advised not to go to the Parliament. Things are in great confusion there. One day everything is broken off, on the next all goes smoothly again. God grant that all may end well.

Things were, indeed, "in great confusion," for the two Houses had just passed, and, after a stormy meeting, had forced the king to give his assent to, the bill known under the name of the Petition of Rights, an Act establishing anew, and recapitulating in detail, all the liberties and securities acquired by the English people; immediately after which Charles prorogued the Parliament, on the 26th of June, 1628. Two months later (23rd of August) the Duke of Buckingham was assassinated.

Lady Strange writes to her sister-in-law, on the 21st of September:

> I am sure, my heart, that, before you receive this, you will have heard of the death of the Duke of Buckingham, who was killed by Felton, the lieutenant of a company, to whom he had refused promotion. Felton might very well have made his escape; but a desire to die, and a gloomy disposition, seem to have led him to commit the act. The duke's wife, (Lady Catherine Manners, daughter of Lord Rutland), is very much to be pitied. He loved her devotedly; and she is very good, and the gentlest of women. The king also appeared greatly distressed by the occurrence, and was a whole day without seeing anybody, and without eating till ten o'clock at night. He heard the news at morning prayers; but he did not rise from his devotions. The next day, Sunday, he attended divine service, and sent word to the duchess that he would be as a husband to her, a father to her children, and a master to her servants. You may judge what a great change this will make at Court. God grant that it may be for His glory, and may lead to a happy peace.

Meantime, the subsidies voted by Parliament were levied. Lady Strange writes to her mother:

> To these subsidies the highest people contribute, each according to his means. My husband's great grandfather, whose income was certainly three times as large as ours, was taxed at four thousand *francs*, and yet we have to give as much as he did. This arrangement is very disadvantageous for the nobility; but the people are relieved by it, and the king has no power to levy these subsidies except when they are granted by the Parliament. This is not done every year, but only on extraordinary occasions.

She takes advantage of this opening to press once more for the payment of her marriage portion.

> If Chateauneuf has the honour of seeing you, he can tell you,

Madame, how much I and my house suffer from not having had this sum of twenty thousand crowns. If I had not so good a husband, this would perhaps arouse suspicions in him, which, however, thank God, it has not done. What troubles me most is that, by entering this family, I see I have only increased its debts and expenses. Several of my husband's friends became security for the money which he borrowed at the time of his voyage (to Holland, on the occasion of his marriage), and this he has never yet been able to repay, which is a great grief to him and to me also, for there is nothing which he hates so much as breaking his word.

But all her anxiety about her fortune and her concern for the public welfare were suddenly swept from Lady Strange's mind by a heavy sorrow which now came upon her, and on her mother and sister-in-law. The Duc de la Trémoille set out for La Rochelle, not to join the Protestants who were defending it, but to take his place in the army of the King, Louis XIII. He was received into the Catholic Church by Cardinal Richelieu, and was immediately afterwards appointed Commander of the Light Cavalry of France.

Lady Strange writes to her mother:

> I was not altogether unprepared for my brother's change of religion, it is a long time since I first heard a report of it; and, indeed, it was told as a certain fact to the queen, who, seeing that you, *Madame*, were counted among the converts, said that she did not believe a word of it. This, however, made me doubt about my brother. God has been pleased to send this affliction to you, *Madame*, and to his family. I feel my part of it keenly; more indeed, than I could have believed. The letter which you were so good as to send me from him certainly shows that he has suffered; but I cannot believe what he says, that worldly motives had not more to do with it than anything else; the Catholics, at any rate, speak of it thus.

And in writing to her sister-in-law, who had just given birth to a little girl, she says:—

> I love and honour you with all my heart; and this makes me feel doubly your husband's change of religion, which has been a great blow to me. I can hardly believe it; but I trust that God will change his heart. Certainly, few people, in times like these, could believe that he has not been led to do it from worldly

considerations. In truth, if one were to think only of these, no one would remain long of our religion. I feel much for the pain it will cost you not to follow the stream; nevertheless, my heart, I doubt not that you will be able to resist. God will give you strength greater than your own, and we shall see you doing double service for His glory, inasmuch as you must henceforth stand alone.

Lady Strange had other reasons to be displeased with the Duc de la Trémoille, for she writes to her mother:—

I have been told that if my brother had had the power, he would have possessed himself of my fortune but that the laws of the country do not permit it. He began by changing towards me. I must confess, *Madame*, that but for my respect for you, I do not know to what lengths I might not be driven in consequence of the ill-feeling which he has shown for us.

She concludes by entreating her mother's pardon for her brother, the Count de Laval, who had been for several years living as a refugee in Holland, in consequence of vicious follies which he had committed in France.

While the ladies of the house of Trémoille were mourning over the fall of its head, the English Parliament met again (January 20, 1629), and this time Lord Strange thought it his duty to be present He took with him to London his wife, who was again pregnant, and his son. Three months had not passed before dissensions more bitter than ever arose between the king and his Commons. Parliament was once more dissolved; and Charles boldly announced his intention of governing alone for the future.

Lord Strange was still in London when his wife gave birth to a little girl, who died soon after, having been smothered in its nurse's bed. Lady Strange writes to her sister-in-law:

This affects and grieves me so extremely, that without God's help I do not know what I should do.

But the child was a mere infant, her little boy was well, and the mother seems to have consoled herself very quickly. She returned to Lathom towards the end of the year 1629, and we meet with no more letters from her till October 1631. She writes then in the deepest grief for the death of her mother, which took place at the Château Renard, in the month of August:

> Dear Sister—It has been a comfort to me in my great affliction to receive the honour of your letters, and above all to know that I retain your friendship, which is one of the things that I desire most in this world. I trust that you will always preserve your affection for me, not that I deserve it, but for the sake of her whom we both deplore, seeing that you do not doubt of hers for me, and that I have always loved you next to herself Now that God has taken her from us I put you in her place and pay you all the respect, duty, and love, that I felt for her God . . . has taken her away to punish us and to make her happy. I never liked the Château Renard; she was so far from all her children, and had no sort of amusement near her; but God intended by this means to wean her from the world. For myself I confess that I no longer find any pleasure here
> You desire me to tell you of my brother the Count de Laval's sorrow: I did not see him till three days after this news reached us: I saw him shed a few tears, but very soon afterwards he was as gay as ever. I must confess, that if I were in his place, I should never be happy again. I cannot tell whether he tries to deceive himself; but at least he expresses no sorrow for the past. He only sees me occasionally, and he shows an impatience in my presence and a desire to escape out of the house. I hear such different accounts of him that I do not know what to believe.

This was written from Chelsea, where Lady Strange had been living for some months. She there gave birth to a little girl, who received the name of Henrietta Maria at her baptism; probably the queen was her godmother, the little Charles not being able to receive that honour because his godfather had been the king. About the same time a second daughter, named Marie Charlotte, was born to the Duchesse de la Trémoille.

Six months passed during which no letters have been preserved; but in March, 1632, we find Lady Strange again in London, on her way to the Hague, probably to arrange the affairs of Charlotte of Nassau. Some differences had lately arisen between the Duc de la Trémoille and the Count de Laval, which caused their sister much distress. She writes:

> I hope your husband will comply with the last wish of her who brought us all into the world. For your part, dear sister, I doubt not that your goodness and generosity will surmount all other considerations.

The generosity and indulgence of the Duchesse de la Trémoille were more than once to be put to the test by the Count de Laval. He had had several children by an Englishwoman, Miss Orpe. In 1634, this person, being in London, set up a claim to be his wife, and assumed the name of Countess de Laval, a proceeding which greatly disturbed Lady Strange, who wrote on the subject to her sister-in-law.

But her chief trouble still continued to be the money from France, which either did not come at all, or reached her only after it had been diminished by exchange. The rents due at Christmas were still unpaid at Midsummer. She writes on the 20th of October, 1638:

> Forgive me, dear sister, for speaking to you so frankly, but I do it because I know you to be too reasonable and just to consent to anything which is neither. I have no doubt that your son has by this time arrived in Holland (he had passed through London, but his aunt had not seen him). He will not find things there so prosperous as usual; God grant that he may have found the Prince of Orange in good health.

Here the correspondence breaks off: from 1638, to 1646, we have only one letter, written in 1640, on the occasion of the death of Mademoiselle de la Trémoille. Letters in these times were often lost on the road; and those which have been preserved in French families have passed through many vicissitudes. Yet this was the most important period of the life of Charlotte de la Trémoille; although in the whole correspondence, stretching over so long a time and continuing for fifteen years beyond this date, not one single allusion is made to those events which have rendered her name illustrious.

She seems simply to have done what she believed to be her duty, without seeing anything extraordinary in it, and, after the work was once accomplished, her thoughts appear never to have gone back to the past. Happily, her story is here taken up by history, and the documents of the time enable us to make up for the silence of Lady Strange, who was now soon to become Countess of Derby.

CHAPTER 3.

The Beginning of Troubles

Since the year 1637, the old Earl of Derby, weary of life, had resolved to relieve himself of the cares attendant on the management of his property; and had resigned everything into the hands of his son. Lord Strange, only reserving for himself a pension of one thousand pounds sterling, to enable him to live in comfort at a country-house which he had purchased on the banks of the Dee, near Chester. In 1640, Lord Strange was associated with his father as Lord Chamberlain of Chester, and in 1642, on his father's death, he succeeded to the title, and Charlotte de la Trémoille, "Madame Strange," as she was called by her relations in France and Holland, took the name which she has made famous—that of Countess of Derby.

Till within a short time of his father's death Lord Strange had continued to live on his estates, far from the Parliament, and the contests that were being carried on there. Taking no part in politics, though faithfully attached to the king and the ancient constitution of England, he spent his time in intercourse with his friends, in hunting, and in maintaining by turns, in his different houses in the counties of Lancaster and Chester, a princely hospitality, surrounded by his hereditary retainers,—by this means preparing, almost unconsciously, the assistance which he was soon to bring to the king.

He had never solicited for himself or for any of his relations either place or favour; nor had he ever profited either by his own connection with the royal family (he was descended from the Duchess of Suffolk, sister of Henry VIII., who had been at one time Queen of France), or by the family ties which the marriage of Lady Derby's cousin, the Prince of Orange, with the Princess Henrietta Maria, had established between that princess and the countess. He wished for no higher position than that of an English nobleman, living on his estates, apart from the court and its favours.

But when the court had no longer any favours to bestow, he left his retirement, and was one of the first who joined the king at York, where Charles then was, making preparations for the war which had now become inevitable. He brought to the royal cause the support of his name and his arms, and was ready to devote to it both the last drop of his blood and the last farthing in his purse. A noble aim and end—to which alas! his devotion did indeed attain.

Up to this time, 1642, negotiations were still being carried on between the king and the Parliament, but the breach between them was becoming wider every day. Many members of both Houses had joined Charles at York, and great numbers of noblemen and country gentlemen had offered him their services. But, notwithstanding the enthusiasm which the cause and person of the king were beginning to inspire, the Parliamentary Commissioners found that there was a growing division amongst the Royalists; for when it was proposed that a royal guard should be levied from among the gentlemen of the neighbourhood, more than fifty, at the head of whom was Sir Thomas Fairfax, refused to give in their names; and at a meeting of freeholders, summoned by the king himself, a petition was circulated beseeching him to banish all thought of war, and to be reconciled with his Parliament, and a copy of this Sir Thomas Fairfax contrived to place on the pommel of the king's saddle, at the risk of being trampled under his horse's feet.

Neither money, arms, nor even provisions were to be found at York; and, while the loan voted by Parliament was carried by acclamation, the king's commissioners had the greatest difficulty in collecting from house to house a few trifling contributions, which scarcely sufficed for the support of the royal household. No actual preparations for war had been begun, but the overstrained cord was nearly broken.

The proposals of accommodation sent by the Parliament arrived at York on June 17, 1642, and at once dissipated all hopes of peace. The Houses demanded the complete abolition of the royal prerogative, and claimed for themselves the sole exercise of power. On reading these propositions the king could not restrain his anger.

> If we were to grant what you demand, we should remain but the image, the sign, the empty phantom of a king, (and he broke off the negotiations.)

The Parliament had been prepared for this termination, and as soon as they received intelligence of it the question of civil war was put to the vote. Only forty-five members voted against it in the House of Commons; and in the House of Lords the Earl of Portland alone protested. The formation of an army was therefore decreed, and the Earl of Essex was appointed Commander-in-Chief

The king, on his side, assembled his faithful subjects about him, and in the foremost ranks of his growing army we find Lord Strange, who had already raised among his own dependants a body of three thousand men, well supplied with arms and provisions; but on finding that the king was destitute of everything at York, and unable to procure arms, he gave up to him at once the whole contents of his arsenals, receiving a promise that he should be supplied afresh from Newcastle, where a magazine had begun to be formed. But this order was never executed; neither did Lord Strange ever receive the sum of money which the king afterwards allowed him as payment for the arms which he had given up.

This faithful servant of the Crown writes:

> I shall only say that this might show the king my good intention in the discharge of a good conscience and the preservation of my honour, in spite of envy and malice. (Seacome's *Historical and Genealogical Account of the House of Stanley*.)

Envy and malice had, in fact, begun to take alarm at the arrival at court of a young man who was so powerful in his county that the people used to say, "Long live the King and the Earl of Derby!"

He was always surrounded by friends and servants, ready to follow him to the field of battle; but says the historian of the house of Stanley:

> Whether this was more to continue a custom, or for the love of his name or person, was hard to say.

The king had resolved to set up his standard, and for the encouragement of his partisans, both nobles and people, had already passed in person through several counties, everywhere earnestly recommending prudence as well as zeal, and proclaiming boldly his attachment to the religion and laws of his country. By two unsuccessful attempts upon Hull and Coventry he had given the Parliamentarians occasion to charge him as the aggressor. But the two parties still hesitated, and, while awaiting the final decision, a meeting was held to fix upon the most convenient place in which to set up the royal standard. At this meeting Lord Strange was present, and, after listening to the arguments put forward in favour of Nottingham, Chester, York, Shrewsbury, and Oxford, he spoke "with a calm and quiet humility," says his biographer.

He hoped that the king would take into consideration the claims of the county of Lancaster, urging that it lay as the centre of those counties which were favourably disposed to the royal cause; that the people were usually very hardy, and made good soldiers; that they were all loyally disposed; that he himself, though the unworthiest of his lieutenants, would, to the utmost of his estate, contribute to his service; that he durst promise 3,000 foot and 500 horse, and that he made no doubt but in three days he could enlist 7,000 men more, thus furnishing to His Majesty, in the county of Lancaster alone, an army of 10,000 men, to which the accesses from neighbouring counties might in a short time arise to a considerable army; and he hoped His Majesty would be able to march to London walls, before the rebels there could form an army to oppose him. (Seacome's *House of Stanley*.)

The personal influence of Lord Strange was evidently very great—so long as he was present. To the dissatisfaction of the court party, who were opposed to him, the king resolved to set up his standard at Warrington, in the county of Lancaster, and commissioned Lord Strange to proceed thither and prepare the people for his reception. He set out, therefore, doubtless seeing Lady Strange at Knowsley by the way, and, immediately on his return to Lancashire, he mustered his friends and the king's adherents in three places—on the heaths by Bury, at Ormskirk, and at Preston,—to the number of at least sixty thousand men, all well-armed.

Having thus seen his hopes crowned with success, Lord Strange intended to have repeated his efforts in Cheshire and in North Wales, where he was lieutenant; but in his absence his enemies had regained their influence over the king, and had urged many reasons against entrusting him with power. It was insinuated that the house of Derby was very powerful in two or three counties; that the old earl was near his end; that Lord Strange was ambitious, and no favourer of the court, but rather a malcontent; that these levies of troops, about which so much noise was made, were intended to conceal his ambitious designs, for he knew too well his near alliance to the Crown; that those of his name had not always been faithful to the side which they seemed to favour, as witness Lord Stanley, his ancestor, who, though he fought with Richard III. at Bosworth, giving him his son as a hostage, yet turned the battle against him, and crowned, on the field, his own son-in-law, the Earl of Richmond.

It was known also that his Uncle Ferdinand had boldly declared his pretensions to the throne, and that he himself had married a French lady, a Huguenot, brought up in the pernicious principles of the Low Countries—of that house of Nassau which had headed the revolt of the United Provinces. All these things were dangerous and of evil example; it was not safe for His Majesty to trust himself in such hands. (Seacome's *House of Stanley*.)

Such arguments as these roused the king's suspicions, and, suddenly changing his plans, he announced his intention of erecting the royal standard at Nottingham; he hastily divested Lord Strange of the lieutenancy of Chester. and North Wales, and associated with him in that of Lancaster, Lord Rivers, who had recently been made an earl.

This news reached Lord Strange in the midst of his preparations for the king's reception, and gave him some trouble and anxiety of mind, says his biographer:

> Yet, agreeable to his great temper, he quickly recovered himself, and replied to the messenger:—
> 'Let my master be happy, though I be miserable, and if they consult well for him, I shall not be much concerned what becomes of me. My wife, my family, and country are very dear to me; but if my prince and my religion be safe, I shall bless even my enemies who do well for them, though in my ruin.'
> Then, with the advice of his friends, whose counsel he always asked in cases of difficulty, he despatched a messenger with letters to the king, (to assure him of his fidelity, declaring that, though his enemies might prevent him from serving his sovereign according to his birth and quality), yet he would never draw his sword against him; that he did submissively resign the lieutenancies of Cheshire and North Wales to His Majesty's disposal, but besought him to take away that of Lancashire also, rather than subject him to the reproach and suspicion of a partner in that government. (Seacome's *House of Stanley*.)

By this frank submission Lord Strange obtained the removal of Lord Rivers, and secured for himself the sole command of Lancashire. But the country gentlemen and the friends and dependants of the house of Derby were not all so high-minded as their chief; the ill-usage to which he had been subjected was highly resented by them, and proved of the greatest prejudice to the king's affairs in the counties both of Lancashire and Cheshire. Many gentlemen retired to their country seats, resolved not to risk their lives and property in the service of a prince who knew so ill how to reward the zeal of his subjects. Others, in great numbers, went over to the Parliament, foreseeing that these counties, being deprived of their hereditary leader, would never take up arms in the royal cause; and that, in the end, the Parliament would triumph in a part of the country which had at first seemed wholly devoted to the king.

The discontent was, indeed, so decided that the Commons offered Lord Strange an appointment in their army, or whatever power he chose in the county; but he rejected the offer with indignation, and prepared at once to rejoin the king, who had set up his standard at Nottingham on the 28th of August, 1642, and who had written to recall him with his own hand.

Although Lord Strange's authority was still considerable in Cheshire and Lancashire, yet the position of affairs had greatly changed within the last two months. He represented to the king that, the Parliament having seized upon Manchester, many gentlemen of the county had joined them, while others had declared their intention of remaining neutral; and that he could not venture upon a general muster of the county even in those parts which had remained faithful, so greatly had he suffered from the suspicions of which he had been the object. He was forced to lie content with raising amongst his own relations, friends, and tenants three regiments of foot and three troops of horse; and these he equipped and armed al his own expense, hastening with them to the king at Shrewsbury as soon as they were ready to march, that he might receive his commands for their disposal.

The king ordered them to attack Manchester, and desired Lord Strange to send the necessary instructions to Colonel Gilbert Gerrard, one of his lieutenants, and an experienced soldier. The rivers were so swollen that the march of the troops proceeded slowly, and Lord Strange (who had now just become Earl of Derby) was despatched to Manchester by the king's express command, with orders to hurry on the assault in person.

On his arrival before the town he summoned the rebels to surrender upon honourable terms; but his proposals were obstinately rejected, and he was preparing for an attack on the following day when letters arrived from Shrewsbury during the night, informing him that the Parliamentary Army was then on its march from London, under the command of Lord Essex; that the king stood in need of all his forces to oppose the rebels:

> That, if the town was not carried, he should not hazard any of them by an assault; that, if the king carried the battle against Essex, those small garrisons would fall of themselves; and that his lordship should, on receipt of these letters, forthwith advance to him with what forces he had. (Seacome's *House of Stanley*.)

Painful as it was to him, Lord Derby did not hesitate to obey the king's commands. To the regret of all his officers and soldiers, he left a place which he felt sure that he could have reduced at the first assault—left it without striking a single blow. He began his march at five the next morning, and in two days arrived at Shrewsbury with his three regiments of infantry and three troops of horse, intending to form them into a brigade for the king's service.

But he had reckoned without his host—not remembering his enemies at court. (The chronicler nowhere betrays the names of these enemies; but pursues them with his hatred under cover of the anonymous.) The king's mind had been already prejudiced against him, and soon after his arrival the command of the troops which he had himself raised, paid, and armed was taken from him, and bestowed upon other officers. Charles gave him no other reason for this act of injustice than that the duties of the earl's office necessitated his presence in Lancaster, whither he was desired to hasten, and do all in his power to watch the movements and check the progress of the rebels in that county.

His biographer says:

> The earl, though a person of great temper, was yet of as great a spirit He was so ruffled at this unkind usage that he could scarce contain himself; but in a little time, recovering from his great surprise and concern, he replied to the king:—
> 'Sir, if I have deserved this indignity, I deserve also to be hanged; if not, my honour and quality command me to beg your justice against those persons who, in this insolent manner, abuse both me and Your Majesty. And if any man living (Your Majesty excepted) shall dare to fix the least accusation upon me that may tend to your disservice, I hope you will give me leave to pick the calumny from his lips with the point of my sword.'
> The king, with a smooth countenance, appeared to entertain no displeasure against his lordship; but said:—
> 'My Lord, my affairs are troubled; the rebels are marching against me, and it is not now a time to quarrel amongst our-

selves. Have a little patience, and I will do you right.' (Seacome's *House of Stanley*.)

The earl was silent, and restrained his anger; but the treatment he had received could not be kept secret. A report of the matter soon spread through the army; his soldiers, draughted into other regiments, bluntly refused to serve; his friends murmured, and he saw that he must interfere. The king had said truly that this was not a time for the Royalists to quarrel amongst themselves. He, therefore, exerted himself to calm the irritation of his friends; and when he left Shrewsbury for Lathom House, he had prevailed on his soldiers to serve the king dutifully, as he should himself do, notwithstanding what had happened.

The Parliamentarians in Lancashire very soon learnt that Lord Derby had reason to complain of his treatment at court, and thinking this a fit moment to make another effort to attach him to their party, they sent him a letter containing fresh offers from the Parliament, in nearly the following words:

> That he could not but be very sensible of the indignity put upon him at Court by the king's evil counsellors; that those enemies were the enemies of the nation; that they struck at religion and all good men, and would permit none but Papists, or people popishly affected, to be near His Majesty; that it was the whole intent of the Parliament to remove men of such desperate and pernicious principles from his person, and to secure the true Protestant religion; and that if his lordship would engage in that good cause, he should have command equal to his own greatness, or any of his ancestors. (Seacome's *House of Stanley*.)

Lord Derby had restrained his anger before the king at Shrewsbury, but he could not contain himself on receipt of this message from the Parliament. Without giving himself the trouble of writing, he said to the colonel who delivered the letter:

> Pray tell the gentlemen at Manchester, and let them tell the gentlemen at London, when they hear I turn traitor, I shall hearken to their propositions; till then, if I receive any other papers of this nature, it shall be at the peril of him that brings them. (*House of Stanley*.)

By this time the Earl of Essex was at the head of his army, while the king was still engaged in raising forces to oppose him. Towards the end of September, the Parliamentary troops numbered about twenty thousand men, and those of the king nearly twelve thousand. Charles gave the command of his cavalry to Prince Rupert, who had just arrived from Germany, and who, daring and unprincipled, brave, and accustomed to the rudeness of German warfare, overran the country, pillaging and ravaging in all directions, and bringing the king's cause into bad repute with the people, without rendering him much service in the field.

Charles had resolved to march direct upon London, and put an end to the war at one blow; Essex, who had advanced as far as Worcester, turned back to intercept him, and the two armies came up with each other at Edgehill, on the 23rd of October, 1642, where a fierce engagement took place, with, however, no decisive advantage on either side. The next day the king found that his army was too much weakened to renew the attack. Hampden, Hollis, and Stapleton pressed Essex to risk another engagement, but their advice was opposed by the military commanders: Essex therefore fell back upon Warwick, and the king established his headquarters at Oxford, of all the large towns in the kingdom the one most devoted to his cause.

For a short time, his affairs seemed to improve: many towns opened their gates to him; at Brentford, only three hours' march from London, a slight engagement took place. But it was now the middle of November; warlike operations were becoming difficult, and the king returned to Oxford, where he took up his winter quarters.

While the two principal armies remained thus inactive, several expeditions of little importance were attempted in various parts of the country. In some places confederations were formed, holding commissions either from the king or the Parliament, according to their several views. In others, influential noblemen or wealthy country gentlemen equipped bodies of men at their own expense, and carried on a warfare in their immediate neighbourhood, in the name of the party which they had embraced.

On one occasion Lord Derby defeated three such companies of infantry, who had advanced within six miles of Lathom on their march across the country to join the Parliamentary Army. This exploit made some noise, and brought reinforcements to the little body of men that he had again gathered together with infinite difficulty; for he had been left entirely without arms and ammunition, after having twice given up his stores to the king.

He now occupied himself in fortifying his own house at Lathom, taking especial care to supply the castle with provisions, and troops for the defence of his wife and children, whom he left there during his distant journeys; for he was obliged to be constantly in the field, forcing the Parliamentarians to remain shut up in the towns which they had seized, the number of which was rapidly increasing.

In the beginning of March, 1643, Lord Molyneux came into Lancashire to recruit his regiment, which had only lately been formed out of the troops brought by Lord Derby to Shrewsbury, and which had been much shattered at Edgehill. Lord Derby immediately applied to him for assistance to besiege the Parliamentary garrisons at Lancaster and Preston. Lord Molyneux consenting, they left Lathom House on the 17th of March, at nightfall, and, after a forced march of about thirty miles, the little army appeared the next morning before the walls of Lancaster. The garrison was summoned to surrender, and indignantly refused; the soldiers hesitated to make a second attack, when the Earl of Derby, seizing a short pike, sprang forward, crying, "Follow me!"

Some gentlemen volunteers immediately joined him, and urged the soldiers on. The assault was made, the city taken, and the fortifications razed. Allowing the troops but a few days for rest. Lord Derby marched on Preston, and reduced it also on the 21st of March. The value of this success was considerably diminished by the obstinate resistance of the town of Manchester, which was occupied by a body of fierce Parliamentarians. Lord Derby had proposed to make the attack while the alarm of the enemy was still fresh, in order to encourage those friends whom the king had in the place. He promised, if Lord Molyneux would continue to give him his co-operation, to take Manchester, or leave his bones there.

Lord Molyneux at first refused; then, yielding; to Lord Derby's arguments, he apparently consented to accompany him, and during the night the little army advanced as far as Chorley; but they had scarcely reached that place when an express from Oxford ordered Lord Molyneux to rejoin the king immediately. Lord Derby, in despair, begged for a delay. Four days would suffice to take Manchester—His Majesty would pardon the detention in consideration of so great a success. But Lord Molyneux and his officers were inflexible. At length, pushed to extremity by the importunity of the earl, they produced their commissions authorising them to recruit their regiments from the troops that the earl had just levied in Lancashire.

The blow was sharp, and the insult evident. Lord Derby saw himself not only deprived of his auxiliaries just when their aid was most needed for the king's service; but, for the second time, the troops he had raised with so much difficulty, equipped and trained at his own expense—those very men who had just given so striking a proof of their valour—were taken from him. There was nothing now for him to do but to retire to Lathom, leaving the Parliamentarians to attack the little town of Wigan, in which he had recently placed a garrison under the command of Major-General Blair, a Scotchman, who had been recommended to him by the king.

Wigan was taken and pillaged—the communion cups even were carried off from the church, and one of the Puritan preachers hung them round his neck as the spoil of idolatry. So much contumely might well have crushed the strongest heart; but a deep sense of duty and of the goodness of his cause upheld the earl. He silenced the murmurs that rose around him against the injustice of the Court, and repeated the fine passage from Tacitus: "*Pravis dictis factisque ex posteritate et fama metus.*"

There was fighting in all parts of the country, though the war could not properly be said to have recommenced, nor the struggle to have yet become characterized by any violent animosity. In the middle of February, the arrival of the queen gave affairs a new impulse. She landed at Burlington, and was received by the Duke of Newcastle, who conducted her to York, where she stationed herself There was much stir at her court. Hamilton and Montrose had returned from Scotland full of schemes for bringing over that kingdom to the king's side; while, at the same time, the queen herself was carrying on negotiations with certain of the Parliamentary leaders who had become weary of their cause. The hopes of the Royalists were reviving everywhere in the North.

Proposals for resuming negotiations of peace were made to Parliament; and, in spite of their secret anger, the Commons were obliged to send five commissioners to Oxford for twenty days to arrange, first, a suspension of arms, and afterwards a treaty of peace. But all this was rendered of no effect by the king's obstinacy, aided as it was by the manoeuvres of those adherents of the queen who wanted no negotiations to be entered into without her sanction. The king finished by declaring to the Commissioners that he was willing to return to the Parliament if they would transfer their place of sitting to twenty miles at least from London. At this repulse, the Parliament recalled their commissioners by so peremptory a message that they had not time to wait for their carriages, but left the same day on horseback. They reached London as Essex opened the campaign of 1643.

CHAPTER 4

The Siege of Lathom House

While the negotiations were going on at Oxford, the Earl of Derby, who had returned to Lathom, and was trying to muster new forces for the king's service, received an express from Charles to the effect that his enemies had formed a project to seize the Isle of Man; that they had a party in the island in confederacy with them, and that without speedy care it was in danger of being lost. The king thanked him for his loyal services in England, and urged him to direct his efforts towards preserving the Isle of Man by proceeding thither as fast as possible. (*House of Stanley*.)

The earl was not deceived with regard to the purport of this advice when he read the despatch. He exclaimed to his wife, with more than ordinary quickness:

> My heart, my enemies have now their will, having prevailed with His Majesty to order me to the Isle of Man, as a softer banishment from his presence and their malice. (Seacome's *House of Stanley*.)

For the first time the earl hesitated to obey he said:

> I, that have, with the few that durst take my part, hitherto kept the greater part of Lancashire in subjection to His Majesty, in spite of his enemies, must now abandon my family, friends, and country's safety to the malice of a wicked multitude, without either mercy or compassion. (*House of Stanley*.)

In the *History of the House of Stanley*, written by Seacome, the steward of Lord Derby, grandson of Earl James, we find at this time some fragments of the earl's memoirs:—

"It being now known, that the queen was at York with great forces, I was advised and requested by the loyal gentlemen then with me, to go to Her Majesty, and represent to her our distressed state, and the necessity of giving us speedy help and relief; which I complied with, leaving the few forces I had in Lancashire under command of Lord Molyneux, who gave me in the end as much trouble as the enemy; and I set out for York."

Essex had taken Reading from the king's troops, and Hampden urged him to besiege Oxford; but the general refused. He had engaged in the war unwillingly, and he was not quite sure of his army.

The king's cause began to look more hopeful. An important plot in his favour had been discovered in London; and, though the persons engaged in it had been severely punished, the fact of the plot existing in the heart of the City alarmed the Parliament. A fresh blow extinguished the confidence and well-nigh the hopes of the whole party. On the 19th of June Hampden was wounded in a cavalry skirmish with Prince Rupert. A prisoner said:

> I saw him quit the field before the action was finished, contrary to his custom; his head was hanging down, his hands leaning on his horse's neck.

Five days after, on the 24th of June, Hampden expired at the age of forty-nine—suddenly cut off from all the hopes, and escaping alike the perils and the crimes, of the future.

> Happy and but too rare fortune, which thus fixed his name for ever on that height whither the love and full confidence of his contemporaries had carried it, and perhaps saved his virtue, like his glory, from the rocks on which revolutions drive and wreck the noblest of their favourites. (Guizot's *History of the English Revolution*.)

With the death of Hampden fortune seemed to desert his party. Lord Fairfax, father of Sir Thomas, was defeated at Atherton Moor, in the North; Sir John Hotham was on the point of surrendering Hull to the queen; Lord Willoughby declared he could no longer defend Lincolnshire against the Duke of Newcastle; Sir William Waller had been twice beaten in one week. The triumphant queen was preparing to join the king at Oxford.

She had promised forces to the Earl of Derby to enable him to hold the county of Lancaster; but the frivolous courtiers who surrounded her had no sympathy with the proud and austere nobleman who was indifferent to their good graces, but served his Sovereigns without favour or baseness. "A vexatious accident," says the earl in his memoirs.

Captain Halsall, (*Journal of the Siege of Lathom House*), to whom we are indebted for the narrative of the siege of Lathom, says:

> The defeat of Lord Goring at Wakefield, prevented the troops from being sent off.

The earl continues:

> In my absence the enemy possessed themselves of the whole country, saving my house and Sir John Girlington's . . . . . and my troops taking a march towards York in hopes of meeting me there, were disappointed: which verified the old proverb, 'Ill fortune seldom comes alone.' For at that time a report was spread that some Scots, intending to assist the Parliament, would land in the north, and in their way endeavour to take the Isle of Man.

The Earl of Derby, however, did not give much heed to this rumour, and retained his desire to accompany the queen to Oxford, where the king was; but His Majesty had other views, as the earl wrote to his son. Lord Strange, in the memoir we have already quoted from:

> I had received letters from the Isle of Man intimating the great danger of a revolt there; for that many people, following the example of England, began by murmuring and complaining against the government, and from some seditious and wicked spirits had learned the same lessons with the Londoners, to come to court in a tumultuous manner, demanding new laws, and a change of the old; that they would have no bishops, pay no tithes to the clergy; despised authority, and rescued some who had been committed by the governor for insolence and contempt. It was also reported that a ship of war, which I had there for a defence of the island, was taken by the Parliament's ships; which proved true. And that it was judged by the queen and those with her, (as Lord Goring, Lord Digby, Lord Jermin, Sir Edward Deering, and many more,) that I should forthwith go to the island to prevent the impending mischief in time, as well for the king's service, as the preservation of my own inheritance.

This resolution, which cost the earl so much, was attributed by his enemies to a cowardly desire to withdraw himself from the struggle. He writes in his memoir, in a letter to his son:

> It has been said that I wished to become neutral, and many such like invidious and malicious suggestions to my prejudice. But I bless God, I am fully satisfied with my own conduct and integrity of heart, well remembering all those circumstances, as well as the wicked insinuations of my implacable and restless enemies.
>
> How others may be satisfied herewith I know not, but think this short relation, for want of time to set things in a fuller light, may rather puzzle the minds of the readers, if any should chance to see it but yourself; but you, my son, are bound to believe well of your father, and I to be thankful to Almighty God that you so well understand yourself and me: as for others, I am unconcerned whether they understand me or not.
>
> Upon the above advice by the queen and friends, I returned to Lathom; and having secretly made what provisions I possibly could of men, money, and ammunition, for the defence and protection of my wife and children against the insolence and affronts of the enemy, prepared for my speedy voyage to the Isle of Man, taking with me such men and materials as might answer those purposes I was sent about.
>
> Leaving my house and children, and all my concerns in England to the care of my wife, a person of virtue and honour equal to her high birth and quality, who being now left alone, a woman, a stranger in the country, and (as the enemy thought) without friends, provisions, or ammunition, for defence or resistance, concluded that Lathom House would fall an easy prey to them; to which purpose they procured a commission from the Parliament to reduce it by treaty or force. (*House of Stanley*.)

The earl had scarcely left England when Lady Derby received proposals from Mr. Holland, Governor of Manchester for the Parliament, which she was called on either to accept, or to surrender her house. Her reply was not what was expected. "It did not suit her," she said, "either humbly to give up her house, or to purchase repose at the price of honour." Lord Derby's efforts, however, had not succeeded in furnishing the house with sufficient provisions and ammunition for a long siege, and the countess therefore asked to be permitted to remain in peace at Lathom, giving up the land entirely to the good pleasure of the Parliament, and reserving only for herself a sufficient garrison of men at arms to protect herself and her household from the insults of the soldiers. She obtained this favour with great difficulty.

For eight months she remained a prisoner in her house and park, rarely going beyond the courts that surrounded the house lest she should meet with some affront. Deprived of the revenues of her estates, attacked by her friends as well as by her enemies,—the first reproaching her for not having defended her property and her liberty, the last blaming her for not giving up to the Parliament the house as well as the domain,—she waited patiently for the time when she should be able openly to resist.

Steadily and secretly she had collected provisions and ammunition, bringing in the men one by one, and the barrels of powder in the night; repressing the zeal of her garrison, who longed to revenge the insults she had to submit to daily; and preparing herself in silence for the siege which she foresaw must come. In so proud a nature as hers, this noble patience resulted from even a higher courage than Lady Derby displayed in the midst of armed attacks—the courage of a woman and of a general who knows how to bear all while awaiting the time to dare all.

Samuel Rutter, the Earl of Derby's chaplain, afterwards Archdeacon, and finally Bishop of Man, writes:

> Lathom House stands on a flat, upon a moorish spongy ground; was encompassed with a strong wall two yards thick; upon the walls were nine towers flanking each other; and in every tower were six pieces of ordnance, that played three one way and three the other. Without the wall was a moat, eight yards wide, and two yards deep; upon the back of the moat, between the wall and the graff, was a strong wall of palisades around; besides all these there was a high, strong tower, called the Eagle Tower, in the midst of the house surmounting all the rest; and the gatehouse was also two high and strong buildings, with a strong tower on each side of it. . . .
>
> Besides all that is said hitherto of the walls, tower, moat, &c., there is something particular and romantic in the general situation of this house, as if nature herself had formed it for a stronghold or place of security. . . . . . The uncommon situation of it may be compared to the palm of a man's hand, flat in the mid-

dle, and covered with a rising round about it; and so near to it, that the enemy in two years were never able to raise a battery against it so as to make a breach in the wall practicable to enter the house by way of storm. (*House of Stanley*.)

The countess's preparations were nearly completed, in spite of the difficulties incessantly put in her way by Colonel Rigby, who commanded the Parliamentary troops in that neighbourhood. It was in vain that he had pillaged the houses of her adherents, and arrested the people who came to seek refuge at Lathom. Lady Derby had succeeded in getting into the house more than three hundred men, and a great abundance of food of all kinds. Ammunition, however, was less considerable, and they were obliged to economize their powder. Lady Derby commanded in chief, says Captain Halsall, but to make up for her ignorance of military matters, she had with her a Scotchman, Captain Farmer, whom she had made major of her house, and six lieutenants chosen from the gentlemen of the neighbourhood who had come to offer their services.

The garrison had been gathered together with so much secrecy that the Parliamentarians had no idea of its strength; and, after a slight engagement between the troops of Colonel Rigby and those of the countess, Sir Thomas Fairfax resolved to deliver the county of Lancaster from this nest of delinquents.

It was decided in the council of war held at Manchester on the 24th of February, 1644, that three colonels—Ashton of Midleton, Moor of Bank Hall, and Rigby of Preston—should attack Lathom House. This was on Saturday; and on Sunday morning rumours of the projected movement reached the countess. She sent in haste to a friend on whom she could rely to obtain full information; and in the meantime hurried forward her final preparations, rendered doubly difficult by the ill-will of some of her tenants who inclined to the popular cause, and considered that the sequestration had released them from all obligation to the mistress of the house and domain.

But it was not in vain that Lady Derby belonged to the proud race of French Huguenots whose power had once kept that of Royalty in the balance; it was not in vain that the blood of William of Nassau flowed in her veins. She was equal to her position; she watched over everything; calm and resolute, she assigned to every man his post, singling out the best marksmen, those who had been accustomed to attend the earl in his hunting, to occupy the towers of the gate-house for the purpose of harassing and annoying the enemy. Then, when everything was arranged, all the soldiers were ordered to disappear from the ramparts, and the countess, apparently alone with her household, awaited the visit that had been announced.

The Parliamentary soldiers had not been made aware that they were marching against Lathom House; perhaps the leaders feared the hereditary attachment of the people of Lancashire to that noble family who had for so many years held an actual court in the midst of them, dispensing a princely hospitality and an inexhaustible charity. While it was known to the countess that the Parliamentary Army was *en route*, by Bolton, Wigan, and Standish, the people believed that they were advancing towards Westmoreland; but those who went to church at Wigan were undeceived, for one of the preachers taking for his text Jeremiah, 1. 14, "*Put yourselves in array against Babylon round about: all ye that bend the bow shoot at her, spare no arrows; for she hath sinned against the Lord,*" compared the Countess of Derby to Babylon, the great city of the Apocalypse, and announced his intention of reserving the following verse: "*Shout against her round about: she hath given her hand: her foundations are fallen, her walls are thrown down,*" for the text of the sermon that should celebrate the victory over her.

On the 27th February the enemy took up their quarters two miles from Lathom, and on the 28th Capt. Markland arrived at the house with a letter from Sir Thomas Fairfax, and an order from the Parliament promising grace to Lord Derby if he submitted. Sir Thomas Fairfax engaged to carry out this promise faithfully, and called on the countess to surrender Lathom House to him on honourable conditions, which he would make known to her. The letter was courteous, as from a gentleman to a lady of high rank and reputation; but the countess felt the necessity of gaining time: her troops were inexperienced, and the training they received from their captains increased their courage and confidence daily. Her reply to Sir Thomas Fairfax, therefore, was to the effect that:

> She much wondered that Sir Thomas Fairfax should require her to give up her lord's house, without any offence on her part done to the Parliament; desiring that in a business of such weight, which struck both at her religion and her life, and that so nearly concerned her sovereign, her lord, and her whole posterity, she might have a week's consideration, to resolve the doubts of conscience, and to have advice in matters of law and

honour. (Halsall's *Siege of Lathom House*.)

Sir Thomas Fairfax probably thought Lady Derby's conscience sufficiently enlightened, for he refused to give her the time she asked, and invited her to go in her carriage to New Park, a house belonging to Lord Derby, situated a short distance from Lathom, in order to have an interview with him and his colonels for the free discussion of the whole affair.

When the countess received this letter, it roused the haughtiness of the great lady as well as the boldness of the heroine, said she:

> Say to Sir Thomas Fairfax, that, notwithstanding my present position, I do not forget either the honour of my lord or my own birth, and that I conceive it more knightly that Sir Thomas Fairfax should wait upon me than I upon him.

Two days passed in letters and in messages; at length the general demanded free entrance to Lathom House for two of his colonels; and the countess promised to allow them to return in safety. They came on the 2nd of March; but the house that lately had the appearance of being peaceably occupied by women and children, with old servants and a few men at arms for protection, had now assumed the appearance of a fortress. Lady Derby had suddenly unmasked her batteries, either from fear of an immediate attack, or to produce an imposing effect on the enemy.

A body of soldiers well equipped, ranged under orders of their lieutenants, formed a line from the first court to the great hall into which the Parliamentary officers were introduced: the towers and ramparts were bristling with men; the cannon were uncovered; everything wore a martial appearance, and throughout perfect discipline prevailed. At the end of the great hall, more imposing than all her forces sat the general of this little army, the Countess of Derby, surrounded by her women, and with her two daughters beside her. She waited for the officers to approach; then, making a sign to them to be seated with the manner of a sovereign who gives an audience she listened to the propositions of Sir Thomas. They were as follows:—

> 1. That all the arms and ammunition of war shall be forthwith surrendered into the hands of Sir Thomas Fairfax.
>
> 2. That the Countess of Derby, and all the persons in Lathom House, shall be suffered to depart with all their goods to Chester, or any other of the enemy's quarters, or, upon submission to

the orders of Parliament, to their own houses.

3. That the countess with all her menial servants shall be suffered either to inhabit Knowsley House, and to have twenty muskets allowed for her defence, or to repair to her husband in the Isle of Man.

4. That the countess for the present, until the Parliament be acquainted with it, shall have allowed her for her maintenance all the lands and revenues the earl her husband within the hundred of Derby, and that the Parliament shall be moved to continue this allowance.

These conditions her ladyship rejected as being in part dishonourable, and in part uncertain; adding withal, she knew not how to treat with them who had not power to perform their own offers till they had first moved the Parliament, telling them that it were a more sober course first to acquaint themselves with the pleasure of the Parliament, and then to move accordingly; but for her part she would not trouble the good gentlemen to petition for her; she would esteem it a greater favour to be permitted to continue in her present humble condition. (Halsall's *Siege of Lathom House*.)

The two colonels did not insist. For some time past Rigby had been eager to take revenge for an insult which he believed he had received from the earl. They had indeed read determination in the lady's eyes; yet they could not let themselves be thus conquered by a woman, and they both thought it necessary to address some representations to her on the error of her ways, and to reproach her with the wrongdoing attributed in the country to her friends and servants. Said the countess gravely:

I shall know how to take care of my ways and those of my house, you would do well to do as much for your ministers and agents of religion who go about sowing discord and trouble in families, whose unbridled tongues do not spare even the sacred person of His Majesty.

Henry Martyn might say to the Parliament, "the ruin of one single family is better than the ruin of many;" and when they asked him of whom he spoke he could answer without hesitation, "of the king and his family;" but the lieutenants of Fairfax knew that their general would not have permitted such language, and "the grave men, being disappointed both of their wit and malice, returned as empty as they came." (*Siege of Lathom House*.)

Sunday was a day of rest for the besiegers as well as for the besieged. While they preached against her in the camp of Fairfax, probably with sincerity equal to her own, the Countess of Derby, with her children and the greater part of the garrison, was present at divine service in the chapel of the house, where four times a day during the siege she made the chaplain offer prayers; she herself always attending, and gathering new strength for her heavy task at the feet of Him who has called Himself the Lord of Hosts.

"On Monday Mr. Ashton came again, alone, with power to receive her ladyship's propositions, and to convey them to his general, which came in these terms:—

> 1. Her ladyship desired a month's time for her quiet continuance in Lathom; and then, for herself and children, her friends, soldiers, and servants, with all her goods, arms, and ordnance, to have free transport to the Isle of Man, and in the meantime that she should keep a garrison in her house for her own defence.
>
> 2. She promised that neither during her stay in the country, nor after her coming to the Isle of Man, should any of the arms be employed against the Parliament.
>
> 3. That during her stay in the country, no soldier should be quartered in the lordship of Lathom, nor afterwards should any garrison be put into Lathom or into Knowsley House.
>
> 4. That none of her tenants, neighbours, or friends, then in the house with her, should, for assisting her, suffer in their persons or estates, after her departure." (*Siege of Lathom House*.)

Fairfax was not deceived by these proposals. He understood that the countess only wished to gain time for victualling her house; and he foresaw that she would elude the clause in which she promised not to bear arms against the Parliament, by referring herself to the Parliament of the three estates—King, Lords, and Commons, then assembled at Oxford. For the last time, therefore, he sent counter-propositions:—

> 1. The Countess of Derby shall have the time that she desires, and then liberty to transport her arms and goods to the Isle of Man, excepting the cannon, which shall continue there for the defence of the place.

2. That her ladyship, by ten o'clock tomorrow, disband all her soldiers, except her menial servants, and receive an officer and forty Parliament soldiers as her guard. (*Siege of Lathom House*.)

A new messenger was the bearer of this new message, Colonel Morgan, a hot-headed Welshman, with a sharp, imperative manner, who was, however, obliged to restrain himself before the pride and dignity of the countess, who sent back this last answer:—

That she refused all their articles, and was truly happy that they had refused hers, protesting that she would rather hazard her life than offer the like again. That though a woman and a stranger, divorced from her friends, and robbed of her estate, she was ready to receive their utmost violence, trusting in God both for protection and deliverance. (*Siege of Lathom House*.)

Negotiations being thus closed, Captain Morgan went off into descriptions of the cannon, mortars, bombs, and artillery, that would be brought against the house, and left the countess to reflect on the danger she had so proudly braved.

The council of war met. Some of the Parliamentary officers advised an immediate assault; others, a regular siege. The person who supported this last proposal most earnestly was a captain who, in his childhood, had been closely associated with the Rev. Mr. Rutter, the countess's chaplain, with whom he had had a conversation on the occasion of the late conference with Lady Derby. From what had passed then he believed that the house was but scantily victualled, for not more than twelve or fifteen days; and that the countess eagerly desired an assault. They therefore resolved on the siege, and on the 7th of March began to open a trench, in which labour the country people were forced to take an active part.

The works went on round the house, and the circle was growing rapidly, when Lady Derby was informed that six of her neighbours of the highest rank desired to speak with her. She ordered them to be admitted, and received them with her customary courtesy.

At the first glance she detected the origin of the petition they brought. It proceeded from the Parliament, and the worthy delegates had been carefully instructed.

In duty to her ladyship and love to their country they most humbly besought her to prevent her own personal dangers and the impoverishing of the whole country, which she might do if she pleased to slacken something of her severe resolution, and to condescend in part to the offers of the gentlemen. (*Siege of Lathom House.*)

The countess did not receive her neighbours with the same haughtiness which she had shown to the emissaries of the Parliament. She explained her reasons for rejecting the preceding propositions, and advised them to address their petition to the men who robbed and spoiled their country, rather than to her who desired no other favour than to remain at home in peace. The good men were satisfied, and had little more to say than "God save the King and the Earl of Derby."

The report they gave of the interview to Sir Thomas Fairfax decided him to send Captain Ashurst the next day to Lathom House with new propositions. Captain Halsall says:

This Captain Ashurst deserves a fairer character than the rest for his civil and even behaviour. His new message to her Ladyship was in these terms:—

1. That all former conditions be waived.

2. That the Countess of Derby and all persons in the house, with all arms, ordnance, and goods, shall have liberty to march to what part of the kingdom they please, and yield up the house to Sir Thomas Fairfax.

3. That the arms shall never be employed against the Parliament.

4. That all in the house except a hundred persons should immediately leave it, and the rest in ten days. (*Siege of Lathom House.*)

Fairfax was evidently unwilling to attack the place, either because he considered the enterprise a difficult one, or because he was ashamed to employ his arms against a woman, defending her children and her husband's house. But the countess showed no fear. The reply she sent to the general was:

That, as she had not lost her regard for the Church of England, nor her allegiance to her prince, nor her faith to her lord, she could not therefore, as yet, give up that house; that they must never hope to gain it till she had either lost all these, or her life in defence of them. (*House of Stanley.*)

Fairfax had now nothing to do but to begin the siege in good earnest. The trenches around Lathom progressed daily, notwithstanding the continual sorties made by the garrison on the men who were at work there. One small detachment of cavalry even fought hand to hand with some Parliamentary troops, and brought back a few prisoners, from whom it was ascertained that the blockade was determined on; Captain Halsall says:

> The commanders having courage to pine a lady, not to fight with her.

The work of the siege was proceeding rapidly, to the great injury of the country people employed in removing the earth, when, on the 20th March, Sir Thomas Fairfax sent the countess a letter, which he had just received from her husband.

Alarmed at his wife's critical position, the Earl of Derby wrote from the Isle of Man asking the general to permit the countess and her children freely to leave the house, in order to spare them the horrors of a siege:

> Especially considering the roughness and inhumanity of the enemy: .... not knowing, by reason of his long absence, either how his house was provided with victuals and ammunition, or strengthened for resistance. He was therefore desirous to leave only the hardy soldiers for the brunt,—'if it seems good to my wife,' added he.

But it did not seem good to the courageous daughter of the Nassaus. Her spirit rose at the approach of danger, and if her heart beat at this proof of the tender solicitude of her husband, she derived from it fresh strength to remain at the post which he had entrusted to her. She bade the messenger, a coarse preacher employed by Colonel Rigby, say to Sir Thomas Fairfax that she thanked him for his courtesy:

"That she would willingly submit herself to her lord's commands, and therefore willed the general to treat with him; but, till she was assured that such was his lordship's pleasure, she would neither yield up the house, nor desert it herself, but wait for the event according to the will of God." (*Siege of Lathom House.*)

She had meanwhile learned that her husband had quitted the Isle of Man, and she had taken advantage of a sortie, which threw the enemy into confusion and put them off their guard, to despatch an express to him at Chester, where he was anxiously and busily collecting forces with which to march in person to the help of his family. But the house was surrounded by 3,000 men, and the earl had barely a handful of soldiers.

Meanwhile the sorties of the garrison of Lathom continued; and the cannon began to batter the walls of the House, but, thanks to the nature of the ground, not very effectually.

The garrison were anxiously watching the erection of a mortar that the enemy was placing on a mound, at the distance of half a gunshot. The first shots passed over the house, to the great relief of the besieged, who had been furnished by the countess with the wet hides of newly-killed animals with which to extinguish any fire that might occur.

Four days of prayer and pious exercises interrupted the operations of the siege; "four days of sleep," says the historian of Lathom, incredulous as to the devotion of Colonel Rigby. At the end of that time the garrison determined to awaken the besiegers by a furious sortie, in which they spiked several of their cannon, and took a great number of prisoners, whom the countess, proud of having scarcely any men left in the hands of the enemy, would have consented to release in exchange for some of the king's friends detained at Manchester, Preston, and Lancaster. Colonel Rigby promised this: but failed to fulfil his engagement, the narrator of the siege, says:

> It suiting well their religion, neither to observe faith with God nor with men.

And then followed at Lathom a melancholy massacre of prisoners whom the countess could neither keep nor set free.

With her children—her two daughters, Mary and Catherine—she watched over everything, arranged for the food of the soldiers—was present at the distribution of the powder—at the nursing of the wounded—was often on the ramparts, and always at chapel at prayer-time. When a bullet fell in her bedroom she smiled disdainfully, and it was only after the same thing had happened three or four times that she would condescend to change her apartment, though still with the "protest that she would keep the house while there was a single building to cover her head."

On one occasion a shell had burst in the dining-room during dinner, which broke the glass and furniture, but injured no one. The children were beside their mother at the time, but they did not move, and scarcely changed colour. The countess merely gave them a look of approbation, and the meal was continued in the midst of the confusion.

On the 24th of April Sir Thomas Fairfax, who had till then directed the siege, grown tired of making war against a woman, left for York, abandoning the enterprise against Lathom House to Colonel Rigby, who had managed to disembarrass himself of Colonel Egerton, hitherto associated with him in authority. The Colonels Moor, Holcroft, Holland, and Ashton were his subordinates; Colonel Morgan was at the head of the engineering. The siege had now changed its character. The countess had no longer to deal with one who, though a sincere patriot, was a gentleman and a man of cultivation and refined feeling. Her present assailant—formerly a lawyer—was a bad man, a robber and a hypocrite. Resolved not to be conquered by a woman, he laid in a new stock of *grenadoes*, which he used so freely that the besieged renewed their ammunition in the trenches; and he announced a grand attack with mortar-piece and cannon.

Before striking this terrible blow, however, Colonel Rigby desired once more to offer the rebels a chance of submission; and on the 25th an insolent message was brought to the countess, ordering her to surrender herself, with her house, her garrison, her arms, and ammunition, to the mercy of Parliament before two o'clock the next day.

She was in the court-yard in the midst of her lieutenants when the messenger arrived. She took the letter and read it; Captain Halsall says:

> Then with a brave indignation calls for the drum, and tells him that a due reward for his pains is to be hanged up at her gates; 'but,' says she, 'thou art but the foolish instrument of a traitor's pride; carry this answer back to Rigby,' (with a noble scorn tearing the paper in his sight,) 'and tell that insolent rebel he shall neither have persons, goods, nor house. When our strength and provision is spent we shall find a fire more merciful than Rigby's; and then, if the providence of God prevent it not, my goods and house shall burn in his sight; and myself, children, and soldiers, rather than fall into his hands, will seal our religion and loyalty in the same flame;' which, being spoken aloud in her soldiers' hearing, they broke out into shouts and acclamations of joy, all closing with this general voice, 'We will die for His Majesty and your Honour—God save the King!' (*Siege of Lathom House.*)

The time had come for acting resolutely; from words it was necessary to proceed to actions. The mortar-piece was the terror of all the garrison. Captain Halsall says:

> The little ladies had stomachs to digest cannon, but the stoutest soldier had no heart for *grenadoes*.

They had tried in vain to spike the mortar-piece, its mouth was too large to be shut. It was in vain that the best marksmen aimed at the artillerymen in charge of the terrible engine; they fell, indeed, but others replaced them immediately. It only remained to attack the mortar itself; and a sortie was arranged for the next day before the firing began.

It was 4 o'clock in the morning when Captain Chisenhall and his eighty men silently left the eastern gate, and before they were perceived they were under the cannon, and after a slight skirmish were masters of the little fort that covered the house. In the meantime, Captain Fox, who had gone out by another gate, had made himself master of the works which defended the mortar, in spite of a deep ditch and a tolerably high rampart. The two main works being thus obtained, the first care of the captains was to level the ditch, while Captain Ogle and his soldiers beat back the enemy who were trying to recover their position.

The servants of the countess had gone out in crowds, every one eager to have a hand on the ropes which had been passed round the mortar, and to help in drawing within the ramparts the terrible enemy that had done them so much harm. Captain Ogle with a detachment of soldiers protected the passage against another company of the enemy.

At length, amid cries of joy from all the garrison, and to the great consternation of the besiegers, the formidable engine was rolled into the courtyard, to the countess's feet. She immediately ordered her chaplain to be called, and gathered her household together in the chapel, to return thanks to God. The soldiers had tried to carry off the large guns, but found them too heavy, and they contented themselves with spiking as many as they could. The enterprise had cost the lives of two of the garrison; the loss of the enemy was more considerable. During the heat of the action the most skilful marksmen placed on the walls of the house had kept up an incessant fire, to the great destruction of the Parliamentary soldiers, who were gathered in crowds round the fort and near the ditch.

The joy within the house was great; their enemy, the monster vomiting flames, which had so often set fire to the old parts of the house, lay there in the court, mute and inoffensive; and every one gave it a kick as if in revenge for the terror it had once occasioned.

An additional zest was imparted to their triumph by the circumstance that Rigby had invited his friends in the neighbourhood to come on this day and see the reduction or the burning of the house.

They were invited for 2 o'clock, and Captain Halsall says:

> His friends came opportunely to comfort him who was sick of shame and dishonour, in being routed by a lady and a handful of men.

After this, discouragement and discontent increased amongst the besiegers; desertion began in their ranks. The sorties of the garrison were so frequent that the Parliamentarians were obliged incessantly to mount a guard. Rigby complained of this in a letter which he addressed on the 1st of May to the deputy-lieutenant of the county of Lancaster, representing that, as the Colonels Ashton and Holland, with their troops, had left him, he was no longer equal to the task which had been given him, he wrote:

> We are obliged to drive them back as often as five or six times in the same night. These constant alarms, the strength of the garrison, and the numerous losses we have had, oblige the soldiers to guard the trenches sometimes two nights running, and always the whole of the two nights: my son does this duty, as well as the youngest officer. And, for my own part, I am ready to sink under the weight, having worked beyond my strength.

In answer to this remonstrance. Colonel Holland was sent from Manchester to Rigby's assistance.

The incessant rains of spring impeded the operations of the besiegers; the earth was loosened, their trench fell in, and they began to lose the hope of cutting off the water from the besieged, which they had been trying to do for a month.

On the 23rd of May, the besiegers, more weary than the besieged of this long and desperate struggle, which brought them neither honour nor profit, made one more attempt to induce the countess to surrender. Captain Mosley presented himself at the gate of the house, bearing a letter to her ladyship from Colonels Holland and Rigby, ordering her, with rather more insolence than had been used to her before, (for "it not befitting Colonel Rigby's greatness," says Captain Halsall, "to abate any of his former demands,"):

> To yield up her house, her arms, her goods, all her servants, and her own person and children, into their hands, to be submitted to the mercy of the Parliament; which being read, Her Ladyship smiled, and in a troubled passion challenged the captain with a mistake in the paper, saying mercy, instead of cruelty. 'No,' says

he, 'the mercy of the Parliament;' when her ladyship quickly and composedly replied, 'The mercies of the wicked are cruel. Not that I mean,' says she, 'a wicked Parliament, of which body I have an honourable and reverend esteem, but wicked factors and agents, such as Moor and Rigby, who, for the advantage of their own interests, labour to turn kingdoms into blood and ruin. That unless they would treat with her lord, they should never have her, nor any of her friends, alive.' (*Siege of Lathom House*.)

The captain gave her to understand that she could obtain the conditions she had at first asked for, if she would leave the house. "Let that insolent rebel send me no more propositions," said she, "or his messenger shall be hanged at my gates;" which words the soldiers heard with acclamations; and the envoy returned without having obtained any other answer, nor a single word from the hand of the countess.

But deliverance was at hand, though Lady Derby did not know it. Shut up within her walls, she knew nothing of the movements of the king or of those of the Earl of Essex: she had scarcely heard of the efforts her husband was making in all parts to bring her help. She had learned from the taunts of the besiegers that Sir Thomas Fairfax had defeated a numerous body of Royalists at Selby; that the Duke of Newcastle was shut up in York; that a new army had been raised in the east under Cromwell; and that Sir William Waller had defeated Sir Ralph Hopton in Hampshire. All these disasters were so many arguments to induce the countess to surrender.

But she did not put much faith in them, and would not even believe when the men in the trench called out the news that Essex was on the point of besieging Oxford; and that the queen, terrified at the prospect of her accouchement taking place in a city surrounded by the enemy, had left the king her husband, to go and establish herself at Exeter. Lady Derby had no sympathy with terrors of this kind, and smiled scornfully when the reports were brought to her. But they were nevertheless true.

While the king's generals were being defeated in various directions, Prince Rupert had succeeded in raising the siege of Newark, and was preparing to march to the aid of the Duke of Newcastle, who was threatened in York by Fairfax, Manchester, and the Scotch Army, which had just arrived under command of the Earl of Leven. The Earl of Derby conjured the prince to pass through the county of

Lancaster, and deliver Lathom House, and his wife and children; and to quicken the march of the army, he promised the soldiers a reward of three thousand pounds, raised on his wife's jewels, which she had found means of conveying to him during the siege.

The Parliamentarians had known for several days that the troops of the Royalists were advancing, when, on the night of the 23rd of May, a few hours after the departure of Captain Mosley, one of the countess's scouts succeeded in stealing into the house (not, however, without having killed the enemy's sentinel), with the intelligence from the earl that Prince Rupert had entered the county of Chester; that report said the Earl of Derby was with him; and that they were both marching to the succour of Lathom.

This unlooked-for news transported the timid with joy, but the strong were unmoved by it. Prayer more fervent than ever rose from the little chapel; but no precaution was neglected, and no advantage given to the enemy.

Gravely and silently the Parliamentarians guarded their trench, no longer shouting out insulting tidings to the besieged, as they had been wont to do. No one now boasted of the successes of Fairfax in the North, or of those of Cromwell in the East; nothing more was heard of taking the king in a mousetrap.

In the evening of the 26th of May, the guard was renewed in such small number that the countess determined to attempt a grand sortie the next day. Captain Ogle and Captain Rawstorne were selected for this service, with two hundred soldiers of the garrison.

The besieged were to attack the trench at three o'clock in the morning; but by one o'clock the enemy had raised their camp, collected their forces, and packed up their tents.

The news that Prince Rupert had entered the county of Lancaster had arrived during the evening. He had forced his way past Stockport, in spite of the resistance of Colonel Duckenfeld, and Rigby, like a brave general, sparing of the lives of his men, determined not to wait for his coming to Lathom. By six in the morning he and his troops were on Eccleston Moor, six miles from Lathom, much puzzled where to turn his steps: Colonel Holland had returned to Manchester, and Colonel Moor to Liverpool.

At length, thinking Prince Rupert was going through Lancashire, and being very desirous of avoiding him, Rigby proceeded to Bolton-le-Moor, little imagining that the Royalist Army was also counting on taking up its quarters there.

When the Earl of Derby ascertained from the scouts that Rigby had entered Bolton, after raising the siege of Lathom House, he urged Prince Rupert to storm the place in revenge of the insults with which Rigby had overwhelmed the countess for so long a time.

The town was small but well-fortified. Rigby had taken into it above 3,000 soldiers, and Colonel Shuttleworth had sent a reinforcement of 1,500 more. The first assault was repulsed with considerable loss. The Parliamentarians massacred in cold blood the soldiers they took on the ramparts. The prince, hot and haughty of mood, and little accustomed to be resisted, and being also akin to the countess, was enraged at the insolence of the clowns who had dared to besiege her in her own house. He yielded readily to the entreaties of Lord Derby that he would make a second assault, being quite sure that, if the Royalist Army retired without taking Bolton, the siege of Lathom would soon be renewed. The earl said:

> Let me have the command of my old soldiers, and give me the charge of the storming party, and if I do not enter the town, Your Highness will find me in the trench.

The prince hesitated; the adventure was a hazardous one to be committed to so important a man. But Lord Derby insisted, and, after a terrible struggle of a quarter of an hour, he was the first to enter the place at the head of his 200 men, and, possessing himself of a flag carried by an ensign, he sent it to the prince, who immediately afterwards entered the town. They were not able to take Colonel Rigby, who managed to escape, but 1,600 of his men were killed on the spot, and 700 taken prisoners.

Captain Halsall says:

> On his first passing into the town, closely following the foot on their entrance, his lordship met with Captain Bootle, formerly one of his own servants, but now the most virulent enemy against his lady in the siege. Him he did the honour of too brave a death of dying by his lord's hand, with some others of his good countrymen who had for three months thirsted for his lady's and his children's blood. (*Siege of Lathom House.*)

The earl was afterwards bitterly reproached with the death of Bootle.

While Prince Rupert was marching against Liverpool, which he reduced on the 26th of June, the countess was at length receiving her husband in that house which she had so bravely defended for him and in his name.

With the earl came Sir Richard Crane, sent by Prince Rupert to present the twenty-two flags taken from the enemy at Bolton to his cousin. A few days before, these very banners had been insolently flourished before her walls. It was with the most profound gratitude to that God in whom she had trusted, that Lady Derby hung them up in the Chapel of Lathom, in memory of the deliverance vouchsafed to her.

After the taking of Liverpool, Prince Rupert came to rest for a few days at Lathom, among the ruined ramparts and bullet-pierced walls. He was full of admiration at the brave resistance made by a woman against a force so numerous and resolute. He ordered new defences to be made to some of the fortifications, and repairs to others, in order to put the place in a condition to sustain a new siege if necessary. At Lady Derby's request he raised Captain Rawstorne to the post of governor of the house, with the rank of colonel, leaving him two squadrons of cavalry. He gave the same rank to Captain Chisenhall, whom he took with him.

Before leaving the countess, the prince advised her to withdraw to the Isle of Man. He knew the jealousy and suspicion which the power and valour of the earl excited amongst the courtiers, and, impetuous though he was, he was well aware how doubtful were the chances of war. Lord Derby had re-established order in the little kingdom of Man, and his wife and children would there find security and repose.

> After the siege of Lathom ... the Countess of Derby willingly resigned to her husband the authority which she had never exercised but in his name; and with her children, under the protection of the earl, retired to the Isle of Man, leaving Lathom House to the care of Colonel Rawstorne. (*Postscript to Siege of Lathom House.*)

Regardless of the glory and renown she had won, her only desire was to live in peace, far from the troubles which distracted her adopted country. She does not appear to have had much ambition, even for her husband: the remarkable heroism of her character and her conduct was only called forth by duty, and she never seemed to remember her own exploits. Not a word, not an allusion in her letters ever recalls the fact that for more than a year, by the exercise of prudence, resolution, and courage, she had succeeded in keeping the enemies of her husband and her king in check, and had finally obliged them to abandon the enterprise they had so much at heart. She now thought of nothing but of bringing up her children. The prince had said:

> Take great care of them. The children of such a father and mother will one day render to their king as much service as yours has received from you.

The services which the Earl of Derby and his wife rendered to the House of Stuart were not, however, yet terminated. Charlotte de la Trémoille did not yet know how much her loyal devotion was to cost her.

When the Earl of Derby followed the advice of the prince and retired to the Isle of Man, with his wife and his three sons and three daughters, the king had quitted Oxford, where Essex threatened to besiege him, and had marched towards the west, where Prince Rupert, newly entered into York, had attacked the enemy who had just raised the siege of that city. They were on Marston Moor.

"What post has Your Highness destined for me?" the Duke of Newcastle had asked.

"I do not count on beginning the action till tomorrow morning," replied the prince, "You can rest till then."

But the duke had scarcely entered his carriage when the firing began, and hurrying to the scene of action, he fought as a volunteer. The most terrible disorder prevailed upon the field. Royalist and Parliamentarian struggled confusedly, without orders and without generals. The squadrons of Cromwell alone remained firm, and secured the fortune of the day. The Cavaliers, misled by the rout of the right wing of the Parliamentarians, returned from the pursuit to find the battlefield occupied by a victorious enemy. Three thousand Royalists were killed; sixteen hundred taken prisoners. The standard of Prince Rupert was in the hands of the Parliamentarians.

★★★★★★

> In the middle of this standard was a lion *couchant*, and behind him a mastiff biting at him; from the mastiff's mouth came a streamer, on which was to be read, 'Kimbolton;' at its feet were several little dogs, beneath whose jaws was written, 'Pym, Pym, Pym;' from the lion's own jaws proceeded these words, '*Quousque tandem abutere patientiâ nostra?*'—*Rushworth*, ii., Guizot: *Hist. of the Eng. Revolution.*

★★★★★★

He and the Duke of Newcastle returned to York without speaking to, without seeing, each other. The next morning the prince went to Chester with the remains of his army, and the duke embarked for the continent, as the Queen Henrietta Maria had done two days before. A fortnight after York capitulated.

While the king, eagerly supported by a resolute and numerous party, was fighting Essex in Cornwall, and obliging him to retreat and to submit to a humiliating capitulation, the Parliamentary forces had recommenced the siege of Lathom; but, deprived of the presence of the Countess of Derby, the heroic defence of the place attracted no more attention. She, who had won the admiration even of her enemies, was in safety in the Isle of Man with her husband and children; but she had left behind her brave men and well-disciplined soldiers, who for six months more held the house for their lord, displaying a courage and a skill above all praise.

Lady Derby's chaplain, the Rev. S. Rutter, who remained at Lathom after her departure, had managed to keep up an active correspondence with her friends in the neighbourhood, and with the king, by means of a woman, who for several months courageously risked her life to take despatches and bring back answers during the frequent sorties made by the besieged. She was at length taken and put to the torture, but she would reveal nothing, and suffered three fingers on both hands to be burnt off before her tormenters, tired out by her invincible fortitude, at length desisted.

Deprived of this faithful messenger they trained a dog to carry the despatches in his collar: they were in cypher, and a friend in the neighbourhood sent them to those to whom they were addressed. For several months the poor animal rendered eminent service, but at last a soldier, in mere wanton ill temper, fired a musket at him just as he had swum across the moat and thus their means of communication with the outer world was again lost.

The garrison of Lathom had held out since the month of July, 1645, hoping for succour from the king. But Charles's affairs were looking darker than ever. He had been defeated at Naseby on the 14th of June, and had turned towards Scotland to put himself at the head of the insurrection raised there by Montrose; but he was beaten in his attempt to raise the siege of Chester, and forced to retreat to Wales, where his friends held the country parts. The rising excited by Montrose had died out like a fire of straw, and the heroic adherent of the king had been obliged to hide himself, and to become, like his master, a wanderer and a fugitive.

The king made it known to the brave defenders of Lathom that he could give them no help, and that their only course was to surrender. The historian of the House Stanley says:

> A melancholy consolation to receive from the master of three kingdoms, to see him unable to succour his children their distress;—a fatal example of the effects of constant division in his councils, and of the habitual irresolution which prevented this unhappy prince from being faithful to his best friends.

Hopeless at last, the garrison determined to accept the propositions which had been often addressed to them. The governor, faithful even in his defeat, stipulated, as the first condition of surrender, the cession to Lady Derby and her children of a third of the revenue of the earl her husband, with the right to remove all her goods to Knowsley House. He also required that the garrison should be permitted to retire with their arms and baggage:

> That all gentlemen in the house should compound at one year's value for their estates, and that every clergyman should enjoy half the revenue of his living without any oath imposed upon them. (*House of Stanley*.)

Two of the Parliamentary commanders had already accepted these conditions; the third still stood out, when an Irish soldier, the only traitor in the garrison, swam across the moat, and communicated to the enemy the deplorable state of the besieged,—that they were at the end of their food and ammunition, and unable to hold out any longer. Upon this information, orders were given to surrender the place to the mercy of the Parliament; and the soldiers determining, in spite of the entreaties of the governor, to hold out no longer, the gates were opened, the house was pillaged, and the towers and strong works were razed to the ground. Two or three little detached buildings alone remained to show where stood the fortress which had been so long and so bravely defended.

Amongst the parish documents of Ormskirk are the receipts for the sale of the planks, beams, and lead of Lathom House, which were all sold by the officers who destroyed the place.

CHAPTER 5

Renewal of Correspondence

We now return to the correspondence of Lady Derby, of which we have lost sight for several years. How deeply interesting would be those lost or stolen letters of hers, particularly any that she might have been able to despatch from Lathom by means of the sorties of her brave soldiers, and those that she wrote on her arrival in the Isle of Man. It is not until the date of August, 1646, that we recover possession of these precious documents, which enable us to see into the very household of the countess, and to be face to face with her anxieties and her joys.

She writes at that time from the Isle of Man in great anxiety. Her son, Lord Strange, of whom we heard nothing during the siege of Lathom—he, as well as his brothers Edward and William, having probably remained with their father—had secretly quitted the island. His mother wrote:

> He stole away from *Monsieur* his father and from me on the 29th of last month, and we know nothing of him since; but we are assured he is in Ireland. The letters he left behind told us he was going to you; and I hope, dear sister, that you will, for my sake, receive him and be a mother to him—all the more because what he has done has offended *Monsieur* his father and me. If he obeys you, he will the more readily obtain our pardon.

The young Lord Strange was really in Paris, and his mother's next letters are full of thanksgivings to God, who had preserved him, and to her sister-in-law, who had received him and treated him as a mother.

The Duchesse de la Trémoille tried to make his peace with his parents; and Lord Derby thus replied to her on the 21st Dec, 1646:—

> *Madame*,—If my son had committed a much greater fault, I would at your request have forgiven him at once; but having now only forestalled my long-cherished wish that he should have the honour of being with you, I consider him most fortunate in having; gained that end. And if, by obeying you as he would myself, he can in any measure merit the honour of your good opinion and friendship, he will gain not only my pardon but my increased affection. This alone can gratify me. It has given me so much happiness to see how you have been pleased to receive him, and what especial care you have deigned to take of him, that I can never offer you sufficiently worthy and humble thanks for it. But if God ever restores to me the power of requiting these deep obligations, you will never, *Madame*, have a more faithful servant than myself, to whom nothing will be difficult by which I can render you humble service, and prove to you with what devotion
> I am, *Madame*,
> Your very humble and very obedient brother and servant,
> Derby.

The earl consoled himself more readily than he had done of old for the absence of his son, for the affairs of the Royalists were now in a desperate condition. Sir Ralph Hopton and Lord Astley, the last who had held out, had been forced to surrender, and the king had just taken refuge at Keltham, the headquarters of the Scotch, accompanied by M. de Montreuil, the French envoy, seeking protection from that people whom in former times his fathers had often led against England.

The distress of the Royalists was very great. Lady Derby wrote to her sister-in-law in a letter in cypher:

> You will know as soon as we what the Scotch have done with the king. What the queen is doing in France is very hurtful to us; but she cares neither for what she says nor does, provided she can recover her position. I hope the gentlemen of the States will instruct their ambassador to assist me if I go to London. You will know what my movements are by what the Scotch do with the king. If they make me write to my son to contract a marriage that is unworthy of him, I beg that he will excuse himself on the ground that he is not thinking of such a thing at his present age, nor of anything so much as seeing the world.

The times had indeed become momentous, and the journey of the countess proved to be most important.

In the propositions submitted to the king by the Parliament, which he had just received at Newcastle, the Earl of Derby found in the list of names excluded from the amnesty his own, standing next to those of Prince Rupert and Prince Maurice. (*Thurloe's State Papers.*) The list consisted of thirty-six persons, of whom the Parliament reserved to themselves the power of condemning seven to death.

The king had not yet accepted these conditions, nor did he ever definitively do so; for such acceptance would have implied the adoption of the covenant, the abolition of the English Church, and the abdication of his power into the hands of the Parliament.

This evidence of animosity towards her husband greatly alarmed Lady Derby, and she resolved to go to London, and do her utmost to get his name erased from the fatal list.

On the 6th of February, 1647, we find her in England, and on the point of starting for London. She writes:—

> Trioche (the confidential attendant of Lord Strange, and much employed by Lady Derby,) met me in England, and is ready to set out for London, where I wish to be as soon as possible, starting, please God, on Monday. I have been in this part of the country, near one of our houses, for a fortnight, in order to get money for my journey. Many of my friends encourage me to hope; others cause me to fear. I am much troubled by all this doubt and suspense, but God will not forsake me. I will not fail to let you know what happens to me, and I will send Trioche back to you. I have told *Monsieur* your brother of his arrival. I have left him and his children very well, but anxious about my voyage. We were forty-eight hours on the sea, in a very bad boat, and in great danger. But if God blesses my sufferings, as I have prayed Him to do, I shall bear everything well.

On the 10th of March she writes from Chelsea:—

> Immediately after my arrival in Lancashire (she spells it Lenguicher) I did myself the honour of writing to you, and I intended to do the same on coming here, but could not; for, besides the fatigue consequent on my journey, the day after my arrival I received the bad news of the death of Monsieur le Prince d'Orange, which distressed me greatly, much more than all my own sad affairs. (Frederic Henri, third son of William the Silent, uncle of the Countess of Derby.) They say he died a

most pious and Christian death; a great consolation to all who loved him.

But you will know more particulars of it than I, who am new to this great world, where I find everything so changed. I must own to you, however, that several people who knew me formerly still show me much affection, and promise to help me. They advise me not to be impatient; but, when it is time, to begin by a request to the House of Peers that the name of *Monsieur* our brother-in-law may be taken from the list of those who are not to hope for pardon. Many say they will help me, and I believe it will be less difficult to obtain this aid from the nobles than from the Commons, who are so much more numerous. I daresay it will be done without much trouble, and God will give me wisdom and prudence.

The king goes on refusing to do what the Parliament require, and will not hear their ministers preach. He is carefully guarded, and seen by very few. May God counsel him for His glory, and give us a safe peace!

I have done nothing yet in our own business. Our friends advise me to take no steps till the propositions of peace are again presented to the king, which will not be till the coming of the deputies from Scotland. At present I do not know what to hope. I wish I had your cleverness; but, besides never having had anything like it, the life I have led since I came to England has been so different from that I am now entering upon, that if God does not give me His powerful help, I know not what I shall do.

By the 25th of March, 1647, the Scotch had betrayed the king into the hands of the Parliament. He had been for a month at Holmby House, in the county of Northampton. The Scotch Army had slowly retired, carrying off their 200,000*l*., the price of their treachery, but humbled and discontented—angry with the king, who would not accept the covenant, and with the Parliament of England, for having made them degrade themselves in their own eyes.

In addition to the anxiety caused by her husband's affairs, the countess had now that of a law-suit, instituted for the recovery of the estate of her brother the Comte de Laval, who had recently died. His effects were claimed by Miss Orpe, who maintained that he had privately married her; and, to the indignation of Lady Derby, this lady's cause was openly countenanced by the queen. The countess writes to her sister-in-law:

> I can assure you that the Queen of England has never seen this woman in my house, she has never entered it except one morning, and when no one was there. When the queen has spoken to me about her, I have always said that I did not believe in any marriage, and that even if there had been such a thing, a clandestine marriage was never held good. Her Majesty does not remember how by her own authority she annulled a marriage that had been contracted by the sister of La Harpe, and one of the nephews of her nurse, and how she threatened an Irish priest with hanging for having; officiated in such an affair.

This nurse of Queen Henrietta Maria had doubtless great influence with her mistress, for it was the circumstance of the marriage of Miss Orpe's brother with one of the daughters of this woman that procured her the royal protection, which, however, was less efficacious in France than in England, for there she could not threaten to hang the judges.

When we see such results from the possession of absolute power, which has fallen into blundering and unscrupulous hands, we can understand how an indignant and outraged nation rises at last into actual rebellion.

The countess said in another letter:

> It is with great astonishment that I have read the proceedings of the Queen of England in connection with our law-suit, by what I can see, she has done more harm to herself than to us, and everyone is ashamed of her. The electoral prince came to see me today, and I could not help telling him what I thought of the conduct of Prince Rupert in this matter.

Notwithstanding these powerful protectors, Miss Orpe was nonsuited, and the property of the Comte de Laval was divided, though not without difficulty, between his brother and sister.

Public affairs now wore a new aspect, but one more troubled and confused than ever. The Parliament, for the time masters of the king, and dreading the growing influence of the generals, had voted the disbanding of the army, with the exception of the forces required for the war in Ireland, and for the safety of the garrisons; but neither the independent party, who derived their strength from the army, nor their able leader, who was beginning to exercise a preponderating authority, would permit this.

From his place in Parliament, Cromwell urged the army to resist, and the Countess of Derby thus relates to her sister-in-law the result of his machinations:—

> The army has refused to be disbanded. Yesterday was the day they were to have begun by disbanding the general's regiment (Fairfax was not to take part in the war in Ireland). The Parliament sent their commissioners to the headquarters of the regiment, but they found no one there, and all the army is assembled. They have chosen two men on whom they can most rely, from every company, and formed them into a sort of council; those of the officers who have refused to do what they want have been disbanded. The general approves of this, and has sent a letter of excuse to the commissioners for not meeting them. They have applied to Parliament for permission to return, and have returned. God knows what will come of it! I pray that it may be for His glory; but I greatly fear the nation is not at the end of its misery. However, we have the consolation of knowing that things cannot be worse.
>
> In times like these one cannot think much of one's own individual troubles, but I am continually assured that, with God's help, our affairs will come right.

On the 2nd of June, when Lady Derby wrote thus to her sister-in-law, Cornet Joyce, in the name of the army, removed the king from Holmby House, and conveyed him to Newark.

The king in the hands of the army! The blow was a terrible one for the Presbyterian party, who saw themselves outflanked by a new power, more resolute and indomitable than themselves.

Lady Derby writes, on the 21st of June, 1647, to the Duchesse de la Trémoille:

> Within a month the face of things here is completely changed. It is almost beyond conception. The people are so much excited against the present government, and show it so freely at the doors of both Houses of Parliament, that many of the members are in great danger; and although the guard has been doubled, that does not protect them from injury, for those who are brought there for their protection mock and urge on the others. It is said that the approach of the army to London has occasioned great confusion and alarm, and many have hastily left the

city, believing that there will be war. The generals are already chosen (Massey, Waller, and Hollis), but the city of London does not side with the Parliament. It desires that the army should be satisfied, but has hitherto prevented any warlike resolution. Each one speaks differently concerning its intentions; but it is thought the City will bring the king back, and have the honour of that, and of making a good peace, in which no distinctions of party will be recognised. I hope it may please God that the arrangement of our affairs should be comprehended in this peace, and that He will direct everything for His own glory.

I have had letters from the Isle of Man, and everybody there seems very pleased, even those most employed in public affairs, which are more uncertain than ever. I consider my son very fortunate in having the honour of being with you.

I have no power of attorney from *Monsieur* his father, only a letter in which he tells me that whatever I may do for his submission to Parliament he will subscribe to, and other similar things that have no relation to our affairs in France.

The king continues with the army; and the frequent changes ordered by the Parliament in his residence—now to one place, now to another—are only attended to by the army as it suits them. They profess that they will respect his person, and they allow him to have his servants and chaplains. The Duke of Richmond sleeps in his bedroom. The Parliament storms against both, but nevertheless gives great support to the orders of the army, which they call *theirs*. They have effaced from their registers all those resolutions against the army which declare they will restore the king and his house to their rights; they promise to maintain the rights of the Parliament and the liberty of the subject; and they say they do not desire the ruin of the king's party.

One result of this is that the Lords have already struck out *Monsieur* your brother-in-law's name from the list of exceptions; and today they are doing the same by others. It passed without any opposition, but the Commons have done nothing, as it has not been sent to them yet from the Lords; but I am encouraged to hope that, with God's help, there will be no difficulty.

I suppose you have already heard how eleven members of the House of Commons have been accused by the army; and the Parliament, in accordance with their desire, have expelled them the House. This change is incredible, for these men (Hollis, Stapleton, Maynard, &c.,) were the most distinguished, and those who led everything; but the alterations in the Parliament are so extraordinary that if I had not seen and heard for myself no one could have persuaded me of them. They are now treated with scorn and hatred, and every day they are so much insulted in their houses and their persons that their guard has been doubled. It is beyond my power to tell what will come of all this, but I am sure the army will not be disbanded till everything is settled, and this Parliament ended and another called. This is all that can be said.

The hopes of the countess with regard to the good-will of the army, though destined to be so cruelly disappointed, were nevertheless not without foundation. M. Guizot says:

> Some of the leaders, Cromwell and Ireton especially, too clear-sighted to flatter themselves that their struggle with the Presbyterians was ended and their victory certain, were uneasy about the future. They calculated all the chances, and, seeking to bring matters to a crisis, bethought them if the favour of the king, raised again by their means, would not be the best guarantee for the safety of their party; for themselves the surest means of gaining fortune and power.

Lady Derby writes:

> The king is still fifteen miles from this (at Eversham). The princes and princesses, his children, went from here yesterday to visit him, and are not to return till tomorrow. Permission for this meeting was asked from the Parliament by Sir Thomas Fairfax, though they had declared anyone who should dare to make such a request the enemy of the public. There are various opinions about his intellect, but no doubt about his courage, and that he is a man of his word. In this matter he acted with the army, which has hitherto made the Parliament do what it likes It is said by some that the design of the army is to put away all those who hold opinions contrary to their own, and to be governed by the remainder of the Parliament.
> The king is allowed every kind of liberty; the ambassadors see him and talk to him as formerly. He has received a visit from the electoral prince. Before he was in the hands of the army it was a crime to think of anything of the kind.

Yesterday, the Parliament passed an act confirming the appointment of Sir Thomas Fairfax to the post of general, which augmentation of rank gives him power over all the forces in the kingdom. Hitherto, he has had the command only of the army that he happened to be with in person; and now he will have the disposition of all the garrisons, the greater number of which have been already under his control.

The king showed great delight at the sight of the princes his children; and there was much tenderness on all sides. The little princess (Elizabeth) paid a very apropos compliment to the general, whom she saw quite unexpectedly, and gave evidence of a great deal of cleverness—which they all have, particularly the youngest (the Duke of Gloucester).

Lady Derby's stay in London was prolonged; but her business did not advance. She was deeply grieved at the loneliness and inaction to which her husband had been condemned for two years. It was doubtless at this time that he wrote for his son a series of very curious instructions for the government of the little kingdom of Man. The earl writes:

> This island was sometimes governed by kings, natives of its own, who were converted to Christianity by St. Patrick, the Apostle of Ireland. And Sir John Stanley, the first possessor of it of that family, was by his patent styled King of Man, as were his successors after him, to the time of Thomas, second Earl of Derby, who, for great and wise reasons, thought fit to forbear that title. And no subject I know hath so great a royalty as this. And lest it should at any time be thought too great, keep this rule, and you will more securely keep it, 'Fear God and honour the King.' When I go to the top of Mount Baroule, by turning myself round, I can see England, Scotland, Ireland, and Wales; and think it a pity to see so many kingdoms at once, which is a prospect no place, as I conceive, in any nation that we know under heaven can afford, and have so little profit from all or any of them.
>
> But having duly considered thereof, I have, as I think, discovered the reason of it. The country is, indeed, better than I was informed of; for which I blame myself that I enquired so little of it; for, indeed, he who seeks not to know his own is unworthy of what he hath. And I am of opinion this island will never

flourish until some trade or manufacture be established in it. But though you invite strangers or natives to become merchants, yet never anything will be done to the purpose until you yourself lead the way, and by your example and encouragement set this people a pattern,

By this, or such like means, no doubt but you may grow rich yourself, and others under you improve the land, and set the people to work, so that in time you shall have no beggars nor no loiterers; and where you have one soul now you shall have many; every house will become a little town, and every town a little city; the sea will abound with ships, and the country with people, to the great enrichment of the whole. (*House of Stanley*.)

To these wise practical counsels, the Earl of Derby added directions for the moral progress of the population, he writes:

Choose for your bishop, a reverend and holy man, who may carefully see the whole clergy do their duty; but not any person already beneficed in England; and oblige him you choose to residence. In a few years, the leases will be all expired, and then the bishopric will be worth having; and, considering the cheapness of the place, I know few bishops in England that can live better than he, the whole being entire, and your prerogative herein very great, to which have a particular regard. . . .

And if you, even as I designed, set up a university, it may oblige the nations round about us, get friends to the country, and enrich the land, which, in time, will bring something to the lord's purse. And, as the place is cheap, yet well-furnished with proper subsistence, and the temptations to idleness or luxury few, education might be had here on the easiest terms. But of this I will tell you more when, please God, I can see you and myself in peace. (*House of Stanley*.)

While the earl was preparing these thoughtful and wise directions for the life-long conduct of his son, the loneliness in which the absence of his wife left him was growing more and more oppressive.

In the month of September, 1647, the Parliament at length accorded to Lord Derby's children what they had at first conceded for their personal maintenance, that is, a fifth of their father's revenue. It was only after two years' application that this bounty was assigned to them on the hereditary manor of Knowsley. Catherine and Amelia Stanley were at once sent there by their father, who kept with him only Lady Mary and his sons Edward and William.

A letter from Fairfax to Major Jackson, who was established with his family in the house, had given instructions for the evacuation of the place, and directions had also been conveyed to the keepers to watch that the said Major Jackson destroyed nothing in the house or park before leaving—an injunction which seems to indicate ill will on the part of the major.

The Countess of Derby was still in London, engaged in her great business. Writing on the 14th of March, 1648, she says:—

> I am advised to go to Lancashire, and try to live on what they have allowed my children, for I receive no money; and I hope my presence may facilitate the means employed for getting it. Being near, and on the spot, we must live economically, and make the best of what we have.

In the same letter she gives a very curious picture of the confusion that prevailed in England on religious questions.

> As for my husband and myself, all that relates to religion is, thank God, so thoroughly engraved on our hearts, that nothing, with His grace, can take it away. If the Parliament had for their end religion and the glory of God, as you think they have, they would not act with the cruelty and injustice which characterize all they do. As for religion, they have so deceived the people that now, when they perceive their errors, and groan under the burden of their tyranny, even those who have been the most attached to their cause deplore our misery and their own. They would find it hard to tell you their creed, where there are as many religions as families.
>
> The test is publicly maintained; books printed which deny the Holy Ghost,—and the persons known to have produced them not punished; the commandments of God and the confession of faith disregarded; the Lord's prayer neglected, and not thought necessary to be said; the sacraments administered according to the fancy of the person administering; the ministry neglected— everyone who thinks he is able to preach, even women, may do so without any examination; baptism is thought nothing of, and not administered to children; and worse things, which make all who have any religion left shudder to see it so abused. As for people who wish ill to us, there are some, but not more than the Lords have who are in Parliament; for the Commons intend

to recognise no more aristocrats, but to have perfect equality, only they do not know how to get it managed.

If you could hear the discontent amongst them, you would hardly believe it. I speak of those who have risked all for the Parliament, and are the greatest enemies of the king's party. This discontent has reached such a height, that if the Scotch come, as it is supposed they may, there will be very few who will not join them. In consequence of this, all the governors who had been most zealous in the cause of the Parliament have been changed, and replaced by men who regard nothing but their party. But although the Parliament has passed this resolution, if the army disapproves, they must change it: thus, one day undoes what the previous one has done. Those only who see what goes on can believe it; and if I myself had not been present, no one could have persuaded me of it.

If I had the honour of talking to you for a couple of hours, you would soon be convinced of the truth, and would deplore the sufferings of the Protestant religion and the profit that the Catholics derive from them. I have no doubt the queen will do what she can for her religion, but I think she ought to consider that she cannot advance it. She is most unfortunate; her own party are much dissatisfied with her, and say she has ruined them. They are no better pleased with the king.

The tragical end of the drama was approaching; all the hopes of the Royalists were about to be crushed by a single blow. The king had spent two months and a half at Hampton Court, at first with his court around him, and freely visited by his children and friends.

Lady Derby wrote, in September, 1647:

I saw the king yesterday, for the second time since it has been permitted to visit him. He is hopeful about his affairs. The princes, his children, see him two or three times a week; they are living only three miles from Hampton Court, the finest of his houses.

Cromwell and Ireton negotiated with the king, to the suppressed wrath of the Independent party. Charles multiplied offers; but, with his incurable duplicity, at the same time negotiated with Scotland, where they still hoped to make him accept the covenant. In a letter to the queen, which was seized by Cromwell, he wrote:—

For the rest, I alone understand my position. Be quite easy as to the concessions I may grant. When the time comes, I shall very well know how to treat these rogues; and instead of a silken garter, I will fit them with a hempen halter.

He added, that he thought he would rather treat with the Scotch Presbyterians than with the army.

Cromwell and Ireton at once decided on the course they would take; and from that time the king's cause was lost, and his life doomed.

Notwithstanding the hopes he built on his secret manoeuvres Charles was alarmed at the changes that were being made about him. His faithful counsellors had been ordered to leave him; his servants even had been withdrawn from him, and his guards doubled. Warnings of assassination reached him every day. He made up his mind, and on the 11th of November escaped from his guards and went to the Isle of Wight, where he was received (not without difficulty) by the governor, Colonel Hammond. The king thought he was safe, and began to negotiate openly with the Parliament, who sent commissioners to him; and secretly with the Scotch, who promised him an army; and even with the leaders of the Independent party, who were uneasy at the Republican tendencies manifested by the soldiers.

Charles alone held the thread of all these intrigues, ready at any time to take refuge on the continent if there was really danger, said he:

I wish to finish with the Scotch before quitting the kingdom, if they saw me out of the hands of the army they would get more exacting.

He concluded his treaty with the Scotch; refused the propositions of the Parliament, and sent back their commissioners. His escape was planned for the following night, when suddenly the servants were all sent away from the island, the doors of the castle closed, and the guard doubled. Charles Stuart was a prisoner: and in Parliament they ventured to speak of a Republic.

Charles had lost his liberty, but the report of his imprisonment raised him up new defenders. There were numerous insurrections in the West as well as in the North; and on the 8th of July the Scotch Army, faithful to the treaty of the Isle of Wight, entered England under the orders of the Duke of Hamilton. The Republican chieftains, in spite of the distrust with which Cromwell inspired them, felt that he, and he only, could meet the danger. He hurried to the North, fought the English insurgents under the command of Langdale on the 17th of August, then, uniting with Lambert, he came up with the Scotch at Wigan on the 18th, cut the rear-guard in pieces, and, continuing to advance, won a last victory at Warrington.

The Scotch infantry surrendered, and Hamilton was taken prisoner as he was trying to escape with the cavalry. Every sign of invasion had disappeared, but Cromwell entered Scotland to take from the Royalist Presbyterians all means of action and their last hope of safety. Three months later he returned in triumph to headquarters; and the king, carried off on the 29th of November from Newport, where the Parliament had guaranteed his safety, was shut up in Hurst Castle by order of the army, in an apartment so dark that torches were required at midday, and under the guard of Colonel Ewers, a fierce and ill-mannered gaoler.

While the unhappy king, with the courage and grave dignity which characterized him in his troubles, was passing through all the tragic stages that led to the final sacrifice, his friends and partisans were paying the price of their devotion to him and his cause.

The Countess of Derby had returned to her husband. She writes to her sister-in-law on the 25th of March, 1648:

> Necessity obliges me to quit this place, and our friends of the Parliament advise me to do it, telling me there is no doubt our business will go on very well. There is a gentleman in the same circumstances as ourselves who has been allowed to treat for his estate after having presented his petition, and they have taxed him so high that he will not consent to pay the money. But I am advised to do nothing; there is so much general discontent that those who are in office say in confidence things cannot be long without change.

CHAPTER 6

Letters After the King's Death

Fifteen months passed, and what changes had taken place! There was not a word from the Countess of Derby to her sister-in-law during that terrible period. She may not have written, or her letters may have been lost. The king's trial, his death, and the first months of the Republic, remain shrouded in melancholy silence. One cry of indignation alone comes from the Isle of Man, and it is from the Earl of Derby.

The Parliament had again tried to shake his fidelity. The king he had served was dead; and Ireton wrote to induce him to surrender the Isle of Man to the Parliament, promising him the free enjoyment of all the rest of his possessions in return. Here is the reply made by the earl:—

Castletown, July 22nd, 1649.

Sir,—I received your letter with indignation and scorn, and return you this answer; That I cannot but wonder whence you should gather any hopes from me, that I should, like you, prove treacherous to my sovereign, since you cannot but be sensible of my actings in His Late Majesty's service; from which principles of loyalty I am no whit departed. I scorn your proffers, disdain your favour, and abhor your treason; and am so far from delivering up this island to your advantage, that I will keep it to the utmost of my power to your destruction. Take this for your final answer, and forbear any further solicitations; for, if you trouble me with any more messages on this occasion, I will burn the paper and hang the bearer.

This is the immutable resolution, and shall be the undoubted practice of him, who accounts it his chiefest glory to be

His Majesty's most loyal and obedient servant,

Derby.

At the same time that the earl sent this haughty reply to General Ireton, he published in London a declaration, consisting of several pages, expressing the same resolution, and ending with this paragraph:—

And I do hereby declare, that, to the utmost of my power, I shall faithfully endeavour to hold out this island to the advantage of His Majesty, and the annoyance of all rebels and their abettors, and do cheerfully invite all my allies, friends, and acquaintance, all my tenants in the counties of Lancaster and Chester, or elsewhere, and all other His Majesty's faithful and loyal subjects, to repair to this island, as their general rendezvous and safe harbour, where they shall receive entertainment, and such encouragement as their several qualities and condition shall require; where we will unanimously employ our forces to the utter ruin of these unmatchable and rebellious regicides, and the final destruction of their interests both by land and sea.

Neither shall any apprehension of danger either to my life or estate appal me; but I shall on all occasions (by God's assistance) shew myself ready to express my duty and loyalty with hazard of both; and this I shall adventure for the future with more alacrity, for as much as, in all my former actings in His Majesty's service, I never did anything with relation to the trust reposed in me, that awakens my conscience to repentance.

Derby.

From Castletown, in the Isle of Man,
July the 18th, 1849. (*State Trials*.)

On the 27th July, 1649, two months after this declaration of war, the Countess of Derby wrote to her sister-in-law:—

I believed, as you did, that our business was accomplished, and the person who hitherto managed it brought us the news with the congratulations natural in the circumstances; his stay here was only for a few days, but when he got back to England he found everything in worse condition than ever, and some of our estates already given away—a thing which has never yet been done. No reason was given for this alteration, but I know it was occasioned by petitions, full of false representations, having been presented to Parliament by low people, and, although numbers know and say how false are these statements, they will not hear reason.

Dear sister, if you had the least notion of the truth, you would change your opinion. The sects of which you speak increase daily, and it makes one's hair stand on end to think of it. The *Koran* is printed with permission. It is common to deny both God and Jesus Christ, and to believe only in the Spirit of the Universe. I am not repeating from report, I have heard these blasphemies; as for baptism, they make a joke of it. I assure you, the hearts of those who have any religion left bleed to talk of these things.

They threaten this poor place; but we will do our utmost, with the grace of God, to defend it. He knows how my husband and I have always sought His glory rather than our own interests, and that we have loved the religion I profess above all others.

How great a consolation it would be if I could tell you what is in my mind, for I am sure you would pity us, and our sufferings would grieve you, and make you hate the malice of our enemies, and those of God and true religion. God will not abandon His Church. The Gospel does not promise temporal blessings as signs of the good cause. It is by tribulation and misery that we are to come to heaven. I prepare myself for it with joy diminished only by the thought of my poor children and their father. But I hope God will help them, and that those to whom they have the honour of belonging will not suffer them to perish; and that, since they cannot help them against their enemies, they will at least have pity on their misery.

Dear sister, forgive the terrors of an afflicted mother, who opens her heavy heart to you, and begs you, in God's name, to give her your help. (Then in cypher):—The only cause of their ill will to us is their desire to have this island, and, when they have got us into their power, to take our lives and our property. My wish is to be protected by some foreign state or prince. But we must implore your aid and advice in the extreme distress in which our poor family is placed. . . The person who brought us the news of our composition, also brought a passport for my husband to return to England; but if he used it his life would be in danger. You may judge by this with what kind of people we have to do, and of the integrity of their intentions.

So much trouble told upon Lady Derby's health. She was ill when she wrote the letter we have just read. A few lines only on the 15th of October show that she was worse. On the 30th of December she wrote:—

For seven weeks I have scarcely taken sleep or nourishment, and I believed God, in His mercy, had made me satisfied to quit this world, having given me the firm assurance of the pardon of my sins through the merits of His son, and perfect confidence in my salvation and in the joys of a future state. But it has pleased Him to keep me longer in this miserable world; and I hope He will give me grace to employ for His glory the life to which He has so miraculously restored me. To have suffered in so good and holy a cause gave me great repose of conscience during my illness; and I would not exchange the least happiness I have experienced for all the joy of my persecutors, since the prosperity of the wicked is only for a time.

I hope, dear sister, that my letters have shown you the truth, and the designs they have in England with regard to religion (the Duchesse de la Trémoille had evidently been led away by the pious protestations of Cromwell); and permit me to say, that nothing has ever so grieved me as to see that you entertained a belief so opposed to what is professed in England and other places where these monsters have power. Not a week passes but some of their people are here; and to hear the blasphemies they utter is almost beyond belief, and how they pervert the Scriptures, declaring that whatever wickedness is done by the elect, is done by the inspiration of the spirit they call Holy; and that everyone may serve God after his own fashion; that Christ and His Apostles had some light, but that *they* were come to restore religion, and that there was more error in the Presbytery than in the Church of England under the government of bishops.

I declare that what I am writing is the least extravagant of their doctrines, in which one can perceive no foundation, since they change according to their fancy, and, provided nothing is said against their tyrannical government, every kind of vice the most monstrous, and of heresy the most execrable and unheard of, are endured. I am assured that, if this goes on, in a few years the Catholic religion will be openly professed in England; it is now very freely tolerated, and the votaries of this religion live peaceably and enjoy their property.

I am troubling you too much, dear sister. It is true, when I am on this topic it is not easy for me to quit it.

Lady Derby's reflections on the progress of Catholicism continued to alarm the Duchesse de la Trémoille; a letter written by her two months before only reached the Isle of Man in January, 1650, and the doubt which she then expressed caused Lady Derby to write without delay on the 20th of that month:—

> I have read what you were good enough to send me in cypher about the king's affairs (Charles II.—who had been proclaimed in Scotland and Ireland at the very time that the Parliament had been forced by Cromwell to proclaim the Republic, and who was still in Holland); but, if you are not mistaken in the cypher for my husband, I believe exactly the contrary; for, by all possible assurances and protestations, you may rest satisfied, dear sister, that he is as true a Protestant as ever, and that he has not the least inclination to become a Catholic; and for this I give you my word.
>
> But, dear sister, how much mistaken they are who tell you there are none such in England. I received a letter yesterday from a person of credit, who has always been of their party, who tells me that one of their ministers, whose name she gave me, and the place where he preached, had said and maintained openly in church that there was no greater divinity than himself, and that, as he was not God, therefore, there could be no God. Someone complained of it to the governor of the town; but the man was not punished, and nobody seemed to consider it strange. If you understood English, I would send you the letter.
>
> One of our people, who returned from Scotland a short time ago, had seen many sorcerers burned, who all declared that they were always present with Cromwell when he fought; and others in England, near Newcastle, say the same thing, our doctor being present at the time; and there is a sorcerer now in prison in Edinburgh, who affirms that he was present when Cromwell renounced his baptismal vow.

What a strange medley of faith and superstition, of strength of mind and credulity! The strict Huguenot and the lady of rank were equally outraged by this burst of mad liberty; in her alarm and contempt she confounds the *Koran*, Catholicism, and sorcerers, with levellers. Atheists, and Pantheists. When we find people speaking of the spirit of the universe and the divinity of human nature in the very midst of the Rebellion of 1649, we are tempted to exclaim, "There is nothing new under the sun."

In the midst of the sufferings and anxieties and the terrible realities with which Lady Derby was surrounded, we are surprised and not a little amused to find several of her letters filled with questions of etiquette. On the Ist of May, 1648, the Prince de Tarente had married Amelie de Hesse Cassel, daughter of the reigning Grand Duke. At the congress of Münster, in 1643, the Duc de la Trémoille put forward pretensions to the crown of Naples, in right of a marriage contracted in 1521, between François de la Trémoille and the granddaughter of Frederic III, King of Naples. Mdlle. de la Trémoille was about to be presented at court, and there was some question as to her "*tabouret.*" The mother therefore applies to the aunt for her reminiscences on this subject; and, from her retirement in the Isle of Man, after having lived for twenty-four years away from France and the court, Charlotte de la Trémoille throws herself eagerly into the discussion.

She refers for a moment to the subject of her own "*tabouret.*" She writes to her sister-in-law:

> You were in Paris when the queen, the king's mother (Marie de Medicis) deprived me of it; and it was that very summer, at St. Germains, that she gave it back to me, saying that she did so with all her heart, for she believed it was my right. The Cardinal de Richelieu, who answered for me, said as much to my mother when she went to thank him; and I have kept it ever since at the court of both queens.

"*Le tabouret,*" or right of sitting on a stool in presence of royalty, was accorded to Mademoiselle de la Trémoille, to the great satisfaction of her aunt.

On the 2nd of June, 1650, Charles II. embarked for Scotland, fifteen days after the execution of Montrose. To acquire a crown, he had accepted the covenant, and sacrificed his own honour and the life of his servant; his father had refused to the end to preserve his crown at such a price.

Lady Derby writes, in May, 1650:

> It is said that the king has certainly concluded a treaty with the Scots, and that he is soon to be in Scotland in person. If this news had been known two days earlier, the life of the Marquis of Montrose might have been saved; within three days he has been condemned and executed. He was to have been commander in Ireland if it had pleased God to spare his life. I pray that this event may not damp people's spirits.

The king was no sooner landed in Scotland than his faithful servants found all their troubles increased—a melancholy foretaste of the sacrifices which they were destined to make in his cause.

On the 8th of June, 1650, Lady Derby writes to her sister-in-law:—

Since my last letter I have received news of your nieces in England which afflicts me not a little; and though I can think of nothing to relieve them, I hope to find some comfort in telling you my troubles, for I know that you will share, and, if possible, remedy them. More than two years ago, when I was in England, and intending to come here, I was advised, with some show of reason, to send for your two nieces, Catherine and Amelie, and to leave them at Knowsley during my absence, that they might keep possession of the house, and receive the income granted to the children of delinquents, for so they call us (the petition putting forward a claim to this revenue is drawn up in the name of the six children of the Earl of Derby), and which was the fifth part of the revenue of their father's estates.

Before I sent for them from this place, I procured passports from the Parliament and the general (Sir Thomas Fairfax), and his protection for my daughters, and they have been there two whole years without any one ever having disturbed either them or their people. But about three weeks ago, a man of the name of Birch, the governor of a small town called Liverpool, took them prisoners, and confined them in the said town, where they are now in custody with their attendants. No reason is given for this, but we hear it is because they are thought to be too much liked, and that people were beginning to make applications to the Parliament in the hope that their father might come to terms, of which I see no chance. They are kept so strictly that no one about them is allowed to go to the distance of even six miles from their residence without permission, running the risk of being shot like a criminal.

They persecute those who belonged to their own party before this horrible attempt against the king, quite as much as those of his party. In all this we acknowledge the righteous judgments of God. Here is all I can tell you, dear sister, on this unhappy subject. I trust in God that He will protect them, and I do not doubt that He will. We hear that they are bearing it bravely, and I have no doubt this is true of the eldest; but my daughter Amelie is delicate and timid, and is undergoing medical treatment, by order of M. de Mayerne. (A medical man in whom Lady Derby placed great confidence.) They are in a wretched place, ill lodged, and in a bad air; but these barbarians think of nothing but carrying out their damnable designs, which could not be worse if all hell itself had invented them.

Bradshaw's hatred of the Earl of Derby had conceived this method of satisfaction; it was easy enough to understand the end he had in view in thus persecuting the earl's children.

Their sufferings continued to increase; the income allowed them by Parliament was not sufficient even to procure them bread; and if it had not been for the liberality of the poor impoverished Royalists, and the fidelity of their own servants, who went about begging for them from house to house, these poor girls. Lady Catherine and Lady Amelia Stanley, would have died of hunger. At length they applied to Fairfax, who had always been kind to them; and he wrote to the Earl of Derby to this effect:

> That if his lordship would deliver the Isle of Man to the Parliament's commands, his children should not only be set at liberty, but he should peaceably return to England, and enjoy one moiety of all his estate. (*House of Stanley*.)

This was more than Lord Derby had reason to expect from the Parliament; yet the Isle of Man was the brightest jewel in his coronet; a safe and peaceful retreat in stormy times; and a place where the authority of the king and the Church was still recognised. He replied to Sir T. Fairfax:—

> I am deeply afflicted for the sufferings of my children. It is not the course of great and noble minds to punish innocent children for their father's offences. It would be a clemency in Sir Thomas Fairfax either to send them back to me, or to Holland or to France; but if he can do none of these, my children must submit to the mercy of God Almighty, but shall never be redeemed by my disloyalty. (*House of Stanley*.)

In addition to her anxiety for her daughters, the Countess of Derby had other troubles. Her son, Lord Strange, had left France, and to her great grief was living in idleness in Holland.

She writes to her sister-in-law:

We have written to your nephew, desiring him to return to France, that he may see a campaign there; for it is shameful for a person of his age (he was under twenty-three,) never yet to have seen anything; he has received some hints of this kind from those about him which have piqued him greatly, and inspired him with a desire to see service, for which I do not blame him.

Young Lord Strange had no very great desire to see service, and other ties kept him in Holland. He had conceived a passionate affection for Mdlle. de Rupa, a young German lady of good family, but without fortune or rank. This new trouble roused in Lady Derby's mind the strongest feelings of anger; her son had often offended her, and in this matter not only were her maternal feelings wounded, but her family pride, accustomed as she was to great alliances, was outraged. She therefore resolved to go herself to Holland to break off the connection.

Charles II. had been a month in Scotland when she wrote from Kircudbright in August, 1650:—

Dear Sister,—I had the honour of writing to you two days before my departure from the Isle of Man, which was on the 26th of last month, (this letter is lost,) when I told you my resolution to go through this country to Holland, to remedy, if possible, this sad business; but finding that the English Army had come here in great force, I could not travel without a passport; I have sent to ask for one, and I shall wait for it in the Isle of Man, to which place I return today, please God; with a fair wind it is but a ten hours' voyage. I have been here fifteen days, suffering every imaginable inconvenience, being reduced to eat oaten bread, and some of us to lodge in the house of the chief person of the place, though I never saw anything so dirty. But this is nothing to the religion.

I fear greatly the result of this war, and I assure you that those who are in power are not so much in favour of monarchy as against the Duke of Hamilton, and his faction. The king behaves with wonderful prudence; he is obliged to listen continually to sermons against his father, blaming him for all the blood that was shed; and those which I have heard in this place are horrible, having nothing of devotion in them, nor explaining any point of religion, but being full of sedition; naming people by their names, and treating of everything with such ignorance, and without the least respect or reverence, that I am so scandalised I do not think I could live with a quiet conscience among these atheists. I shall do my utmost to make out my journey from the island; if my passport comes, as I have reason to hope it will, I shall certainly attempt it.

But if it does not, look with compassion, dear sister, on this unfortunate affair, which is of so much consequence to my poor distressed family; have pity on an unfortunate mother, distracted with grief, for I know not what to do. If my passport is refused, I see no means of breaking off this affair by personal interference, unless you would take it in hand, with that prudence and skill with which you manage whatever you are pleased to undertake.

The passport did not come, and all Lady Derby's anger could not prevent the marriage of her son with Mdlle. de Rupa, for which she never forgave him to the end of her days.

It was no doubt by his wife's advice that the Earl of Derby, in drawing up his will before his departure from the Isle of Man, wrote these words:—

> I give and bequeath to my most gracious sovereign and liege Lord Charles, the second of that name, one cup of fine gold of the value of one hundred pounds, humbly beseeching His Majesty, if God shall call me out of the world before I see my estate settled by his grace and favour, my chief honour and estate may descend upon my son Edward and his issue male, and in default of him upon my son William and his issue male, or in default of any such issue upon my daughter Mary and her two sisters Catherine and Amelia successively; and this by reason of my just sense against Charles, my eldest son, for his disobedience to His Majesty in the matter of his marriage, as His Majesty well knows, and for his going to join the rebels of England at this time to the great grief of his parents, by which he hath brought a stain upon their blood if he were permitted to inherit.

The father spoke harshly when he styled the proceedings of his son an adhesion to the rebels: Charles Stanley had written to the Duchesse de la Trémoille in December, 1650:—

> Some days ago I received letters from the Isle of Man in which I am desired by my father and mother to address myself to M.

de la Trémoille and to you, and to receive your orders as if they came from my parents themselves, a command which I am very willing to obey. Some people in England have sent me word that, if my father did not make his peace with the Parliament within two months, neither he nor any of his race after him should enjoy his estates in that country; urging upon me that, since they were sure the Parliamentarians would never come to terms with my father, I should do well to go over and make terms with them on my own account, which being done, my father might enjoy his property in my name.

I do not wish to say anything about this to my father and mother until I have your approval of it. I hope you have not so bad an opinion of me as to think that in this matter I look to my own profit so much as to the good of our house; whatever advantage I may reap from this negotiation, my chief desire is that I may bring back the waters to their source.

The Duchesse de la Trémoille could scarcely have advised "this negotiation," entirely opposed as it was to the wishes and principles both of Lady Derby and her husband. Yet it seems probable that Lord Strange disregarded her silence or disapproval, for he certainly went to England; we find, indeed, no trace of his stay there, but we may presume that he lived quietly at Knowsley. To the last his mother never forgot his offences.

"I give to my son, Charles, Earl of Derby, the sum of five pounds," she writes in her will. She was poor, no doubt, but even the smallest token of remembrance would have been less cruel than this bequest, evidently intended as it was to disinherit him. Forgiveness was not one of Lady Derby's virtues.

While her letters were thus filled with indignation against her son, and especially against "the Delilah," as she constantly calls her daughter-in-law, who had drawn him into a marriage so highly disapproved by all his family, events were hurrying on rapidly in Scotland. Cromwell had entered that country on the 22nd of July, 1650, almost at the same moment as the king, with an army of about fifteen thousand men. As soon as he had crossed the borders of Scotland, he addressed his army, exhorting them:

> As Christians and soldiers, to be doubly and trebly diligent, to be wary and worthy, for sure enough we have work before us! But have we not had God's blessing hitherto? Let us go on

faithfully and hope for the like still.

Cromwell might well be hopeful, for the king, against whom he had come to fight, was already half vanquished. Treated as a prisoner in the country which had just recalled him, Charles was not even present at the councils where his affairs were discussed. While surrounding him with all the pomps of royalty, they never took the trouble of consulting him. Lady Derby writes:

> The king gains everybody's affection, though he is treated very shamefully. The Church wished to keep him away from the army, but he presented himself to them, and they received him with the greatest joy; the Church, fearing that he would become too popular, sent him away again. Cromwell, who is general of the English Army, has sent in a declaration along with that of the Parliament, and the Church has replied, on its own authority, without consulting either the king or the Council of State. The Pope himself never assumed such authority.

This Church of Scotland, for which Lady Derby had conceived such an aversion, or rather for the fanatics in it who were stirring up the people, required the king to sign a declaration, acknowledging and deploring the evil deeds of his father, his mother's idolatries, and the sin which he had himself committed in treating with the Irish rebels. For the first time since he entered Scotland, Charles allowed his indignation to appear.

"I could never again look my mother in the face if I were to sign, such a paper," he exclaimed. But they insisted, and the declaration was signed.

Meantime, Cromwell continued his march into Scotland, through a desolated country, the people having retired before him, and destroyed all the crops as they went. Finding neither provisions nor enemies, he withdrew to Dunbar, closely followed by the Scottish Army, under command of Sir Alexander Leslie, whom he attacked, and completely defeated there on the 3rd of September, 1650. Six days afterwards he was master of Leith and Edinburgh, the castle alone holding out against him.

Charles had been taken to Perth, where he heard without regret of the defeat of the fanatics, and the disorganisation of the Presbyterian party. On the 1st of January, 1651, he was crowned at Scone, and his position began to look more hopeful. The Royalists were active in England, and the Scotch Parliament was entirely in the hands of the moderate party, who, with Hamilton and Lauderdale at their head, invited the king to assume the command of his army.

While these favourable changes were taking place in the king's affairs, Cromwell fell dangerously ill, and was at one time thought to be dying. But the strength of his constitution and of his will prevailed over the disorder, and in July, 1651, he reappeared at the head of his forces, laying siege to Perth, and threatening to deprive Charles, who was encamped with his army at Stirling, of this the chief seat of his government.

The king suddenly determined to break up his camp, and to carry the war into England. He believed the Royalists only waited for his appearance to rise in his favour, and that all who were weary of the tyranny of the army would join him, and he counted on his Scotch subjects proving their loyalty by sharing his fortunes. Many of his friends disapproved of this bold measure, but few dared to speak out. Argyle alone tried to dissuade him; but, having failed, and being too proud to enter England in the train of the Duke of Hamilton, he withdrew from the expedition, and retired to his castle of Inveraig.

On the 31st of July, Charles set out for Carlisle at the head of an army of from twelve to fourteen thousand men, with David Leslie as his lieutenant-general. Eight days afterwards Cromwell also left Scotland, and advanced in the king's rear.

As soon as Charles set foot in England, he sent for the Earl of Derby. Lady Derby, writing from the Isle of Man on the 1st of September, 1651, says:—

> We are still existing here, by the goodness of God, who has permitted my husband to reach the king, his master, in safety, with a considerable force. He took with him ten ships, which nothing but God's help could have brought here safely; for since his departure we have been harassed by the enemy's ships. He left this on Wednesday the 13th of last month, and landed in England on the 15th, in a part of Lancashire called Wyrewater. I hear that the king received him with great joy and with every mark of affection. I wait impatiently for further particulars, which I much fear will not arrive soon on account of the enemy's ships which infest this coast.

Here the letters cease for six months. The Countess of Derby said little in times of sorrow; the great epochs of her life are marked by silence.

Chapter 7

The Last Days of a Noble Life

On the first summons from the king the earl had left the Isle of Man to join the Royal Army, Charles assuring him that not only the Royalists but the Presbyterians also had promised to rise in his favour. But on reaching Lancashire with three hundred gentlemen, he found that the king had already passed through that county, and had left Major-General Massey at Warrington to receive him. On the night of his arrival he had an interview with some of the Presbyterian party. Lord Derby said:

> Gentlemen, I am come to do His Majesty all the service in my power. The king has given me assurance under his own hand (he showed them the king's letter,) that you are all disposed to join with him; to that end I am ready to receive whoever are pleased to come to me, and with them to march immediately to His Majesty.

To this, one of their ministers, in behalf of himself and his brethren, replied:—

> We hope that your lordship will put away all the Papists that you have brought from the Isle of Man, and that you will take the covenant with us; after that we will follow you willingly.

"Sir, I hope this is only your own opinion," said the earl; "and therefore I desire that the gentlemen present will be pleased to deliver their own sentiments."

"His Majesty has taken the covenant," they replied, "and has thereby given encouragement to all his subjects to do the same. If your lordship will not put away all Papists, and enter publicly into the solemn league and covenant, we cannot join you."

Lord Derby said:

> Upon these terms I might long since have been restored to my whole estate, and the blessed martyr Charles I. to all his kingdom," "I am not now come to dispute, but to fight for His Majesty's restoration, and will, upon the issue of the first battle, humbly submit myself to His Majesty's directions on that point; I will refuse none of any persuasion whatsoever that come up cheerfully to serve the king; and I hope you will give me the same freedom and latitude to engage whom I can for His Majesty's preservation; I am well assured that all those gentlemen I have brought with me are sincere and honest friends to His Majesty's person and interest. (*House of Stanley*.)

Major Massey seconded Lord Derby with the strongest arguments in his power, but the Presbyterians obstinately insisted on their demands. The historian of the House of Stanley says:

> The old leaven had taken too much effect, and soured them too far to be sweetened by any arguments or reasonings whatsoever.

Then Lord Derby rose, and ended the conference with these words:—

> Gentlemen, if you will be persuaded to join with me, I make no doubt but in a few days to raise as good an army to follow the king as that he has now with him, and, by God's blessing, to shake off the yoke of bondage resting upon both you and us; if not, I cannot hope to effect much. I may, perhaps, have men enough at my command; but all the arms are in your possession, without which I shall only lead naked men to slaughter. However, I am determined to do what I can, with the handful of gentlemen now with me, for His Majesty's service, and if I perish, I perish but if my master suffer, the blood of another prince, and all the ensuing miseries of this nation, will lie at your doors.

He then took horse, accompanied by the gentlemen he had brought with him from the Isle of Man, and some few of the royal party who came in to him. (*House of Stanley*.)

Resting for a few days at Preston, he found that the secret warrants which he had caused to be dispersed in all the chief towns of the county were beginning to produce their effect; a number of cavaliers had already joined him, and he was hoping for further reinforcements, when he learned that Colonel Robert Lilburn, despatched by Cromwell to repress the movements by the Royalists in the West, had come to Manchester with a considerable body of troops. Lord Derby had with him only six hundred horse, whom he had had no time to train; he, however, gave orders upon this to march to Wigan, a town devoted to the king, where he hoped to add to his numbers; but before he could reach that place, Lilburn came up with him in a narrow lane, where his cavalry fought at a great disadvantage. The brilliant courage of Lord Derby and his cavaliers was forced to give way before the numbers and the regular discipline of the Republican troops.

At the head of his vanguard the earl twice forced a passage through the whole body of the enemy. He had two horses killed under him, but was both times remounted by a faithful servant, a Frenchman, who helped him at the peril of his life. At the third charge, after seeing his best friends fall by his side, he fought his way through the fugitives, with six gentlemen of his party, and having reached the town, he leaped from his horse at a door which stood open, and immediately shut it behind him before the enemy could come up. The woman of the house contrived to keep the door locked long enough to give him time to escape by the back, and take refuge with one of his friends. He was found to have received seven shots on his breastplate, fourteen cuts on his helmet, and five or six slight wounds in his arms and shoulders, while his friends were nearly all left dead on the spot.

When his wounds were dressed, Lord Derby procured a disguise, and set out to join the king. Charles had by this time reached Worcester, after having forced a passage across the Mersey in face of Lambert's troops. He had gained very few recruits; only a small number of cavaliers had joined him, and these were scantily attended: though he was received with acclamation by the people, they did not rise in his favour. Religious and national animosity cooled the enthusiasm of the English, whether Catholics or Anglicans, for the cause of a king who came surrounded by Scotchmen and Presbyterians. The Royalists were disliked even by the English Presbyterians, and the Scotch felt that their cause was bad, Leslie himself was grave and dispirited.

"How can you be sad, general," said the king to him as they approached Worcester, "when you are at the head of so brave an army? Do you not think they look well?"

"Sir," answered Leslie, in his ear, "I am melancholy indeed, for I well know that army, how well soever it looks, will not fight." (Clarendon, *History of the Rebellion.*)

The troops of Lambert and Harrison were scouring the country, and arresting all suspected travellers, when Lord Derby, in disguise, and with only three attendants, left Wigan at nightfall to join the king at Worcester. They dared not keep the high road, but made their way with difficulty from house to house, and from cottage to cottage, lying concealed by day, and travelling during the night. Reaching the borders of Shropshire and Staffordshire, near Newport, he was received by a Royalist family, who directed him to a place of safety, where he might take a few days' rest.

His wounds, though not dangerous, were very painful, and he could scarcely keep his seat on horseback when he arrived at the castle of Boscobel, a small country-house belonging to the Giffards, a Catholic family, who themselves lived on their property of Chillington, to which Boscobel was attached. The situation was wild and solitary, on the summit of a hill, and completely surrounded by thick forests. The charge of this place was entrusted to a family of Catholic peasants, the Penderells, whose name became afterwards so well known for their devotion to the person of the fugitive king.

In this refuge, intended for the concealment of proscribed priests, the earl might hope to defy the pursuit of his enemies; and here he rested for two days. On the 31st of August, 1651, he continued his journey to Worcester, which he reached on the 2nd of September. The fatal Battle of Worcester was fought on the following day, when the Royalists were completely routed by Cromwell, the king scarcely escaping with his life. A little band of Royalists, Lord Derby, Lord Cleveland, and Colonel Wogan, by surrounding and protecting him with their swords, contrived to force a passage for him through the ranks of the enemy, they themselves remaining behind to cover his retreat.

At the end of the day, they rejoined him at some distance from the town, and, Lord Derby advising his concealment at Boscobel, Mr. Charles Giffard, who was present, offered to conduct him thither. Accompanied by his faithful servants, Charles marched all night, and arrived early next morning at the castle of White Ladies, which also belonged to the Giffards. Some hours afterwards he left this house, conducted by William Penderell, to whom Lord Derby had particularly commended him, parting from the friends who had served him so faithfully, in order that he might reach the coast and embark for France.

The perils through which he effected his escape are well known. Some of his followers shared his fortunes; but Lord Derby, attempting, with Lord Lauderdale, to enter Cheshire or Lancashire, fell into the hands of a troop of horse, accompanied by a regiment of foot, commanded by Major Edge, who were marching towards Worcester to join the Parliamentary Army. The earl and his companions, making themselves known, asked for quarter, which was granted on condition that they gave up their arms and surrendered themselves prisoners. Lord Lauderdale was sent to another part of the country, and his life was spared. The Earl of Derby was immediately conducted to Chester, from which place, soon after his arrival, he wrote the following letter to his wife:—

> My dear Heart,—It hath been my misfortune since I left you not to have one line of comfort from you, which hath been most afflictive to me; and this, and what I now further write you, must be a mass of many things in one.
>
> I will not stay long on particulars; but, in short, inform you that the king is dead or narrowly escaped, in disguise, whither is not yet known; all the nobles of the party killed or taken, save a few; and it matters not much where they be. The common soldiers are dispersed, some in prison, some sent to other nations, and none like to serve any more on the same score. I escaped a great danger at Wigan; but met with a worse at Worcester, being not so fortunate as to meet with any that would kill me, and thereby have put me out of the reach of envy and malice. Lord Lauderdale and I, having escaped, hired horses, and, falling into the enemy's hands, were not thought worth killing; but had quarter given us by one Captain Edge, a Lancashire man, and one that was so civil to me, that I and all that love me are beholding to him.
>
> I thought myself happy in being sent prisoner to Chester, where I might have the comfort of seeing my two daughters, and to find means of sending to you; but I fear my coming here may cost me dear, unless Almighty God, in whom I trust, will please to help me some other way. But whatsoever come of me, I have peace in my own breast, and no discomfort at all but the afflictive sense I have of your grief and that of my poor children. Colonel Duckenfeld, Governor of this town, is going, according to his orders from the Parliament, General to the Isle of Man, where he will make known unto you his business.
>
> I have considered your condition and my own, and thereupon give you this advice. Take it not as from a prisoner, for, if I am

never so close confined, my heart is my own, free still as the best, and I scorn to be compelled to your prejudice, though by the severest tortures. I have procured Baggerley, who was prisoner in this town, to come over to you with my letter. I have told him my reasons, and he will tell them to you; which done, may save the spilling of blood in that island, and it may be of some here, dear to you. But of that take no care; neither treat at all, for I perceive it will do you more hurt than good.

Have a care, my dear soul, of yourself, and of my dear Mall, Ned, and Billy; as for those here, I will give them the best advice I can. It is not with us as heretofore. My son, (Lord Strange, who, as we have seen, had come some time before to England, in spite of all his mother's efforts to prevent it), with his spouse, and my nephew Stanley have come to see me. Of them all, I will say nothing at this time, excepting that my son shows great affection, and is gone to London with exceeding concern and passion for my good. He is changed much for the better, I thank God, and would have been a greater comfort to me if I could have left him more, or if he had provided better for himself.

The discourse I have had here of the Isle of Man has produced the enclosed, or at least such, desires of mine as I hope Baggerley will deliver to you upon oath to be mine; and truly, as matters go, it will be best for you to make condition for yourself, children, and friends, in the manner as we have proposed, or as you can further agree with Colonel Duckenfeld, who being so much a gentleman born, will doubtless, for his own honour, deal fairly with you.

You know how much that place is my darling; but since it is God's will to dispose in the manner it is, and of this nation and Ireland too, there is nothing further to be said of the Isle of Man, but to refer all to the will of God, and to procure the best conditions you can for yourself and our poor family, and friends there, and those that came over with me; and so, trusting in the assistance and goodness of God, begin the world again, though near to winter, whose cold and piercing blasts are much more tolerable than the malicious approaches of a poisoned serpent, or an inveterate or malign enemy; from whose power the Lord of Heaven bless and preserve you.

God Almighty comfort you and my poor children; and the Son of God, whose blood was shed for our good, preserve your lives,

that, by the goodwill and mercy of God, we may meet once more on earth, and at last in the kingdom of heaven, where we shall be for ever free from all rapine, plunder, and violence. And so, I rest everlastingly,
   Your most faithful,
      Derby. (*House of Stanley*.)

Lord Derby was fully aware that his life must be sacrificed; he knew how many enemies he had in the town where his trial was to take place. Bradshaw contrived that his son should be one of the judges. Amongst them were also Colonel Birch, who had seized the earl's daughters at Knowsley, and who never forgot that Lord Derby had once "trailed him under a hay-cart at Manchester," which had procured for him the name of the Earl of Derby's carter; and Colonel Rigby, still smarting under the recollection of his defeat before Lathom House. These three were seconded by Sir Richard Houghton, a son of Sir Gilbert Houghton, formerly a friend and follower of the earl.

This "rebellious son of a very loyal father" united with Bradshaw in representing to Cromwell how very unsafe it would be to suffer so powerful an enemy to live; and a commission was appointed to try him by a pretended court-martial, composed of twelve sequestrators for the county of Chester, under the presidency of Colonel Mackworth, of Shrewsbury. This tribunal was also intended to try Sir Timothy Featherstonehaugh and Captain Benbow, who were both taken, like Lord Derby, with arms in their hands.

On the 1st of October, 1651, the earl was brought before his judges, accused of a breach of the Act of Parliament passed on the 12th of August, and addressed in the county to Major-General Mitton, prohibiting all correspondence with Charles Stuart or his party, which constituted the crime of high treason, and entailed the punishment of death. When Lord Derby heard the word treason, he exclaimed,—

"I am no traitor; neither—"

"Sir," replied the president, "your words are contemptible. You must be silent during the reading of the act and your charge." (*State Trials*.)

The earl conducted his own defence, for he was allowed neither books nor counsel. He pleaded that, having received quarter, and not having committed any other offence since then, he ought not to have been brought before a court-martial; and he demanded to be tried by a civil court; insisting, at the same time, that, as he was still in the Isle of Man at the date of publication of the act cited against him, he had not and could not have any knowledge of it, and was, therefore, not responsible for having violated it.

No importance was attached to this last plea; but a long and serious discussion took place on the question of the quarter received, and his appeal to the civil court. By his judges he was already condemned; but it was necessary to give some colour of justice to the trial. They maintained, therefore, that quarter for life could be granted only to such as were *hostes*, that is, enemies, not to such as were *perduelles*, or natives; that, as such, taken with arms in his hands, fighting against his country, the Earl of Derby was guilty of high treason, and merited the punishment of death; which sentence was accordingly passed on the 11th of October, and was ordered to be carried into effect at Bolton, on the 15th of the same month.

By allowing him so short an interval between his sentence and his execution, the judges intended to render impossible any appeal to Parliament; but Lord Strange, whose horses had been kept ready saddled for two days, set off for London as soon as his father's condemnation was known, and, by travelling day and night, reached the end of his journey in twenty-four hours, and sent in his petition to the House through the Speaker, Mr. Lenthal. The appeal was an affecting one. The noble character of the earl pleaded strongly in his favour; the Royalist party was so completely crushed as no longer to cause the government any uneasiness, and the majority of the members present were inclined to mercy.

At this critical moment Cromwell and Bradshaw rose and left the House, carrying several of their friends with them; and, the numbers left not being sufficient to form a House, the petition could not be put to the vote, and the question was thus decided silently, and without appeal.

Lord Strange rode back to Chester, where his father still was, and carried the fatal news to him himself. The earl embracing him, said:—

> My son, I thank you for your duty, diligence, and best endeavours to save my life; but since it cannot be obtained, I must submit.

And, kneeling down, he said—"*Domine, non mea voluntas, sed tua.*"

His chaplain, Mr. Baggerley, who has left us an account of these last hours of the earl's life, was present when Lord Strange returned.

Lord Derby said:

> Colonel Duckenfeld wished to persuade me yesterday evening that my life was not in danger. I patiently heard him discourse,

but did not believe him, for I was resolved not to be deceived with the vain hopes of this fading world.

He then repeated his instructions to Mr. Baggerley, to whom he had intrusted his letters for the Isle of Man, touching particularly on those articles which he had communicated to the countess for the surrender of the island:

> Discoursing with affectionate protestations of his honour and respect for my lady, both for her high birth and goodness as a wife, and much tenderness of his children there, especially my Lady Mary; and was going on, when suddenly came in one Lieutenant Smith, a rude fellow, with his hat on, who told my lord he came from Colonel Duckenfeld, the governor, to tell his lordship he must be ready for his journey to Bolton. My lord replied,—
> 'When would you have me to go?'
> 'Tomorrow, about six in the morning," said Smith.
> 'Well,' said my lord, 'I thank God I am readier to die than for my journey. However, commend me to the governor, and tell him by that time I will be ready for both.'
> Then that insolent rebel Smith said:—
> 'Doth your lordship know any friend or servant that would do that thing your lordship knows of? It would do well if you had a friend.'
> 'What do you mean?' replied my Lord. 'Would you have me to find one to cut off my own head?'
> 'My Lord, if you could get a friend—'
> 'Nay, sir,' answered my Lord, 'if those men that will have my head will not find one to cut it off, let it stand where it is. I thank my God my life hath not been so bad that I should be instrumental to deprive myself of it, though He hath been so merciful to me as to be well resolved against the worst of terrors death can put upon me. As for me and my servants, our ways have been to prosecute a just war by honourable and just means, and not those barbarous ways of blood, which to you is a trade.' (*Narrative of Mr. Baggerley, in State Trials.*)

When Smith withdrew, Lord Derby wrote the following letters to his wife and those of his children who were with her in the Isle of Man:—

Chester, October 12th, 1651.

My Dear Heart,—I have heretofore sent you comfortable lines, but, alas! I have now no word of comfort, saving to our last and best refuge, which is Almighty God, to whose will we must submit. And when we consider how He hath disposed of these nations and the government thereof, we have no more to do but to lay our hands upon our mouths, judging ourselves and acknowledging our sins, joined with others, to have been the cause of these miseries, and to call on Him with tears for mercy. The governor of this place, Colonel Duckenfeld, is general of the forces which are going now against the Isle of Man, and however you might do for the present, in time it would be a grievous and troublesome business to resist, especially those that at this hour command three nations; wherefore my advice, notwithstanding my great affection to that place, is, that you would make conditions for yourself and children, servants, and people there, and such as came over with me, to the end you may go to some place of rest where you may not be concerned in war; and taking thought of your poor children, you may in some sort provide for them; then prepare yourself to come to your friends above, in that blessed place where bliss is, and no mingling of opinions.

I conjure you, my dearest heart, by all those graces which God hath given you, that you exercise your patience in this great and strange trial. If harm come to you, then I am dead indeed; and until then I shall live in you, who are truly the best part of myself. When there is no such as I in being, then look upon yourself and my poor children; then take comfort, and God will bless you.

I acknowledge the great goodness of God, to have given me such a wife as you; so great an honour to my family, so excellent a companion to me, so pious, so much of all that can be said of good. I must confess it impossible to say enough thereof I ask God pardon, with all my soul, that I have not been enough thankful for so great a benefit, and when I have done anything at any time that might justly offend you, with joined hands I also ask you pardon.

Baggerley and Paul (Moreau) go by my directions to tell you my further reasons for the delivery of the island, according to these desires which you will see under my hand.

Oh, my dear soul, I have reason to believe that this may be the last time that ever I shall write unto you. I thank you for all your goodness to me; for Jesus' sake forgive me when at any time I have not been good to you. Comfort yourself the best you can. I must forgive all the world, else I could not go out of it as a good Christian ought to do; and I hold myself in duty bound, and in discretion, to desire you to forgive my son and his bedfellow. She hath more judgment than I looked for, which is not a little pleasing to me, and it may be of good use to him and the rest of our children. She takes care of him, and I am deceived much if you and I have not been greatly misinformed when we were told ill of her. I hope you will have reason to think so too.

It will be necessary that the writings concerning the estates be sent over, to the end my son may put in his claim betimes. Oh, my dear, again I ask you to take comfort; when you so do rejoice thereat I beseech you, as doing me a great favour; and for my sake, keep not too strict, too severe, a life, but endeavour to live for your children's sake, which by an over-melancholy course you cannot do, but both destroy them and yourself, and neglect my last request. The world knows you so full of virtue and piety that it will never be ill thought of if you do not keep your chamber, as other widows who have not reached to that reputation which you have, and than which there is not a greater upon earth. I draw near the bottom of the paper, and I am drawing on to the grave, for presently I must away to the fatal stroke, which shows little mercy in this nation, and as for justice the Great Judge judge thereof.

I have no more to say to you at this time than my prayers for the Almighty's blessing to you, and my dear Mall, Ned, and Billy. Amen: sweet Jesu.

   Your faithful

                Derby.

(Printed entire, for the first time, in the publications of the Cheetham Society, vol. lxvii. p. 227.)

My Dear Mall, Ned, and Billy,—I remember well how sad you were to part with me, but now I fear your sorrow will be greatly increased to be informed that you can never see me more in this world; but I charge you all to strive against too great a sorrow; you are all of you of that temper that it would do you much harm. My desires and prayers to God are that you may have a happy life. Let it be as holy a life as you can, and as little sinful as you can avoid or prevent.

I can well now give you that counsel, having in myself, at this time, so great a sense of the vanities of my life, which fill my soul with sorrow; yet I rejoice to remember that when I have blessed God with pious devotion, it has been most delightful to my soul, and must be my eternal happiness.

Love the archdeacon (the Rev. Mr. Rutter); he will give you good precepts. Obey your mother with cheerfulness, and grieve her not; for she is your example, your nursery, your counsellor, your all under God. There never was, nor ever can be, a more deserving person. I am called away, and this is the last I shall write to you. The Lord my God bless and guard you from all evil: so, prays your father at this time, whose sorrow is inexorable to part with Mall, Ned, and Billy. Remember

Derby.

While Lord Derby wrote these simple farewell words to his wife and children, his son and daughters who had the sad satisfaction of being with him at Chester, were still hoping against hope. As early as the 9th of September, Lady Catherine had written to her aunt, the Duchesse de la Trémoille, as Lord Strange had also done from London, on first hearing the rumour of his father's arrest, even before he had ascertained it as a fact:—

Lord Strange wrote:

I hear that he is certainly taken, if it is true, there is no hope for him, humanly speaking, but in the Isle of Man, and scarcely even there. The party now in power laugh at that idea, regarding the place as one that is sure to follow the rest of their conquests. Those who have made themselves masters of three kingdoms may well laugh at a refuge like the Isle of Man; all this makes me despair. If there could be an ambassador sent here to treat of a peace between France and this country, with instructions to speak in favour of my father, perhaps, with God's help, some good might be done. I am sure that your goodness of heart will incline you to do what you can for my father, who has the honour of being so nearly related to you.

The daughter's cry of distress was more tender and pressing:—

Madame,—The honour of my relationship to Your Highness emboldens me to implore your help in the extremity into which our whole family has been plunged by the arrest of my father, who is now a prisoner in the hands, of the Parliament. About five weeks ago he came to this kingdom in the service of His Majesty of Scotland, who also came here in person at the head of an army, which has been completely routed: no one knows what has become of the king; but my father with many others, of every rank and condition, has been brought to this town, where my sister and I, after two years of imprisonment, have seen him in so miserable a condition that our own is rendered a thousand times more grievous and sorrowful, from our apprehensions of his danger.

The thought of this is killing us, and will certainly be the death of my mother when she hears of it, unless she can be assured, at the same time, of his safety. She is in the Isle of Man, and I fear she will not obtain permission to come and help him, which makes me humbly implore my uncle, and you, *Madame*, to have compassion on our sorrow, and to do what you may judge expedient for my father's preservation and deliverance: by doing which you will uphold a falling house, and restore life to my mother and to all her family, who will never cease to pray to God for the preservation and prosperity of Your Highnesses. I am, and will be all my life,

Madame, your very humble, obedient,
and faithful niece and servant,

Catherine Stanley.

But Cromwell's judges allowed no time for the sending of embassies, or for slow diplomatic intervention; before Madame de la Trémoille could reply to these letters, Bradshaw had accomplished his revenge.

After writing his last letters to his wife and children, Lord Derby divided what jewels he still possessed, wrapping them up in several papers, and addressing them to his friends and servants.

Mr. Baggerley says:

At night about six, I went to him again, and as we were talking, the governor sent him a second message that he was to be ready to start at seven o'clock next morning.

'I shall not have occasion to go before nine o'clock,' replied his lordship; 'tell the governor I shall be ready at that hour; if he has earnester occasion he may take his own hour.'

The earl wished to take the communion before setting out. His daughters were with him and he desired to enjoy in peace the last moments that he had to devote to his children. He also permitted his daughter-in-law, Lady Strange, to come to him, as her husband wrote a few days afterwards to the Duchesse de la Trémoille:—

> My wife and I have had the consolation of receiving my father's blessing and his pardon for what we have done without his sanction; and much more than a simple pardon, for before his death he showed as much affection and tenderness for my wife as if she had been his own daughter, and one that he loved dearly, who had never done anything to displease him."

Lord Derby's indignation against his son's marriage had never, indeed, been so great as that of his wife, and in his last hours he was willing to forget all the past.

> Forgive us our trespasses as we forgive those that trespass against us.

When his children had left him, he remained alone with Mr. Baggerley, to whom he repeated his instructions and advice.

He said:

> I hope they that love me will never forsake my wife and children; God will be a master to them and provide for them after my death.

Then, giving the chaplain his letters for the Isle of Man he said:

> Deliver these with my most tender affection, to my wife and sweet children, which shall continue with my prayers for them to the last minute of my life. I have instructed you as to all things for your journey; but as to that sad part of it with respect to them, I can say nothing. Silence, and your own looks, will best tell your message. The great God of heaven direct you, and prosper and comfort them, in this their day of deep affliction and distress.

On the morning before his execution, after taking the sacrament. Lord Derby spent some time alone at his devotions, as was his custom. His chaplain has preserved the following prayer, which he was in the habit of using every morning:—

> O Almighty Lord God! thou that hearest prayer, assist me now in my devotion. By the help of thy blessed spirit, make me to have so right a sense of my sins that I may be humbled before thee, and of thy mercy that I may be raised and comforted by thee. O Lord, make me tremble to consider thee a most mighty and terrible God; and make me again rejoice to know thee a most loving and merciful Father. Make me zealous of thy glory, and thankful for thy bounties; make me know my wants and the frailties of nature, and be earnest in my prayer that thou will forgive all my misdeeds; make me in my address to thee to have a present mind, and no cares, wandering thoughts, or desires elsewhere, or separate from thee; make me so to pray, that I may obtain of thee mercy and the relief of all my necessities; for the sake of thy blessed Son and my Redeemer, the holy Jesus. Amen.

When he left his closet. Lord Derby took leave of his companions in misfortune, Sir Timothy Featherstonehaugh, Mr. Crossen, and three other gentlemen, who were condemned like himself, he said

> Gentlemen, God bless and keep you. I hope now my blood will satisfy for all that were with me, and that you will in a short time be at liberty. But if the cruelty of these men will not end there, be of good comfort; God will strengthen you to endure to the last, as he hath done me; for you shall hear that I die like a Christian, a man, a soldier, and an obedient servant to the most just and virtuous of princes.

He then rode out of Chester, "the people weeping all round him," About half a mile from the town, the earl, meeting his two daughters, alighted from his horse, "and with an humble behaviour and noble carriage, kneeled down beside the coach and prayed for them. Then, rising up, took his leave, and so parted."

Mr. Baggerley says:

> This was the deepest scene of sorrow my eyes ever beheld; so much grief and so much concern and tender affection on both sides, I never was witness of before.

As they drew near to Leigh, where they were to spend the night, Lord Derby said to his chaplain:—

When you come into the Isle of Man, commend me to the archdeacon there; tell him I have not forgotten our conversations on death. I often said to him the thoughts of death could not trouble me in fight with a sword in my hand, but that I feared it would somewhat startle me tamely to submit to a blow upon a scaffold. But tell the archdeacon from me, that I do find in myself an absolute change as to that opinion, and I bless God for it, who hath put such comfort and courage into my soul, that I can as willingly lay down my head upon a block as ever I did upon a pillow.

As he lay down in bed with his face resting upon his hand, he said:

Methinks I lie like a monument in a church; and tomorrow I shall really be so.

The last day, Wednesday, 15th of October, had now arrived, when his journey was to end at the foot of the scaffold. He said to Lord Strange, who held the Order of the Garter, which had lately been sent to the earl by Charles II., before his departure for Holland:

Put on my order once this day, and I will send it to you again by Baggerley; pray return it to my gracious sovereign, when you shall be so happy as to see him, and say I send it with all humility and gratitude, as I received it, spotless and free from any stain, according to the honourable example of my ancestors.

When he was dressed, he went to prayers, and had the *Decalogue* read to him, making his confession at the end of every commandment; then received absolution and the sacrament; after which he called for pen and ink, and wrote his last speech.

Before starting "he drank a cup of beer to the health of all he loved," and would have walked into the church, but he was not permitted, "nor even to ride that day upon his own horse; but he was set upon a little galloway," the guards fearing that the people would rescue him.

On the way, observing that the wind was easterly, cold, and sharp. Lord Derby turned to his chaplain and said:—

Baggerley, there is a great difference betwixt you and me now, for my thoughts are fixed, and I know where I shall rest tonight, but you don't; for every little alteration of wind or weather moves you of this world. You must leave me, and go to my wife and children in the Isle of Man; but do not leave me, if possible, until you see me buried as I told you, and acquaint my dear wife and family with our parting.

About twelve o'clock Lord Derby arrived at Bolton, accompanied by two troops of horse and one company of foot, the people everywhere praying and weeping as he went.

He was taken to a house in the town—for the scaffold, which was built in great part of timber from the ruins of Lathom House, was not quite ready, the people of the town having refused to strike a nail or give any assistance to it, many of them saying:—

> We have suffered many and great losses since the war began, but none so great as this, that the Earl of Derby, our lord and patriot, should lose his life here, and in such a manner.

He spent the time till three o'clock praying and conversing with his friends; telling them how he had lived, how he had prepared for death, and how God had strengthened him against the terrors of it; then after giving some good instructions to his son, who had come with him thus far, he desired to be in private, where he continued on his knees in prayer for a good while. he then called his friends again, and told them he had no fear of death:

> Only the care and concern he had what might become of his wife and children after his death was often in his thoughts, and sat heavy upon him; but now he was satisfied that God would be a husband and a father to them, into whose hands and Almighty protection he committed them.

And so, taking leave of his son, he embraced him, saying:—

> I charge you, upon my blessing, to be ever dutiful to your distressed mother, and ever tender how you in anything grieve or offend her.

Then turning to an officer, he told him he was ready.

As he approached the scaffold, which was erected on the site of the old cross, he said:—

> *Venio, Domine.* I come to fulfil thy will, O my God; this must be my cross! blessed Saviour, I take it up willingly, and follow thee.

He walked with a firm step through the people, who prayed and wept aloud. He said:

Good people, I thank you all, and I beseech you still to pray for me. The God of mercies bless you; the Son of God establish you in righteousness; and the Holy Ghost fill you with all comforts."

At the foot of the scaffold he said:—

I am not afraid to go up here, though to my death: there are but these few steps between me and eternity."

Then kissing the ladder, he went up; and after saluting the people, and taking a few turns up and down, he seated himself at the east end of the scaffold, and made this address to the people, who pressed about him:—

Christian Gentlemen and People,—
Your business hither today is to see a sad spectacle, a peer of the land to be in a moment unmanned, and cut off by an untimely end. And though truly, if my general course of life were but inquired into, I may modestly say there is such a moral honesty upon it, as some may be so peremptory as to expostulate why this great judgment has fallen upon me. But know that I am able to give them and myself an answer, and out of this breast (laying his hand upon his heart) to give a better account of my judgement and execution than my judges themselves or you are able to give.

It is God's wrath upon me for sins long unrepented of, many judgments withstood, and mercies slighted; therefore, God hath whipped me by His severe rod of correction, that he might not lose me. I pray join with me in prayer that it may not be a fruitless rod; that when by this rod I have laid down my life, by this staff I may be comforted and received into glory.

As for my accusers, I am sorry for them—they have committed Judas's crime; but I wish and pray for them Peter's tears, that by Peter's repentance they may escape Judas's punishment; and I wish other people so happy they may be taken up betimes, before they have drunk more blood of Christian men, possibly less deserving than myself.

It is true there have been several addresses made for mercy; and I will put the obstruction of it upon nothing more than upon my own sin, and seeing God sees it not fit (I having not glorified Him in my life), I might do it in my death, which I am content to do. I profess, in the face of God, no particular malice to any one of the State or Parliament; to do them a bodily injury I had none.

For the cause in which I had a great while waded, I must needs say my engagement or continuance in it hath laid no scruple upon my conscience. It was on principles of law, the knowledgment whereof I embrace, and on principles of religion, my judgment satisfied and conscience rectified, that I have pursued those ways, for which, I bless God, I find no backwardness upon my conscience; nor have I put it into the beadroll of my sins.

I will not presume to decide controversies. I desire God to honour Himself in prospering that side that hath right with it, and that you may enjoy peace and plenty when I shall enjoy peace and plenty beyond all you possess here. In my conversation with the world I do not know where I have an enemy with cause, or that there is such a person to whom I have a regret; but if there be any whom I cannot recollect, under the notion of Christian men, I pardon them as freely as if I had named them by name. I freely forgive them, being in free peace with all the world, as I desire God, for Christ's sake, to be at peace with me. For the business of death, it is a sad sentence in itself if men consult with flesh and blood; but truly, without boasting, I say it; or if I do boast, I boast in the Lord, I have not to this minute had one consultation with the flesh about the blow of the axe, or one thought of the axe more than as to my passport to glory.

I take it for an honour, and I owe thankfulness to those under whose power I am that they have sent me hither, to a place, however, of punishment, yet of some honour, to die a death exceeding worthy of my blood, answerable to my birth and qualification; and this courtesy of theirs hath much helped towards the pacification of my mind.

I shall desire God that those gentlemen in that sad bead-roll to be tried by the High Court of Justice, that they may find that really there that is nominal in the Act, an high court of justice, a court of high justice, high in its righteousness, though not in its severity. 'Father forgive them, and forgive me as I forgive them.' I desire that you would pray for me, and not give over praying till the hour of death, nor till the minute of death, for the hour is come already; that, as I have a very great load of sins, so I may have the wings of your prayers, to help those angels that are to convey my soul to heaven, hoping this day to see Christ in the presence of the Father, and myself there to rejoice with all other saints and angels for evermore.

One thing more I desire to be clear in. There lieth a common imputation upon the king's party that they are Papists, and under that name we are made odious to those of the contrary opinion. I am not a Papist; but renounce the Pope, with all his dependencies. When the distractions in religion first sprang up, I might have been thought apt to turn from this Church to the Roman; but was utterly unsatisfied in their doctrine, in point of faith, and very much as to their discipline. The religion which I profess is that which passeth under the name of Protestant, though that be rather a name of distinction than properly essential to religion.

But the religion which was found out in the Reformation purged from all the errors of Rome, in the reign of Edward VI., practised in the reigns of Queen Elizabeth, King James, and King Charles, that blessed prince deceased; that religion before it was defaced, I am of, which I take to be Christ's Catholic, though not the Roman Catholic religion; in the profession and practice whereof I will live and die.

Good friends, I die for the king, the laws of the land, and the Protestant religion—

At these words, a soldier called out,—

We have no king, and will have no lords."

This raised a sudden tumult amongst the soldiers, who rode up and down the streets, cutting and slashing the people as they pressed round the scaffold.

"What is the matter, gentlemen?" said the earl. "Whom do you seek? I fly not, and here is none to pursue you."

The soldiers desisted; but quietness could not be restored. Lord Derby tried to continue his address; but finding it impossible, he turned to one of his servants, and gave him the manuscript, saying:—

I will speak to my God, who I know will hear me; and when I am dead, let the world know what I would have said.

Then he called to the headsman, and asked if he was ready.

"Not quite, my lord," replied the man, with a surly air.

"I am not angry with thee, friend," said the earl; "thou art not the hand that throws the stone."

The bystanders called to the executioner to ask his lordship's pardon, but he seemed unwilling; upon which Lord Derby said:—

> Friend, I give thee the pardon thou wilt not ask.

Then, handling the rough furred coat the man had on, he said:—

> This will be troublesome to thee. I pray thee put it off as willingly as I put off this garment of my flesh, that is now so heavy for my soul.

The executioner made his preparations so slowly that the earl murmured:—

He said to one of his chaplains, whom he saw moving about amongst the crowd:

> How long, O Lord, how long! You see I am ready, but the block is not," "When I am got into my chamber (pointing to his coffin), I shall then be at rest, and no longer troubled with such a guard and noise as I have been.

Then, turning to the crowd, he said:—

> Good people, I thank you for your prayers and your tears; I have heard the one and seen the other; the God of heaven hear your supplications for me, and mine for you, through the mediation of Christ our Saviour.

He caused the block to be turned towards the church, saying:—

> I will look towards thy sanctuary whilst I am here, and I know that in a few minutes I shall behold my God and my king in thy sanctuary above. Under the shadow of thy wings shall be my rest till this calamity be overpast.

On seeing the block:—

> That methinks is very low, and yet there is but one step betwixt that and heaven.

Then taking the axe into his hands he kissed it, and said:—

> Thou canst not hurt me, for I fear thee not.

He then removed his doublet, and asked how he should place himself. He said:

> I have been called a bloody man, yet, truly, I never yet had that

severe curiosity to see any put to death in peace.

The executioner told him to put up his hair, and he knelt down and prayed privately a good while; after repealing the Lord's prayer, aloud, he rose and said smilingly:—

> My soul is now at rest, and so shall my body be immediately. The Lord bless my king, and restore him to his right in this kingdom, and the Lord bless this kingdom and restore them to their rights in their king, that he and they may join hand to hand to settle truth and peace. And the Lord bless this country, this town, and this people. The Lord comfort my sad wife and children, and reward all my friends with peace and happiness, both here and hereafter. And the Lord forgive them who were the cause and authors of this my sad end and unjust death; for so it is as to mankind, though before God I deserve much more. But I hope that my sins are all washed in the blood of Jesus Christ.

Then laying his head upon the block, he said to the executioner:—

> Wait till I give you a sign. The Lord bless my wife and children; the Lord bless us all. Blessed be God's gracious name for ever and ever. Amen. Let the whole earth be filled with his glory. Amen.

He lifted his hand, but the executioner either did not observe it or was not ready; and the earl rose again, saying:—

> Why did you keep me from my Saviour? What have I done that I die not, and that I may live with him?

And, placing his head again upon the block, he repeated the same words; then, lifting up his hands, the axe fell, and separated his head from his body. (*House of Stanley. Narrative of Mr. Baggerley. State Trials.*)

There were no sounds of triumph; the soldiers dispersed silently, and nothing was heard but the sobs of women and children, for the grief of the men was dumb, like their anger.

CHAPTER 8

Widowhood

While Mr. Baggerley, faithfully carrying out Lord Derby's instructions, was accompanying his son to Ormskirk, to see his body placed in the tomb of his ancestors, Lady Derby was still in the Isle of Man, ignorant of the blow about to fall upon her. Communication with the island was carried on with difficulty, and news travelled slowly. Before she had received her husband's first letter telling her of his capture, he was already dead.

She had been making preparations for the defence of the island which was so dear to them both, and had fortified the castle of Russen, a place situated upon a high and almost impregnable rock, where was kept the leaden crown, the distinctive mark of the independent royalty of the Isle of Man, when, one day. Captain Young arrived on board the frigate *President*, one of those ships of the enemy which, as she had written to the Duchesse de la Trémoille, harassed their coasts, and summoned her to surrender the Isle of Man in the name of the Parliament.

She replied:

> I hold it by commission from my Lord, and I will not give it up without orders from him, being obliged by my duty to obey the instructions of my husband.

Before any such instructions reached her, she heard of his death. We do not know who undertook to carry her the mournful intelligence; whether she learnt it from Mr. Baggerley, or whether her son ventured to bring the news to her himself. From a sentence in one of her letters, dated the 22nd of March, 1652, we are rather led to infer that she learnt her misfortune only on the arrival of her enemies, and from their lips. However this may be, she continued to hold the Isle of

Man, and when Colonels Duckenfeld and Birch, with a commission from the Parliament, arrived on the coasts and demanded the surrender of her little kingdom, she replied that she held it for the king, and would not give it up to his enemies, without his orders.

It was now about the end of October; Charles II. had taken refuge in France, and the Royalist cause seemed lost without hope of recovery. All towns and castles holding for the king had surrendered to the Parliament; but the intrepid daughter of the Trémoilles and the Nassaus still held her islands in the king's name, and refused to give them up without his authority.

She placed herself and her children under the protection of Sir Thomas Armstrong, who had been appointed governor of Russen Castle by Lord Derby. His brother commanded Peele Castle, and the forces of the Isle of Man were intrusted to Captain William Christian, a native of the country, and a son of Captain Edward Christian, who had formerly held a high place in Lord Derby's esteem. He had, in fact, for some time been governor of the island; but Lord Derby had reason to be dissatisfied with his services, and had appointed Captain Greenhalgh in his place.

He, however, continued his favours to the family of Christian, and after the father's death he intrusted to the son, William Christian, the charge of such troops as he left behind him in the island when he went to join Charles II. in England. But the son proved as ungrateful and faithless as the father. The malice of Lord Derby's enemies was not satisfied even by his death; Bradshaw desired the destruction of his family, and Rigby hoped to be revenged on the heroine who had humbled him before Lathom. They succeeded in gaining over Christian, who permitted the Parliamentarian troops to land on the island during the night. The soldiers had been bribed and offered no resistance; and on the following day the garrisons of both the castles revolted against their governors, who were taken prisoners by Christian, and, with the countess and her children, were delivered into the hands of the Parliamentarian commissioners.

"These, *Madame*, are the conditions under which Captain Christian has delivered up the island," said Birch, ironically, offering Lady Derby a paper, in which no mention was made of her rights nor of her son's rights over this hereditary kingdom of the Derbys. Glancing at it, she said, with her accustomed courage:—

No place is mentioned here but the Isle of Man; the neighbouring islands have not surrendered; permit me to retire to Peele Castle (on one of the adjacent islands) with my children, that I may rest there until I can pass over into France or Holland, and find a place to lay my head.

This, which she asked as a favour when she might have claimed it as a right, was not granted; the Isle of Man, of the hereditary possession of which she and her children were to be deprived, was to be their prison for two months longer; and it was only in the following December, as we learn from a letter of her son to the Duchesse de la Trémoille, that she at length obtained permission to go to England, where she hoped to find shelter and sympathy.

The historian of the House of Stanley says:

She who had brought fifty thousand pounds sterling of dowry to this nation, had not even a morsel of bread to eat, and owed everything to the favour of friends almost as distressed as herself.

The first letter which we have from Lady Derby after her long silence is dated from London on the 25th of March, 1652:—

Dear Sister,—In all my heavy trials I have desired nothing so much as the honour of your letters, which were so full of friendship for this unhappy one, and of compassion for the misfortunes I have suffered, that, I confess, if my grief were not inconsolable, you would have relieved it. But alas! dear sister, there is nothing left for me but to mourn and weep, since all my joy is in the grave. I look with astonishment at myself that I am still alive after so many misfortunes; but God has been pleased to sustain me wonderfully, and I know that without his help I could never have survived all my miseries. To tell you all would be too distressing; but, in short, dear sister, I have endured all the sharpest sorrows that could be conceived, and they were announced to me by the destroyers of my happiness, with all imaginable particulars to overwhelm me.

It is in this that I have experienced the wonderful assistance of my God, that I did not despair as, humanly speaking, stronger minds than my own might have done; but His providence supported me, and led me in my misery to adore His goodness towards me; and to magnify Him in my sorrow for the noble end of that glorious martyr who showed such wonderful constancy—nothing shaking him in the least but the thought of the wretched condition in which he foresaw I should be. In his last letters he gave me far greater proofs of his affection than I had any right to expect, and his last request was that I would live and take care of his children.

This thought alone sustains me in my afflictions; for my son the Earl of Derby does nothing to comfort me, both he and his wife showing great bitterness of feeling towards me. But this is the will of God to wean me altogether from the world, and to show me its vanities. If I were not obliged for my children's sake to look after my affairs, which are in such an uncertain state, I should no longer have any concern with the world. It is true that in one of their courts, after incredible trouble, I have succeeded in getting my marriage contract allowed, which settled on me, besides my dowry, certain estates bought with my own money, which is all that I have for my five children. I must, however, obtain the authorisation of another of their courts, in order to receive the revenue of the estates, and it is here that my enemies endeavour to prove me guilty; if this should happen, it will be necessary to present a petition to Parliament, which is a very difficult and tedious thing.

But I have reason to think that I shall obtain what I desire; the most influential people tell me to hope. God has hitherto blessed my endeavours, and has given me both friends and means of subsistence; for I have lost all my personal property, having had only 400 crowns worth of silver plate allowed me to bring me here from the Isle of Man, and nothing more since that. You see, then, the unhappy condition to which my life is reduced; I wish to end it with you, but I cannot yet tell what will become of me. . . . If I could get the produce of what has already been granted to me, I should have the means of bringing up my children in a manner befitting their birth, my two youngest sons, (both died young and unmarried), being of great promise, healthy, tall and well-grown for their age, and studious, especially the younger, who, I think, will be a good scholar. If it please God to bless them and make them worthy of their father, they will doubtless feel how much honoured they are by their connection with so many illustrious persons.

A good and virtuous reputation counts for something even in human affairs. Lady Derby's next letter proves that her embarrassed circumstances did not prevent her from marrying her children "according to their birth."

I have something very different to tell you of, that is, a suitor for your niece Catherine: thus, you see that God does not forsake His children. I was very far from thinking of such a marriage in our poverty, or indeed of any marriage. The gentleman is the Marquis of Dorchester. He has been married before, but has only two daughters. He is a Protestant, aged forty-four; sensible, clever, accomplished, and rich, having fourteen thousand a year, his brothers and sisters provided for, and ready money in his purse. The best and highest alliances in England have been offered to him, and yet he has sought us out. I shall not be able to give her anything until my affairs are settled; but this alliance will help us not a little.

The business was concluded in three days, and I was obliged to promise to keep it secret till everything was arranged, otherwise I should have been unwilling to conclude it without your consent, and that of *Monsieur* my brother. I crave your pardon for this, but you know, dear sister, what risks letters run in these times; and if the matter had been discovered before all was concluded, many difficulties would have been put in the way. Certain people have attempted this, especially his next brother, who has sons, and who believed that he would never marry. God has sent this good fortune to us; and I implore His blessing on them both: they will be married, I think, in a month.

He has given her a ring and a bracelet-clasp, worth ten thousand crowns. She will be a rich woman. Her father was so intimate with him that they called each other brother; but I never saw him before. I hope that God will provide as well for the others who are in my charge. I know of nothing in them but what is good and agreeable. As for my eldest, I cannot say as much for him; he is worse than the prodigal son: and I often think of what that martyr said to me about him before he went to France,—that he had no good opinion of him; 'for,' said that sainted soul, 'he has no shame for his faults, and I never saw him blush for anything that he did.' Alas! I deluded myself; but his father knew him better than I did. There never was so malignant a nature as that woman's, who has nothing good or pleasant about her.

We willingly excuse Lady Derby's joy at seeing her daughter "a rich woman," for she herself had suffered all her life from embarrassed circumstances, although occupying so high a position, and she was now reduced to actual poverty. But if her friend, M. du Plessis-Mornay, had been still alive, he would have reminded her that:

> Wealth was the last thing that should be thought of in a marriage. What is most important is the moral character of the person with whom one's life is to be spent; and, above all, that he should fear God.

The Marquis of Dorchester was possibly without this fear of God, for his wife was not happy. Only three months after the marriage, her mother wrote :—

> I have not made her so happy as I expected; I was led to hope for better things: but what consoles me is that she behaves with admirable wisdom and patience; and, certes, she is gaining an unexampled reputation.

Lady Dorchester had only one daughter, who died in infancy.

While Lady Derby was thus occupied with her daughter's marriage, war had broken out between France and Holland. The struggle was obstinate, and skilfully conducted by the ablest men of their time—Blake, Van Tromp, Ruyter, Corneille de Witt; but it was carried on with very unequal resources in the two countries; and, after two years of mingled reverses and successes, Holland confessed herself beaten.

Corneille de Witt said, in July, 1653, in a full assembly of the States:—

> Why should I hold my tongue any longer? I am here in the presence of my rulers. It is my duty to tell them that the English are now masters of us and of the seas.

A few months later the States-General obtained from Cromwell an honourable peace. On one point alone he was not to be moved: he would have no ally of the house of Stuart in power in Holland; and he demanded that the young Prince William, and the whole house of Nassau, should be excluded for ever from the *Stadtholdership*. The States resisted this insolent attempt to regulate the internal affairs of their country. Cromwell persisted in demanding from Jean de Witt at least the special consent of the province of Holland, believing that this province was strong enough to force its opinions upon the other members of the confederation. After much hesitation, the States of the province of Holland acceded to Cromwell's demands, and the treaty was concluded on the 5th of June, 1654.

Cromwell had now possessed himself of absolute power in England. On the 30th of April, after a violent scene in the House of Commons, he drove out the members, bidding them begone, for they were no longer a Parliament; and, locking the doors behind him, he said to the officers who surrounded him:—

> I did not think to do what I have done today; but I felt the Spirit of God so strong upon me, that I could no longer give ear to flesh and blood.

He had long been striving to free himself from all restraints to his power, and he now elected no new members, but called together, by his own warrant, a council composed of 139 persons, whom, at the end of a few months, he dismissed as they had been convoked. Four days after the dissolution of December, 1654, he received from the army the title of Lord Protector of England, Scotland, and Ireland, a title which he accepted without eagerness, and by which he became virtually Sovereign of Great Britain.

Lady Derby had just sent her second son to her sister-in-law in France.

On the 14th of May, 1654, she wrote:—

> I send you, in this dear child, one of the best parts of myself; I pray that God will bless him, and make him acceptable to you. He is very anxious to please you, and I have commanded him to obey, reverence, and love you as he does myself. He is gentle, and of a good disposition, brave, but without pride, a very common vice of his nation. His *valet-de-chambre* is a gentleman whose father is so much attached to our poor family that he desires his son should be with him, rather than in another position where he might have greater external advantages. He has some knowledge of mathematics, painting, and surveying. His footman is a very useful person, and will do, well whatever is given him to do."

In later times, during the French Revolution, it was not usual for the members of the great fallen families to be so well attended. Lady Derby's reasonable complaints must not prevent us from rendering justice to her enemies. The correspondence which is here published absolutely refutes those traditions, which have become almost historical, concerning the treatment to which Lord Derby's family were subjected after his execution.

It has been said and printed everywhere that the countess was kept a prisoner in an unhealthy dwelling in the Isle of Man; that she there lost two of her children; and that she was not released from captivity till the restoration of Charles II. So far from this being the case, we see, from the indisputable evidence of her own letters, that although poor, and deprived of all the luxuries natural to her rank, she was at least free, living in London, demanding justice, and in a measure obtaining it, sending her son to Paris with suitable attendants, and marrying her daughters in a rank worthy of their birth.

On the 12th of March, 1655, Lady Derby wrote:—

> I think your nephew will have told you of his sister's marriage, (Lady Mary Stanley married the Earl of Strafford), about which she and her brother wrote to him last week. With God's blessing I have every reason to hope for the greatest comfort from it, he being a very worthy man, who has an unbounded affection as well as the highest esteem for his wife; she is, I think, very happy. I am sure that if my daughter Strafford had the honour of being known to you, she would also have that of pleasing you. She is quite a French woman, speaks French better than I do, and writes it as she does English. I pray that God may bless them all.

The narrowness of her means very soon obliged Lady Derby to leave London and return to Knowsley.

She writes on the 1st of June, 1655:

> You may believe, dear sister, how changed I find everything in this place, never having been here since my troubles; and how cruelly it recalls to my mind my past happiness, and makes my present sorrows press more heavily than ever upon me. God, however, will not forsake me; but will strengthen me of His goodness. In the midst of my sadness He has been pleased to send me the good news of the birth of your grandson, for which I thank Him, and pray that you may derive from it all the happiness that I wish you. As for my affairs they are in so bad a state, my debts being so great, that I am obliged to live here, and to reduce my expenses to suit my poor condition, in order to pay them if possible.

And some months afterwards:—

> I know not if you have heard of the Protector's last proclamation, in which new taxes are imposed on all those whose estates have been in the hands of the Parliament, and who have paid large sums to recover them. I had hoped that in the poor condition to which it has pleased God to reduce me, and by not interfering in anything whatever but what regards my own little property, I should not to be reckoned in that number; but I am assured that I am one of them, and everything I have in the world is mortgaged to pay my debts. The sum now demanded is the tenth part of the value of the estates, and the fifteenth part of the personal property; but I hope I shall not have to pay for more than I possess, which is next to nothing. The good God will not forsake me; as He has had compassion on me in all my troubles, so He will continue to befriend me.

This measure of Cromwell's was a general one; M. Guizot says:

> It was an act of political excommunication against the Royalists, whether as actual conspirators, or because of their avowed hostility and secret connivance with conspirators.

Lady Mary Stanley had written to her aunt in the preceding year:

> They accuse my mother of speaking against the government of this country, and always shut the mouths of those who feel pity for her condition and ask for some kind of justice for her, by telling them that she has defied their authority, without being able to prove anything of the kind, and without listening to those who could and would vindicate her.

At the same time, all who had served the late king or his sons were obliged to leave London, and many Royalists of condition were thrown into prison.

Lady Derby wrote:

> Every day new people are suspected, and the prisons receive fresh inmates. In my present condition I dare not venture to make any inquiries. God grant that all may turn to His glory, and give me grace to submit to whatever He pleases to send me. The loss of my property has never been so hard to bear; but it is my irreparable losses that overwhelm me.

Lady Derby's greatest anxiety at this time was for her youngest sons. In her letters to her sister-in-law she speaks of her concern about the one who was in France, who seems to have been treated harshly and without consideration by his *valet-de-chambre*, who was also, to some extent, his tutor. She wrote on the 16th of November, 1655:

> I am in constant anxiety about him and his brother, the latter is clever and intelligent; he learns well, and conducts himself with discretion. May the Lord preserve them and look on them with compassion; and may you, dear sister, look kindly on him who has the honour of being with you. He is of a gentle and somewhat melancholy disposition; and if he is frightened, as Daguedel tells me he is, and does not dare to speak, I fear he will become incapable of doing anything. I am afraid there is some want of discretion on Daguedel's part; and all who see his letters think as I do.

At length she sent her faithful Trioche to France, who dismissed Daguedel, and found for his young master a less arrogant *valet-de-chambre*.

Trioche will tell you that my affairs are in a very bad state, so that I am unwilling to trouble you with them. I have been taxed on 8,000 *livres* more of rent than I receive. The major-general, the person who manages everything in the provinces where he is in command, would not listen to my agent, or to anyone who, like him, had received the rents from the time that they were in the hands of the Parliament. He asserted that I had great estates beyond the sea (as he expressed it), and many jewels and other imaginary things, and would hear nothing in my behalf, nor treat with anyone who came from me. We have reason to hope that commissioners will be appointed in London, with power to redress these abuses, and also to exempt from payment those whom they had supposed it necessary to tax. I have presented a petition to the Protector, but it has not yet been answered.

Many people of large property, who are good Catholics, have been exempted. Everything, however, would be endurable if they had left us the free exercise of our religion; but that is most strictly forbidden. It is the same religion as that professed in the time of Henry VIII., and of his daughter Mary, who made all suffer martyrdom who adhered to it; and my mother believed it to be that of the primitive Church. She never failed to attend prayers, and had the English liturgy translated into French, and commanded me to conform to it, and to the administration of the sacraments; as I have done, and will continue to do, with God's blessing, to the end of my days. And it was one of the last wishes of my husband that his children should be brought up in this creed.

Cromwell had, in fact, been forced by the passions of his party, against his own will and personal feeling, to forbid absolutely the exercise of the Anglican worship. For his own part, indeed, he was inclined to protect the Anglican Church: "its political maxims and strict discipline suited him." He, therefore, allowed his order against chaplains and preceptors to be almost entirely neglected;

> Though he could neither refuse it to the fanaticism of his party, nor publicly revoke it in the name of that liberty of conscience which it was his glory to sustain. (M. Guizot, *La Republique et Cromwell*.)

Another family trouble now distressed Lady Derby. Her nephew, the Prince de Tarente, was a warm adherent of the Prince de Condé, and had been formerly attached to his suite in the Fronde. When his brave leader was thrown into prison, he left France, and entered the service of the Low Countries; but returning home in 1655, he was himself arrested, whilst the Prince de Condé was fighting against his country in the Spanish Army.

The countess wrote:

> I have heard with great sorrow of the imprisonment of your son. I have since learnt from Trioche that his life is not in danger, for which I bless God. . . . I do not doubt that, with God's help, for which I pray, he will soon recover his liberty.

M. de Tarente was detained for several years in prison, only recovering his liberty in 1660.

Cromwell had now reached the summit of his greatness; one step alone remained to be taken, and for this he prepared with his accustomed prudence and vigour. Several Parliaments had met and been dismissed without the fitting occasion presenting itself in which to attempt the final blow. At length, in 1657, he believed that the opportunity for which he waited had arrived. A petition was presented to him by the House, modestly entitled, "A humble petition and advice," entreating him to accept the title of king, and to take upon him the entire government of the country.

Conferences were held between Cromwell and the Parliamentary Commissioners, all the proceedings of which were public. It was not the Parliament alone, but the country, that had to be convinced—that party who had effected the Revolution and raised him to his present power. Even in his own family, the measure was vehemently opposed by his brother-in-law, Desborough, and his son-in-law, Fleetwood, who would not admit the advisability of the step. The excitement in the army was increasing and becoming serious.

It was said that Cromwell was resolved to take no notice of it, and to proceed, when Parliament was called at Whitehall to receive the final answer of the Protector. He accepted all the power which the petition offered him, but refused the title of king, that "feather in his cap" which he had so longed for, and without which he knew neither his work nor his family could take root in England. Once more his hopes were disappointed; his natural caution had arrested him on the edge of the precipice, but his indomitable perseverance never renounced the hope of attaining the object of his desires.

Lady Derby writes, on the 17th of July, 1657:

> You have seen by the papers what they have added to the power of the Protector. It is said his own party are not satisfied. For my part I know nothing about it.

The new political organisation proposed in the petition, and adopted on the 7th of May by Cromwell, demanded the construction of an "Other House," as it was styled by those who still hated the title of Lords.

The Protector at once busied himself in forming it, summoning some of the old peers, a certain number of members of the House of Commons, a few of the highest of the general officers, a few country gentlemen and rich citizens; in all sixty-three persons. But these did not all respond to the call. The Commons, so lately all-powerful, reluctantly accepted this division of the authority that was henceforth to be shared by the three orders of the State, while Cromwell's declining health gave occasion for a formidable opposition to arise.

Lady Derby writes, in February, 1658:

> There are so many different opinions about the Parliament that I know not what to think of it. The House of Commons vigorously opposes the other House. It is said the army is approaching London. God will guide all for His glory and for the good

of those who desire it.

She did not know that before she wrote this Cromwell had dissolved the Parliament. (4th of February, 1658.)

The argument he employed in explaining his conduct was, that dissensions in the government were dangerous to the safety of the Republic, now, more than ever, threatened by the friends of Charles Stuart. This danger was doubtless intentionally exaggerated to further his own interested schemes; he said, "there are nothing but Royalist plots in all parts of the kingdom."

Lady Derby wrote, in April 1658:

> We know little news, as it is dangerous to ask for any. We live in times in which the most insignificant person may do harm, and very few have the power to do good. The Scotch rumours have come to London, but I think they are without much foundation. They say another Parliament ought to be called there. Meanwhile numbers of people are thrown into prison, and amongst them, it seems to me, are many who need not, and do not, think of anything but living peaceably at home; but everyone is suspected."

A large number of arrests and eight executions had just given evidence of the vigilance and the alarm of Cromwell. The tears of his favourite daughter, Lady Claypole, could not extract from him the pardon of Sir Henry Slingsby, or of Dr. Hewitt, a distinguished Anglican minister, whose preaching she had frequently attended in secret. This favourite daughter died on the 6th of August, and grief for her loss, operating on Cromwell's already shattered health, threw him on a bed of sickness. All England was startled by the news.

Even to his enemies Cromwell was the representative of organised power and public order. If he should die, the country, they believed, would fall back into a state of anarchy. It was not even known if he had appointed his successor. Many prayers for him rose up; his own were very fervent. His religious faith had seldom arrested him in his resolute course towards any precise object; he had often employed pious expressions or religious motives as a potent means of working upon men; nevertheless he believed, and at the last moment, as Archbishop Tillotson says, " religious enthusiasm took the place of hypocrisy." He was dying, in spite of the confidence of those who had prayed to God to cure him. He felt it himself, but the desire to live surmounted every other feeling in his breast. He prayed aloud:

> Lord, though I am a miserable and wretched creature, I am in covenant with Thee through grace. And I may and will come to Thee for Thy people. Thou hast made me, though very unworthy, a mean instrument to do them some good, and Thee service; and many of them have set too high a value on me, though others wish and would be glad of my death; Lord, however Thou do dispose of me, continue to go on to do good for them.... Teach those who look too much on Thy instruments to depend more upon Thyself. Pardon such as desire to trample upon the dust of a poor worm, for they are thy people too. And pardon the folly of this short prayer, even for Christ's sake. And give us a good night if it be Thy pleasure. Amen.

Part of this prayer was granted. The day dawned.

It was the 3rd of September, the anniversary of his victories at Dunbar and Worcester. When they offered him something to drink, said he:—

> It is not my design to drink or sleep, but my design is to make what haste I can to be gone.

By four o'clock he was dead.

CHAPTER 9

The Year Before the Restoration

Lady Derby was but little disturbed by this great event, which threw all England into confusion; she did not see in it the omen of the restoration of the king; she did not perhaps understand that the feeble hands of Richard Cromwell were unfit to wield the heavy sceptre bequeathed to him by his father. She lived retired and alone, and was, besides, at this time much occupied about a negotiation for the marriage of her daughter Amelia with the Earl of Athol.

Cromwell died on the 3rd of September, 1658, and it was only on the 5th April, 1659, that the Countess of Derby wrote:

> The news about the Parliament is changed. It speaks with little respect of the late Protector, and has liberated all those whom he put in prison. I know not yet what will come of it.

And then she turns at once to the subject nearest her heart:

> Two days ago, this Scotch nobleman arrived here. He is the Earl of Athol. I think him good-looking and agreeable. I do not yet know your niece's opinion of him. She is so obedient and gentle that I know she will do what I wish; but I would desire nothing that she disliked. God will direct me for her good. This-gentleman has a rent-roll of 30,000*l*. M. d'Athol was made an earl by James I. of Scotland, and the house has been allied with the royal family. His surname is Maure, and he is the head of this family; in which there are several noblemen. (The family name of the earls afterwards Dukes of Athol is Murray. Lady Derby is confused in her mind about proper names.)

The countess returns several times with tender pleasure to the charms of her daughter, she says:

"She is an agreeable-looking brunette, with an equal and patient temper. She has plenty of intellect, and will never vex those to whom she owes respect."

The marriage was at length accomplished. The Countess of Athol lived happily, and had several children; but she resided in Scotland, and henceforward her mother saw less of her than of her other children.

The affairs of the family were at last partially settled. In 1657, the Parliament had ratified an Act passed by the Barebones Parliament, which secured to the Earl of Derby a revenue of *500l.* sterling, for himself and his heirs. Another Act decreed him forests in Ireland of the value of nine or ten thousand pounds.

Major Brooke had said during the discussion:

This noble family is among the most unfortunate in England.

Lord Broghill said:

Justice and charity invite you to confirm this Act. The poor gentleman has suffered sufficiently, and for the faults of his father; for I never heard that he himself had committed any crime.

The Master of the Rolls said:

The family is in great distress. It would be right to pass the Bill, if it were only for the consolation of the lady, a foreigner, who belongs to an honourable family.

The recommendation of the Master of the Rolls doubtless referred to Charlotte de la Trémoille, and not to Helen de Rupa. The Bill was passed; but the Countess Dowager does not speak of it. She remained a stranger to the affairs of her son, who was living at Lathom, which he had in part rebuilt. She still loved him, however, as we shall very soon see.

In the month of May, 1659, the army demanded from Richard Cromwell the dissolution of the only freely-elected Parliament that England had possessed since the death of Charles I. The power gained by the father escaped from the feeble hands of the son, and the remainder of the Long Parliament, driven out by Cromwell without having ever accepted its dissolution, came back to sit at Westminster, passionately resolved to re-establish that Republic for which it had risked and suffered so much. It counted on the support of the army, which had recalled it, and which was soon to prove its master.

The weakness and disunion of their enemies reawakened the hopes of the Royalists, so long crushed under the powerful hand of Cromwell. A formidable conspiracy had spread its meshes all over England, and the king and the Duke of York held themselves in readiness to cross the Channel as soon as the plot was ripe; but the treachery of one of its agents rendered it abortive. The Royalist leaders, alarmed by the precautions that had just been taken by the government, remained quiet. One Presbyterian gentleman of the county of Chester, Sir George Booth, alone took up arms as he had promised. The Earl of Derby, Charlotte de la Trémoille's son, engaged with him in this movement, and was, like him, defeated by Lambert, whom, notwithstanding their recent disagreements, the Parliament had placed at the head of their troops. The two Royalist leaders were taken as they were trying to escape, and thrown into prison.

Lady Derby said to her sister-in-law on the 16th of September, 1659:

> It is only a few days since I performed the duty of writing to you. I thought you were at Thouars, as you had been pleased to tell me. I told you about the troubles we have had, and how they were relieved by the diligence of Mr. Lambert, who has used his victory most gently. I addressed my entreaties to you for my son Derby, who had been engaged in that unfortunate affair unknown to me, for I have for long been a stranger to everything that concerns him. You know, dear sister, how he has failed in his duty to me, but the tenderness of a mother is easily aroused when her children are in danger.
> What fills me with anxiety for my son now is that he is a prisoner in the Castle of Shrewsbury, and in some danger, I am told by his sister Dorchester, who helps him in the management of his affairs. Only two days before he was taken his wife was confined with her ninth child, four of whom are living. She is with him at present, which prevents her from doing anything in his affairs. They write me from London that if a letter of recommendation could be sent to M. (le Bordeaux it would do much for the preservation of his life, which makes me humbly beg you to have it done for us. Many people give us great hopes that there is no danger, but others fear the contrary, and in this uncertainty I am not myself.

And some days after:

> The governor of Shrewsbury has received orders to take my

son to London, where he is just arrived with his wife. He has had permission to dine with his sister Dorchester, two miles from London, with his guards. He has not been placed in the Tower of London, but in another prison. What they will do with him after he is examined, I do not know. It will be a good sign if they return him to the same prison. He is in no way surprised, and his sister tells me he is in the same mind that he was in before his misfortune. There are no judges appointed yet for any of them, which makes us hopeful for him and the others; there are a great many prisoners, amongst whom is the son-in-law of the old Protector (Lord Falconbridge) whose wife is with him in the Tower. My son's wife has not done the same, as it was thought she would be more useful in acting outside with my daughter Dorchester and our other friends, than in being with her husband.

I have not been advised to go to London, or I would have done my utmost for the journey. My friends have prevented me, for, dear; sister, besides my age and the infirmities attending it, I have no equipage; the few horses that my youngest son had have been taken. I have had no carriage since my return from London, where I have never had the means of keeping more than two horses. Two of his children are here with me, and I shall have the others in a few days, for the little he had for their support will be taken from them; and, as things are at present, he cannot do without help from me.

I have just had news from my daughter, who tells me her brother has not been examined yet. The delay has been caused by the Parliament and part of the army being of different opinions; and the City of London has presented a petition to the Parliament for the right of exercising their privilege of choosing a mayor. The Parliament had directed that the last year's one should be continued, which the said city believes to be contrary to the custom of all former times, when absolute power to choose their mayor was given them. It is reported that Mr. Lambert is displeased at not having received the thanks his services merit.

On the 13th of October, 1659, Lambert drove the Long Parliament from Westminster, as Cromwell had done six years before. But this time it was not a step in advance; the power of the Revolutionists did not increase, and the internal disorganisation of the Republican party made rapid progress.

Lady Derby wrote:

> Affairs in this country are not yet as they ought to be.

But the darkness was soon to be made light.

Before its fall the Parliament had passed an Act, which threw the Royalists into great anxiety with regard to that remainder of their possessions which many successive confiscations had left them.

Lady Derby wrote on the 4th of October, 1659:

> I have learnt by this post, a thing which, if it is true, will quite ruin me and more than six thousand persons. It is an act which the Parliament has passed rendering null all the compositions made by Cromwell's Parliaments. And it is ordered that all my revenue is to be seized, and that we shall be forced to buy it anew, without any regard being had to the money that has been already paid; and it is not even certain that I shall be permitted to buy it again. I never heard of such a thing! God will put His hand to it, and take care of a poor persecuted creature.

She writes on the 21st of October:

> They have done what they projected. The commissioners have been here taking an estimate of everything in and out of the house, and they have given orders to all my tenants to pay me no more rent. The cause of this is my having made my composition with the Parliaments that Cromwell called. This injustice has no sooner been executed than the leaders of the army have broken up the Parliament, who thought they had entire power over them. They have chosen Mr. Fleetwood for their head. What government they will establish is not yet known. The changes are so sudden, and everything is so uncertain that it is very difficult to form any judgment about the future. They assure me my affairs will improve presently. May God watch over them, and turn everything to His glory, and to the good of those who put their trust in Him.

Another change, and a more serious one than the oscillations of power between the various shades of the Revolutionary party, was silently approaching. For several years the position of General Monk had been quietly growing in importance. He had been a faithful, but not an enthusiastic, adherent of the Long Parliament and of Cromwell, and, since the death of the Protector, he had kept himself secluded in his government of Scotland, taking no part in any intrigue, and not committing himself to any party.

His prudent course had attracted the attention of all thinking people. Politicians of every party paid court to him, but he was impenetrable and cold to all. He had been on the point of declaring himself at the insurrection of July, but on the defeat of Sir George Booth he resumed his reserve. When Lambert drove out the Parliament, Monk openly sided with the civil power, from which he held his own appointment.

Lady Derby wrote, on the 2nd of December, 1659:

> You have seen how the Parliament has been broken up by the army. General Monk, who commands the army in Scotland, has since that opposed himself to the army by a declaration, and has seized Berwick, a sufficiently strong town on the frontier, it is said, where he is now negotiating some kind of treaty with Lambert; but people say they find it hard to agree. Monk has written to the City of London, which, report says, is divided. The governing body at present consists of twenty-three persons, mostly officers of the army, and one lawyer. God in His goodness will bring out order from our disorder.
>
> As to my personal affairs, I have been allowed to receive my rents, on giving other security jointly with my own; but only with much difficulty."

Monk's negotiations with Lambert came to nothing, and he took the road to London, without having declared himself, protesting that he was devoted to the Parliament. Fairfax, who had just raised the County of York in the same cause, supported him. At Coldstream Monk learnt that the English Army, alarmed by his progress, and weakened by internal dissensions, had recalled the Long Parliament. Almost at the same time he received the formal thanks of the restored Parliament, but without any invitation to come to London. He nevertheless continued his march, not, however, allowing his plans to transpire. On the 11th of February he led his troops into the City, and announced to the lord mayor that he had come to take up his headquarters there, said he:

> I have written this morning to the Parliament to request that they will issue orders in a week for the elections to take place that will fill the vacant seats, and that they will dissolve on the

6th of May, to give place to a free and complete Parliament. I have resolved, meanwhile, to remain with my army amongst you until I have seen my letter obeyed, and the wishes of the City and of the nation accomplished.

A week after, on the 20th of February, Monk himself caused all the members excluded in 1648, to return to the House; and on the 16th of March the Long Parliament, for twenty years the real sovereigns of England, voted its own dissolution and the opening of the new Parliament on the 25th of April.

Monk had now decided on his course. In reply to a letter which Sir John Grenville brought to him from the king, he wrote on the 20th of March, demanding in return for his services a general amnesty, with the exception, at the most, of four persons; the recognition of the sales of confiscated property; and liberty of conscience for all his subjects.

All over the country the Royalist reaction burst out spontaneous and ungovernable. Those who were persecuted yesterday became the persecutors of today, recovering, weapon in hand, the houses and lands which had been taken from them, and at the same time seizing the horses and furniture which they found there. Cromwell's widow fled from London. Everywhere the Revolutionary party were struck with the same terror with which they had so long inspired their adversaries. The self-imposed government of the country had not yet spoken; but the excitement of the people, bursting the bounds of moderation and prudence which Monk and the Parliament would have imposed, declared itself on every side.

On the 1st of May, Sir John Grenville presented himself at the door of the House of Commons, and was immediately admitted, said he:

Mr. Speaker, I am ordered by the king, my master, to hand you this letter, in order that you may read it to the House.

The letter was dated from Breda, "the twelfth year of our reign," and was addressed to "our trusty and well-beloved the Speaker of the House of Commons." While the House, standing with uncovered heads, listened to the king's letter and the declaration of his political intentions, Grenville carried the message for the Lords to their House, where he was received by the forty-one peers present, who came with the Chancellor to meet him; and the thanks of the House for the gracious message he had brought from the king were immediately given him. The same day the whole Parliament, at the suggestion of the Lords, declared that, "according to the fundamental laws of the kingdom, the government resides, and ought to reside, in the king, lords, and Commons."

On the 7th of May the countess writes thus:—

My letter of the 12th of last month (which is lost) would tell you of the hope we had of the restoration of the king. This one will tell you that, by the grace of God, the Parliament has done justice, and recognised His Majesty. On the 1st of this month the Houses of Lords and Commons unanimously consented to it. All are delighted, and have given evidence of their repentance for their past conduct. This change is so great, I can hardly believe it. The king has written three letters—to the two Houses, and to General Monk, who has conducted this affair with a prudence that will cause him to be esteemed for all generations. It is true that this passes human wisdom, and that in all humility we ought to recognise in it the hand of the Eternal; it is beyond our understanding, and can never be enough admired.

Neither can it be believed, except by those who have seen all that has happened during the past year. Lambert, after escaping from the Tower, tried to carry out his bad designs, which were at once defeated. He has now been again consigned to the same prison, but he is more strongly guarded.

My son Derby has taken his place in the House of Peers, according to his rank. His younger brother has been elected to the other House, but with much opposition; however, by the grace of God, he was successful. My second son is with the king, his master, who, they tell me, does him the honour of liking him; and I have the hope of seeing him soon, if I can, please God, make preparation for going to London. I should be already there if I could have found the means of accomplishing it, but my poverty is very great; yet I must make an effort, for the good of my children depends on it.

You may believe that the sight of the great world and the joy therein will call up many and opposite thoughts, and the contemplation of my own misfortunes in the midst of so much happiness will revive very bitter recollections.

Forgive me, dear sister, if I occupy you so long with subjects so little pleasant; but the knowledge that you do me the honour to be interested in all that concerns me, makes me take this liberty.

I will not, however, trespass longer on your patience, and will only assure you that no one can be more devoted to you than I—who can never be anything else to my dear sister than her very humble and very obedient sister, and very faithful servant.

The work of pacification was not yet completed. Not only did numerous delicate questions remain unsettled, but doubts and uncertainties of various kinds arose in the minds of many good people. Already the general amnesty which the country had been allowed to hope for seemed to be limited. The Bills intended to secure religious liberty, and to confirm the sale of confiscated property, remained suspended, impeded in their course by the Cavaliers.

The king was at Breda, waiting for the commissioners of the Parliament. Crowds of visitors flocked to him every day.

> Cavaliers, Presbyterians, Republicans, Cromwellians came in their own interests to boast of their fidelity, or to excuse their errors; to recall their past services, or promise new ones; and to seek their rewards, whether already earned or by anticipation. When Grenville arrived, bearing the gift voted by the House of Commons, with 30,000*l.* in gold and in letters of change, the happy king sent for the Princess of Orange and the Duke of York, that they might see this treasure, to which their eyes had long been so little accustomed, before it was taken out of the valise of the messenger. (M. Guizot, *Protectorate of Richard Cromwell.*)

The commissioners from the two Houses at length arrived, and with them came the Presbyterian ministers, who obtained from the king nothing but vague promises of personal liberty, without any concessions on the subject of the ceremonies of the Church of England.

The English fleet, in command of Admiral Montagu, had just cast anchor in the Bay of Schevelengen, in sight of the Hague, and Charles was urged to take possession of his throne. After taking leave of the States-General, and thanking them for their magnificent hospitality, he recommended his sister, the Princess of Orange, and Prince William, his nephew, to Jean de Witt, Pensioner of Holland, assuring the States that he would be as grateful for evidences of their good affection shown to them as if he should receive it in his own person. Jean de Witt replied, in the name of the States of Holland, by:

> A discourse which exceeded in respectful and friendly profes-

sions all that had been hitherto said to the king by the Dutch authorities. As politic as he was wise, the Dutch patrician, who contended in Holland against the House of Orange, desired to be at peace with England, whatever might be the government of that country, and sought with some anxiety the friendship of her new master. (*Protectorate of Richard Cromwell.*)

On the 23rd of May, 1660, the king embarked at the Hague, on board a vessel which had hitherto been called the *Naseby*, but to which he now gave the name of the *Royal Charles,* and landed at noon on the 25th at Dover, where Monk awaited him, surrounded by an immense crowd. On the 29th he entered London, after receiving at Blackheath the address of the army, which was submissive, but cold. In London, the satisfaction was animated and hearty. Evelyn writes in his *Journal*:

> I stood in the Strand, and beheld it, and blessed God. All this was done without one drop of blood shed, and by that very army which rebelled against him. But it was the Lord's doing, for such a restoration was never mentioned in any history, ancient or modern, since the return of the Jews from the Babylonish Captivity.

The king himself expressed some ironical surprise at this satisfaction.

> It is certainly a mistake, that I did not come back sooner, for I have not met anyone today who has not professed to have always desired my return.

CHAPTER 10

Life at Court

Lady Derby wrote on the 26th of May:

Our good news is so public that I have no doubt you know it. We may well say God has done wonders, for which may His name be for ever blessed.

The countess was then about to start for London, whence she wrote, on the 16th of July:—

I have been here for six weeks, and the king has done me the honour to treat me with great kindness and sympathy in my heavy afflictions. Nothing, however, has yet been done for me. Such confusion prevails in the court and in public affairs that it would require much more cleverness than I possess to see my way through all this disorder. The king is overwhelmed with business, and has promoted some who have not hitherto done him good service, and cannot, it seems to me, ever be of much use to him: I am sure it is against his own inclination, but his advisers think it is good policy to govern in this fashion.

I hope that, after working so many miracles to bring His Majesty back to us, God will strengthen his throne and give him grace to re-establish his church, and deliver it from schism, of which it is now so full. For the last week the Marquis of Argyle has been, with several others, a prisoner in the Tower, which shows us the vanity of this world. He has had his day, and in the end, he will receive the punishment which he so justly merits.

I am engaged, dear sister, in pursuing the pretended judges of *Monsieur*, my late husband, and I hope to have justice on them, which I do not desire so much for my own satisfaction as to draw God's blessing on the king and his people, by the punishment of those who spilt that dear and innocent blood with so much cruelty. I have already made some progress in the matter, and I hope tomorrow to have the issue as I desire it. I leave all to God, and I shall at least have the consolation of having done my duty. Many who have undergone similar losses have followed my example.

Strange blindness of human passion! This true Christian hopes to draw the blessing of Heaven upon the king and the people by pursuing an act of personal vengeance, not less at variance with the amnesty proclaimed by the king than with the words of pardon pronounced by Lord Derby upon the scaffold:—

Forgive me as I have forgiven them.

Soon after the restoration of Charles to the throne of England, Louis XIV. terminated the wars that had so long desolated Europe, by the treaty of the Pyrenees and his marriage with the Infanta Maria Theresa of Spain, who had just arrived in Paris when Lady Derby wrote on the 13th of August:

If your young queen resembles the queen her mother-in-law, and if she has the advantage of complexion, she cannot but be a very charming person; she seemed to me very beautiful. It is thought our queen will not come this winter, fearing the climate, which is not good for delicate lungs. The princess royal (Princess of Orange) is preparing for the journey. The gentlemen of the States, to whom she has recommended her son, have been informed of it; and she has offered to help them with the king, her brother. Thus, we shall have a court of ladies, which will be a great comfort in enabling us to speak to the king, who always treats me as I would desire.

I shall be very glad if M. de Ruvigny comes; I was acquainted with him before, but I did not know he was so much attached to you, and I will do as you wish. Some people have hoped that *Monsieur*, your brother, (the Duc de Bouillon), would come to renew the alliance. *Monsieur*, your father, held the same office under King James: *Monsieur*, my brother, accompanied him on this journey.

She wrote on the 12th of September:

The princess royal is expected with the first fair wind. The Duke of York has gone to receive her, and has ordered my youngest son to follow him; the one who has the honour to be known to you has remained with His Majesty, who does him the honour to like him. Parliament should be adjourned, but there is so much business, that they have prolonged their sittings from day to day. The army ought to be entirely disbanded (a great business) which will surely be accomplished, and then we shall be able to judge what we are to do. Everything seems to me in great confusion. May it please God in his goodness to give wisdom for the re-establishment of his church, and the prosperity of the king and his people!

The Duke of Gloucester has been ill with smallpox, but by the grace of God, the worst is over. He is a prince of great promise.

She adds on the 17th:

We lost His Highness, the Duke of Gloucester, yesterday, after all the doctors had judged him out of danger, from the smallpox. It is a great loss; the prince had a mind that cannot be too highly valued. May God turn this affliction to our amendment.

Things fell out as the countess had anticipated. She writes on 4th of October:

The army is disbanded, but with much difficulty. I hope, with God's blessing, all will go well.

The king had resolved to get rid of the sombre faces which had produced so uncomfortable an impression upon him on the day of his entrance into London; and Monk offered no resistance to this measure, which stripped him of all power. The discontent was extreme, and various plans had been formed for assassinating the general. The soldiers were not all disbanded when an insurrection broke out in London, headed by Venner, a Fifth Monarchy man, who went out in the night with about fifty enthusiasts, crying, "The sword of the Lord and of Gideon!" They made a most heroic resistance; and the regiment of Guards which was called out to repel them behaved so well on the occasion that their conduct furnished a pretext for retaining them, although Monk would not make the demand. (This is the regiment of Coldstream Guards, so named in memory of Monk's entrance into England by Coldstream; it became the germ of the standing army.)

Lady Derby wrote on the 7th of January, 1661:

> We have had a great alarm tonight. The Anabaptists and other of these discontented sects rose last night, and possessed themselves of some of the gates of St. Paul's Church; but, thank God, all is quiet now: the king's guards and the London Militia repelled the fanatics, as they are called. Some were killed, and others wounded. The mayor has testified his zeal and his diligence, as well as much spirit, in suppressing these disorders. His Royal Highness (the Duke of York—the king was absent) had given his orders beforehand; but he never left Whitehall; and he was right."

And on the 11th of January she wrote:

> These fanatics are to be tried tomorrow. They have confessed their designs, which are the most odious imaginable. They call themselves Fifth Monarchy men, and consider our Saviour Jesus Christ their King, and the author of all their crimes; and a thousand blasphemies of this nature. It is thought that Lambert and Vane have had some share in their schemes, from which may God, in His goodness, preserve the king."

The fanatics were executed immediately; Lambert and Vane were not sentenced till the following year; and Vane alone was destined to perish on the scaffold. A sad ending for a man of such remarkable character and so much elevation of mind! Though a visionary, he was a sincere and fervent Christian, whose indomitable devotion to his theories was unshaken by even the prospect of martyrdom.

A curious and amusing change appears now in the correspondence of Lady Derby, as well as in the subjects which engaged her attention. After more than thirty years passed in the country, away from courts; after severe afflictions and acts of rare heroism, the spirit of the "*grande dame*" suddenly re-awakens in Charlotte de la Trémoille. The atmosphere of the Court resumes its influence over her. The movements of the king and the queen, their little favours, their good graces, the marriage of the king, the affairs of the Duke and Duchess of York, the countess's expectations of personal advancement at the court, all assume supreme importance in the eyes of the widow, who had lost her husband, her fortune, her position; whose life for ten years had been passed in sorrow and privations, and whose only wish had been to die.

She, on the 22nd of September, wrote:

> The princess royal arrived yesterday. She was on the sea when

she learnt her bitter loss, which is one of the greatest the king and his people could sustain; and we all individually feel it deeply, for the prince honoured my two youngest sons with his liking. He had very remarkable qualities, which would have rendered him one of the greatest men of the age.

I hear nothing of the king thinking of marrying a woman of an opposite religion. All his most important advisers say it would be his ruin. They speak of the Princess of Denmark; but, in my belief, there is nothing that the king has yet thought seriously about. May God put into His Majesty's heart what will be best for his peace and his glory. If he thinks of riches, he could not have more than with *Mademoiselle* (de Montpensier; the great *Mademoiselle*): which I would wish with all my heart; but I fear that, having been despised in his poverty, he would be unlikely now to contemplate such a match. M. de Ruvigny has been twice to see me, but I had gone to visit the princess, who has received me very kindly, and my daughter Strafford with much feeling. The two others will go to her tomorrow....

No proposal has been made for the Infanta of Portugal; everybody is desirous that the king should marry (but I see no appearance of it), and above all that he should marry a Protestant. It is said that many wish Mdlle. d'Orange, but I do not know if this is true. I hear her figure is fine, and not at all spoiled. Prince Rupert has been here for two days, and lodges in the apartment of His Late Royal Highness. The princess, his sister, occupies that of the queen, her mother, who, they say, has borne the loss of the prince with great fortitude.

I beg you will tell me what you think of our young princess (the Princess Henrietta), who, they say, is to marry *Monsieur*, although many wanted her to have the emperor....

She writes on the 8th of October:

I went yesterday to present myself to the princess, but the king was only a minute with her. She told me that the queen, her mother, is to come as soon as possible, and before the marriage of the Princess Henrietta, whom she will bring with her. Everyone tries to guess the reason of this sudden change; for, two days before, it was said she would not come till spring, and that she was afraid of the winter air of this country, which is injurious to delicate lungs. People think that Prince Rupert has brought proposals for the marriage of the emperor and the princess. Others say (in cypher) that the daughter of the chancellor is *enceinte* by the duke, the uncle of the young Prince of Orange. *She* says there is a contract: *he* denies it absolutely. The queen, who does not like the chancellor, is coming to work his downfall. Everyone hates him.

Edward Hyde, afterwards Earl of Clarendon, had, in fact, made nearly all the courtiers his enemies. He had been the most faithful as well as the most able of the counsellors of both father and son, in good and in bad fortune. Before the Restoration he had steadily opposed the Presbyterians, who regarded him as too much attached to the English Church, and he was not more acceptable to the dissolute and unprincipled of the court party, who dreaded his austere demeanour and his high principles. The king, however, had always remained faithful to him, in spite of the annoyance which the chancellor's remonstrances often occasioned him.

But the secret marriage of his brother, the Duke of York, with Anne Hyde, the Earl of Clarendon's daughter, endangered more seriously the father's favour at Court. He felt, or pretended to feel, so much anger that he asked the king to put the bride in the Tower, and, on the rather ironical refusal of His Majesty, he himself imprisoned his daughter in her apartment. The Duke of York for several days denied the marriage, but the birth of a daughter reconciled him to the wife whom he had allowed to be calumniated.

Lady Derby wrote on the 30th of October:

> In her father's house the girl is called duchess, but everything is put off till the coming of the queen.

She writes a few days later:

> I have to beg you a thousand pardons, for not having told you before of the arrival of the queen, which took place last Friday, to everybody's delight, with the acclamations of the whole nation. I saw her on her arrival, and kissed her hand. She met me with much emotion, and received me with tears and great kindness. You may imagine what I felt. Her Majesty charms all who see her, and her courtesy cannot be enough praised. She has constantly received visitors since she came, without having kept her room. Our young princess is all you said she was.

What an interview must that have been between the two widows, both French, and both brought to England to undergo the severest afflictions of life! Henrietta Maria's natural frivolity had cut her off from the highest happiness of conjugal life; but the Countess of Derby had enjoyed it all, and had lost it for the husband and the son of that queen whom, by a miracle, after more than a dozen years of separation, she again met.

Honours now rained on the countess, though she had to wait long for more substantial benefits.

She wrote, on the 3rd of December, to her sister-in law:

> I told you about my illness. I can tell you now that I am better, thank God! But it is not so much for that I trouble you, as to tell you the surprise I had last night. I had only my daughter Strafford with me, when suddenly they told me the king was on the stairs, attended only by the Marquis of Ormond. He did me the honour to assure me that he wished to take charge of my children and me, and he told me that that little matter was done which I spoke to you about; and that it was his own business which had prevented him from doing me this honour before. It must be owned that he is the most charming prince in the world! I have not been to court for a week or ten days, but I am going after dinner.

The king had paid the countess a visit. This—in return for twenty years of affliction, the loss of all her property, and the death of her husband! Was he not truly "the most charming prince in the world?"

Events followed one another rapidly at court. The countess, who was silent during the siege of Lathom and in the Isle of Man, has always something to tell her sister-in-law. Now it is a death and now a marriage.

She wrote, on the 24th of December:

> My last told you of the illness of the princess royal, and now, with much grief, I have to tell you she is at the point of death, and I fear she may have passed away by this time. Good people will be glad to know that on the third day of her illness, feeling some weakness that the doctor said was occasioned by seasickness, she asked for a cordial, in order that she might have more strength to receive the sacrament, of which she partook with great devotion, and perfect confidence in her salvation; and when the king burst into tears, she spoke of death without

fear or emotion. She recommended to him her son, for whose sake alone she wished for life, if it was God's will.

And, the cordial having given her a little strength, she desired to make her will, which she did with great patience and in a very Christian spirit. This was on Friday at five o'clock in the morning; she was better on Saturday, and on Sunday they thought her out of danger. The queen has not seen her since Wednesday, which made me sure she was out of danger; but what induced me to believe the contrary is that the doctors have never agreed as to whether it was measles or smallpox. Her women and others tell me that bleeding her three times so reduced her that Her Royal Highness had not strength enough to throw out the virulence of the disorder. The queen, her mother, selected the doctors who were to attend her, and who were her own—Mr. Colloden and Dr. Fraser; the latter was formerly in France about the king's person, and is in some disgrace with His Majesty.

The queen, his mother, is very much vexed that the marriage of the duke (of York) is absolutely recognised, everyone openly paying court to the duchess. The king brought about the reconciliation, carrying the duke, his brother, to *Madame*, his wife. I pray God that He will give His blessing to this marriage, and grace to us to humble ourselves under our chastisements, which seem to me very grievous, for, in truth, our princess was an excellent person: all the good and rare qualities she possessed were natural endowments, for she had had her own way from childhood, those about her having thought more of their own interests than of what was good for her, or proper for her position.

I had a thousand things to tell you that I cannot write, I do not know if this affliction will accelerate or retard the queen's journey. The princess (Henrietta) changed her lodging from Whitehall to St. James's, where she is at present, and was very well yesterday. All these losses in the Royal family grieve and shock their friends. May it please God to withdraw His hand, and preserve those who remain to us, and protect the king and guide him through all dangers. That which threatened his safety has been discovered, and every day people concerned in the conspiracy are arrested. . . . The princess died at noon, and, when she was not in convulsions, was quite sensible. I have just come from visiting the queen, who is much distressed. I saw her. May

God withdraw His judgments from us!

After this death come the court reconciliations.

> I thought of writing to you, dear sister, on Thursday, the day after the departure of the queen, and of our adorable princess, but I was so tired with having been to court, which is always attended with inconvenience to people of my age, that I could not indulge in that pleasure, and tell you of the reconciliation of the queen and the duchess, which took place the evening before the departure of Her Majesty. There was a great crowd, and so much noise that one could only see their actions; as for their words, it was impossible to hear them: those of the duchess were very humble; she knelt on both knees, and then the queen, kissed her, and afterwards the princess, and they saluted one another.
>
> I am sure she will describe it all to *mademoiselle* your daughter, whom she greatly likes. The queen immediately directed the princess to retire, for she feared that in so great a crowd there might be danger from smallpox; but I think it was for some other reason that Her Majesty led the duchess from her bedchamber to the ante-room, where she made her and the Duke of York sit down. They say that the next day the queen was kinder to *Madame* her daughter-in-law than the night before. In short, it has gone off very well, and Her Majesty has managed well in the matter of the arrangement she desired. (Henrietta Maria always intended to come to England, in order to see all her children together, and to get the matter of her dowry settled.—*Clarendon*.)
>
> The king says she will return soon, though I doubt it He has gone to take her to Portsmouth; but the duke, who is not very well, remains here. People are apprehensive about the journey of the king, as it is to a part of the country where he is not liked; but he has no fear, though he has heard some ugly rumours.
>
> There is much talk of the marriage with the Infanta of Portugal: great advantages in the Indies, and much wealth here are offered; as to religion, she is to be under no restraint; the king will place whoever she likes about her. An ambassador from Portugal is expected very soon. I only know all this from hearsay. May God in His grace preserve our good king and guide him for His honour and the advancement of His glory. . . .

I have a request to make to you, which is, to direct one of your women to buy me the most beautiful doll to be had, that will undress; it is for a little girl whose parents I greatly wish to oblige, as they have been attentive to me. Forgive me for this liberty.

I forgot to tell you that our princess had a wager with my daughter Strafford, and Her Royal Highness has lost; she has done my daughter the honour of promising her a portrait of herself If *mademoiselle* your daughter should find an opportunity of reminding her of it, she will oblige her cousin

Every day, as we remember her merits, the loss of our princess is more and more felt. The king, her brother, has accepted the guardianship of *Monsieur* her son, according to her desire. His Royal Highness has felt her death more than might have been expected from a child of his age. The queen his grandmother has taken away with her all the jewels belonging to him, which Her Royal Highness had left to him, as coming from the house of Orange. Her Majesty thinks she should take care of them, and that they are safer with her .... The grief of princes does not last long; they have so many things to occupy them that they soon forget their sorrows Everyone has been as much astonished as you have been at the reconciliation of the queen (with the duchess,) but I believe it is only in appearance, and that it has helped her and many of her servants to get their affairs settled.

I have given six *jacobuses* to la Pierre for his journey, which will pay for the doll; if more is wanted order them to advance it. It is for the chancellor's grand-daughter.

Eleven regicides had perished on the scaffold, paying with their lives for a crime inspired by the violent passions of the time. But the most important amongst them had hitherto escaped punishment. The accomplices in the king's murder had indeed suffered for their deed, but the leaders of the Revolution were beyond the reach of earthly vengeance. Human wrath, when expended in vain, becomes puerile and contemptible, but executed on a corpse, it is not merely despicable but odious. The Countess of Derby seemed to feel this, in spite of the inextinguishable vengeance that she nourished. She wrote on the 31st of January, 1661:—

There was a fast yesterday in memory of the death of the late king, of glorious memory, which was observed throughout His Majesty's dominions. An Act of Parliament had been passed ordering that the bodies of Cromwell, Ireton, and Bradshaw, should be disinterred the day before, dragged on a hurdle through the town, hanged on the common gibbet (at Tyburn Gate), and buried under it. Nothing makes me recognise so clearly the vanity of the world, and that we have no hope but in the fear of God. It will be said with reason that it would have been better for this man if he had never been born!

All this wickedness, these murders, this Machiavellian policy (Machiavelli was Cromwell's favourite author,) have marked him and his family with eternal infamy. The thought that it is better to be poor and be at peace with one's conscience, makes me patiently bear my miserable condition and that of my children; for though this pension will help me a little to live, yet, having received nothing for them but that, I do not know what will become of us. A great deal is promised, but the fulfilment is long in coming.

Was it, indeed, the body of the great Protector that the king and the two Houses of Parliament had thus exposed to outrage? Strange rumours were current even then, which may now be read in the *Harleian Miscellany*. The story ran that, as a protection against a revolution in human affairs which might disturb the repose of his remains, Cromwell, by his own order, had been secretly interred on the battlefield of Naseby, the scene of his great and decisive victory over Charles I.; and that, by a subtle precaution, which cruelly defeated itself, the embalmed body of King Charles had been substituted for that of Oliver Cromwell in the coffin bearing his name, which was deposited in Henry VII.'s Chapel at Westminster.

It is added that, when the body was hung on the gibbet at Tyburn, and Royalists went to feast their eyes on the dreadful spectacle, they perceived with horror that the corpse bore traces of decapitation, and they even thought they recognised in its disfigured face the features of the king. However this might be, the immediate interment of the body was ordered. This strange story, improbable though it sounds, confirms a statement made by Clarendon himself, to the effect that, at the Restoration almost all the witnesses of the burial of King Charles I. were dead, and that those who survived found their memories so confused by the alterations made in the chapel at Windsor, that the exact spot in which the body of the king had been placed could never be positively ascertained, so that, necessarily, all idea of removing it, or of performing any funeral ceremony, had to be relinquished.

Charles II.'s marriage was still pending; but his own thoughts and leisure were occupied with other matters.

Lady Derby writes, on the 14th of February, 1661:

> They say the king's marriage with the *Infanta* is broken off. An Italian alliance is now talked of; but I do not know who the lady is, and many say the queen is busying herself with this negotiation. It is not the cardinal's niece.

★★★★★★

> *Note*:—The marriage of Charles II. with one of the nieces of Cardinal Mazarin, had been on the *tapis* at the time of Sir George Booth's insurrection. When this was put down the cardinal retired.

★★★★★★

> The report is abroad that the Earl of Bristol is really going on this business, though he says it is on his own private affairs. Whatever may come of it, I pray God it may be for His glory and honour, and the advantage of His Majesty. (In cypher:—) All the good folks are greatly shocked to see the king employ so wicked a person, and one so unfit to represent him at a foreign court.
>
> People here are talking of your great preparations for war, and say it is to be with Venice; but it is feared there may be an understanding amongst the Catholics, and that they are brewing mischief against us. Tell me what you think, and it shall be private.

Court intrigues multiplied. The Spanish ambassador, M. de Wateville, employed every device in his power to prevent the Portuguese alliance, which was supported by Louis XIV., for two reasons, as he tells us in his *Memoirs*:

> The first, to help the Portuguese, whom I else saw in danger of soon yielding; the second, to give me more means of assisting them myself if necessary, notwithstanding the treaty of the Pyrenees, by which I am forbidden to do so.

Lady Derby says, on the 17th of February:

> The king's marriage is still talked of, and M. de Bristol is gone

about it. There are so many different reports that one cannot tell what to believe. May God give him a queen who will be agreeable to him, and a blessing to His Majesty and his people. I think he will make as good a husband as His Royal Highness; and there never was such a one as he is. He even surpasses the king his father. You may judge of the rest.

Where you are nothing is talked of but marriages, and here nothing but the king's coronation, which is to take place on the 23rd of April. Those who have the means are making preparations for great display. We are not of this number. The Knights of the Garter will be installed two or three days before. They have discovered the name of a member of the House of Duras-Gaillard, Seigneur de Duras. I hope yet to find out the year in which he entered the order. The description you sent me of their arms has not been understood, for you say nothing of the field or of the posture of the lions. I should think that, knowing the name, they will be able to find the rest in their genealogies. I believe it was when the English possessed Guienne. I am sorry to be of so little use to my relations, for there is no one who desires more to be of service to them. (The Duras were allied to the Bouillons.)

And on the 25th she adds:—

They say M. de Bristol is to bring back a queen to us, one of the daughters or sisters of the Duc de Mantone. For the present it is a great secret. The Parliament of Scotland has declared the covenant to be criminal, and opposed to the divine right and authority of His Majesty. And on these heads, they are proceeding with the trial of the Duke of Argyle, who, it is believed, will suffer as he deserves; for I think he is one of the most wicked men in the world, and that he has committed unheard-of cruelties.

Plays are often acted at court, and the king and Their Royal Highnesses have been present at two this evening, at the Duchess of Buckingham's. It is not usual, in the absence of one's husband, to take part in such gaieties. Her sister-in-law has declared herself a Catholic; she has never had much religion, so it is no great loss. May God in His goodness support the true faith in this kingdom, which is oppressed on all sides!

Prince Maurice of Nassau will soon be here. I have heard nothing upon the subject of his embassy, but it is supposed to relate to the Prince of Orange, to whom the king is guardian. (The embassy of Prince Maurice concerned Charles II.'s marriage, rather than his guardianship of the young Prince William.)

Lady Derby, on the 14th of March, wrote in cypher to her sister-in-law:—

> I greatly desire the marriage of *mademoiselle*, but the king has an aversion to it on account of the contempt she has shown for him Since the coming of Prince Maurice, people speak a great deal of Mdlle. d'Orange. The Spanish ambassador takes that side, in order to oppose Portugal. Nothing now will content this people but a Protestant marriage. It seems to me that the chancellor ought to desire *mademoiselle* more than anyone else. Would to God I could serve her! it would be with all my heart. I have spoken of her to the Marquis of Ormond, but I meet with small encouragement. If I knew whom the queen favours, I could act to more purpose. I thought *mademoiselle* was to marry the son of the Florentine.

She adds in ordinary writing:—

> At last you have lost *M. le Cardinal*; everyone is wondering what will happen next. They say that *Monsieur* your brother is to be one of the first ministers of the State. I am sure he will use his power for the benefit of good people.

The Countess of Derby continued to be on bad terms with her eldest son. In right of her marriage settlement she possessed the estate of Knowsley, in Lancashire. She writes to her sister-in-law:—

> The Isle of Man was restored to my son Derby immediately after the arrival of the king. *Monsieur* his late father gave it to me for twenty-one years; and my son, without saying a word to me, after I had helped him in prison, and maintained him and all his family, has treated me in this manner! Our friends advise me strongly to come to some agreement by which I should have half the revenue. But I do not believe I shall get anything, except by force. His wife is a person without a single good quality. What shocks me most of all in her is, that she never speaks the truth, and that she makes her husband do things that are quite unworthy of him, which, however, I fear, he is

too much inclined to do; and I apprehend there will be complaints of him from the Parliament, for not acting legally in his government of the provinces of Lancashire and Chester, having raised money and overtaxed the people; but I cannot help it, as I am quite a stranger to his proceedings . . . . . As for that sword which has been restored to my son, I cannot tell what it means; for *Monsieur* his father never had any carried before him in the Isle of Man. It is a piece of his wife's vanity to have it put in the *Gazette*.

The Earl of Derby had never made a display of those insignia of royalty to which the possession of the Isle of Man entitled him, and he had advised his son to follow his example, having written in his last instructions to him:—

> Some might think it a mark of grandeur that the lords of this island have been called kings, and I might be of that opinion if I knew how this country could maintain itself independent of other nations, and that I had no interest in another place. But herein I agree with your and my great and wise ancestor, Thomas, second Earl of Derby, and with him conceive, that to be a great lord is more honourable than to be a petty king.
> "Besides, it is not for a king to be subject to any but the king of kings, nor doth it please a king that any of his subjects should affect that title, were it but to act it in a play; witness the scruples raised, and objections made, by my enemies in His Majesty's council, of my being too near allied to royalty to be trusted with too great power, whose jealousies and vile suggestions have proved of very ill consequence to His Majesty's interests and my service of him. There never was a wise subject that would willingly offend his king; but if offence were given from the prince, would rather humble himself before him as the only means to recover his favour, without which no subject can propose to live with honour or glory.
> To complete this counsel, take it for granted that it is your honour to give honour to your sovereign; it is safe and comfortable; therefore, in all your actions let it visibly appear in this Isle; let him be prayed for duly; let all writings and oaths of officers and soldiers, &c., &c., have relation of allegiance to him. (Seacome's *House of Stanley*.)

The countess was actuated by the same modesty and unswerving fidelity which had governed her husband's conduct. She readily forgot the king's wrongs and offences to herself; and when she was once more at court she felt in her natural element.

She writes to her sister-in-law in the month of March:

> A lady who thinks she knows the news has just told me the queen is coming back to London, and I am advised to entreat you, and all those to whom I have the honour of belonging, to ask Her Majesty to do me the honour of making me one of the ladies of her bedchamber. M. de Ruvigny knows what M. de St. Albans said to him on this subject. If the proposal is made in the right way, I think it will succeed. It would give me the opportunity of talking to the king, of serving my friends, and advancing my children; and I should be able to retire when I liked. Think about it, dear sister, whose I am entirely.

And on the 8th of April following, she wrote:—

> His Majesty is going to Windsor in a week to install the Knights of the Garter, who were created while the king was in exile. He has created four within the last week, of whom my son-in-law, the Earl of Strafford, is one. They are still talking of the marriage with the Infanta of Portugal. And then (in cypher), I have learnt that the Portuguese marriage is not yet arranged. I have had *mademoiselle* proposed, and I have some hopes, provided they are sure of the religion. May God give us a queen who will be a blessing to the king and the people. All over the country they are electing persons friendly to the king's service, who desire the good of the people. Thank God they have not followed the example of London, where they have returned men who, it is believed, will not be admitted into Parliament. (The elections of the City of London had been hostile to candidates of the Church of England.)

The king's coronation had been delayed for several months. It took place at length on the 23rd of April, 1661. The Countess of Derby thus describes it to her sister-in-law:

> I did not write to you by the last post, as it was the day on which the king was to make a kind of entry into London. He went from the Tower to Whitehall on horseback, with all the peers of the realm, a most magnificent sight, and His Majesty

looked very noble. His good looks and his courtesy are beyond description. The Duke of Northumberland was Lord High Constable, and the Duke of Ormond Lord High Steward on this occasion; the latter is always of His Majesty's household.

The day before yesterday was the day of the coronation, which is a most august ceremony. The Bishop of Worcester preached the sermon, which was excellent, and showed us our duty, not forgetting that of the king. His text was from Proverbs,—'May God enable us to follow what he has taught us.' M. Brevient knows this person, and can tell you how good his life is, and how orthodox his doctrine. The Archbishop of Canterbury placed the crown on His Majesty's head, and was assisted by the Bishop of London, on account of the archbishop's great age. The ceremony was long, and I saw both it and the dinner, without any inconvenience, with the Duchess of York. I have no doubt it will be all published.

The most curious part of the ceremony was when the Lord High Constable, the Earl Marshal, and the Lord High Steward, came on horseback into the hall, the Lord High Constable carrying a dish—and remaining so all dinner time; after which two of them went away, and the Lord High Constable only remained; then the two returned, bringing with them the King's Champion all in armour, with his spear and target carried before him, to the sound of trumpets and drum, and at the same time the heralds proclaimed the king sovereign of these kingdoms, not forgetting that of France; and then the Champion threw down his gauntlet, saying if anyone denied it he was there to maintain it with his sword.

The king and the Duke of York dined at one large table, and the lords at another in the great hall, and the mayor, the judges, and the sheriffs at a third. All this ceremony lasted seven or eight hours; and it was a very grand and imposing sight, the lords in the robes proper for the occasion, which are very becoming. It is the last thing of the kind I shall see; and I have greatly desired to witness it, having prayed with tears to be permitted to behold this crown on the head of His Majesty. May he and his posterity long wear it, and may God accord to him and to us the grace of never forgetting His miraculous blessings.

CHAPTER 11

Last Letters

While the court and the people of London were enjoying the festivities of the coronation, the Marquis of Argyle, who had so lately placed the crown on the king's brow at Scone, was at Edinburgh, awaiting his sentence of death.

The Countess of Derby wrote, on the 30th of May:

> It is thought that Argyle will be condemned in Scotland, where he will be beheaded.

But at this time Argyle was already dead. Accused of having delivered King Charles I. to the English Parliament, and of having caused the loss of Montrose, he claimed the benefit of the amnesty granted by Charles II. at Stirling; but the charges were numerous, and the most important of them related to events subsequent to the amnesty, he had received 12,000*l.* sterling from Cromwell, had favoured the invasion of Scotland by the English, had taken his seat in Richard Cromwell's Parliament, and voted the deposition of the Stuarts. It was said that throughout he had sought only the aggrandisement of his own family and the gratification of his personal ambition, at the expense of his country and his sovereign. Argyle defended himself with ability. His trial lasted four months, and his fate was still in suspense when the Scotch Parliament were informed of the arrival of a courier from London.

> From the haste of the messenger, who was accidentally discovered to be of the clan Campbell, it was believed he brought either a pardon or a respite. But when the packet was opened, it was found to contain Argyle's letters to Monk—a proof of the inefficiency of human prudence. (M. Guizot, *Fall of the English Republic.*)

These letters were full of professions of attachment to the government of the Protector, and more than sufficed to take away his last chance of life.

When solicited to give them up. Monk wished to wait till they were absolutely necessary; and then being informed, he says, of what was required to complete the evidence against the duke, he hastened to give them into the hands of the Parliament. They removed all hesitation. The next day Argyle was condemned; and Monk, doubtless, received the congratulations and the thanks of the court with his accustomed humility. (*Fall of the English Republic.*)

Argyle, when he heard his sentence, exclaimed:

I have given him a royal crown, and this is my reward! However, he only hastens my course to a better than his, and he cannot deprive me of that eternal amnesty of which you will all have need.

Said he, on mounting the scaffold:

As I hope to be saved from my birth to this day I have never had part, in any manner, either by counsel or by knowledge, in the death of the late king. And I pray God to preserve His Majesty, to spread His blessing over him and his government, and to give him good and faithful counsellors.

The sentence was executed, and his head set up on the gate of Edinburgh, replacing that of Montrose, to whose remains a superb funeral was given.

Lady Derby wrote on the 3rd of June:

The news came yesterday that Argyle was beheaded, and two more, of the same country (Guthrie and Gowan), were also hanged. They all well deserved what they have suffered; and we see, from his end, that the prosperity of the wicked is but for a time.

The Portuguese marriage was at length resolved on. French policy had counterbalanced that of Spain; and preparations were being made for the reception of the *Infanta*.

Lady Derby wrote on the 3rd of June:

They say that the fleet is not to set out till the end of this month, and with a favourable wind it takes three weeks to go there, and as many to return; so that she cannot be here for three months. The Catholics are very strong in her household. M. d'Aubigny is her grand almoner. I do not know how he has been able to get that place, for he stood very well with the Ambassador of Spain, and not so very well with the chancellor. Parliament is going on as usual. They ordered a holiday on the birthday of the king, which is the same day as that of his entrance into London: he has now been back a year. There were sermons in every church, and bonfires at night. This order is to be regarded in future as an Act of Parliament, and this observance is to be always made.

The Parliament has had the covenant burnt here as well as in Scotland. Money for the king is to be asked for; they will refuse nothing to His Majesty, although I believe this will be a year of famine, for we have had the strangest weather in the world.

I have sent my young children to offer a petition to Parliament representing their miserable condition; both theirs and mine is to be deplored. And I know not what will become of me, overwhelmed with debts as I am. If they would do anything, I would make up my mind to spend little, and leave the remainder of what I have to pay my debts.

And on the 20th of June following:—

The bishops are recalled to Parliament, where the Catholics are being discussed. I fear they will make an oath for them expressly, and that they will have a great deal of liberty; it seems to me that everything is tending to that.

The oath, however, was not modified, in spite of the king's liking for the Catholic religion. The time for toleration had not yet arrived.

Madame de la Trémoille was deeply occupied with the marriage of her only daughter, whose religion had from her birth limited the number of eligible matches for her in France.

Lady Derby wrote in cypher on the 21st of July:

I should like to know what you would think of the Duke of Richmond for the daughter of M. de la Trémoille. He is the fourth person in England, is related to the king, and is rich. You saw him in France before the death of his cousin. Tell me what she will have on her marriage. He has a daughter by his wife, who was an heiress, and he will have all her property for his life.

Doubtless he could aspire to the highest posts at court.

Mdlle. de la Trémoille was in great favour with the Princess Henrietta.

Her aunt writes, on the 31st July:

> I am very glad to learn that your health allows you to go to court; it is right that you should do so on account of *mademoiselle* your daughter. For many reasons she must keep up the interest that *Madame* takes in her. Nothing pleases me better than to know that the princess continues to conduct herself with so much discretion and virtue. You will have heard the conclusion of His Majesty's marriage with the Infanta of Portugal. The king sends over to her a Master of Requests, who speaks Spanish, and knows the language spoken at this court. It is said that she does not understand French. The ambassador of the king, her brother, says she is quite a devotee, and had so strong a desire to become a nun that it was very difficult to change her resolution.
>
> Some of the court here are going to drink the waters; and the Duchess of York wishes very much that my daughter Strafford should go with her. It must be confessed that she (the duchess) has a great deal of modesty, and makes much of all persons of virtue; she is passionately attached to His Royal Highness, and he to her. The Liturgy, (the prayer-book, newly revised, had undergone some modifications), has not yet been read, but it is hoped that it will be next Sunday. The time of the future queen's arrival is not yet exactly known. I do not know if the queen (Henrietta Maria) will remain long at Fontainebleau. If she goes to drink the waters of Bourbon she will not be there long. It is still said that she is coming here, and if so, she will be much pleased to find that she (the new queen) is of her religion. May God guide all for his glory.

Lady Derby's interest in the arrival of the two queens was not unconnected with her hope of obtaining a place at court. She wrote on the 8th of July:

> When I told you, dear sister, of my desire to be with the queen, it was thought that Her Majesty's return was certain, and the king's marriage was not at all so. I have a project, which I will tell you of if it succeeds. The Portuguese ambassador is gone. A

French tailor has been sent to make dresses for the queen that is to be, the king not finding those she wears to his taste. For my part, I think the old Spanish dress was much more becoming than what is now worn. The king has been to the Parliament, and passed two bills, one an act of benevolence, and the other a general pardon. I thought the chancellor would have been unable to be present. He was not well yesterday, after having been bled; but that did not prevent his being there.

The Queen of Bohemia continues very well, and still able to keep about. Rumour says that *Monsieur* is very jealous of *Madame*, and that he makes her a very bad husband, which I cannot believe. The Duke of York is very much the reverse; there never was his equal, he and his wife being inseparable.

And on the 9th of September:—

I went the other day to the Queen of Bohemia. She has plays performed at her house, and never misses one, being of as youthful a disposition as if she were a girl of twenty. She tells me that she has been informed that the eldest of the Dukes of Limbourg has gone to France with a great retinue, and that he intends to pay his addresses to *mademoiselle* your daughter. They say he would be a great match, only that he is married to his cousin-german, who refuses to live with him. His theological advisers, indeed, assure him that he can obtain a divorce; but I do not approve of this proceeding.

I thought it well to let you know of this; and also that (the king has promised to give me the appointment of governess to his children) (these words are in cypher), an important place, which will enable me to confer favours, and do much good Yesterday, we had the English Liturgy read in French in the chapel which His Majesty has given them (the French Protestants?) We had two excellent sermons, from M. Duret in the morning, and from M. Le Conte in the afternoon. The Duke and Duchess of Ormond were there in the morning, and many others, who came away highly pleased.

The Earl of Sandwich, at the head of a numerous fleet, had just cleared the Mediterranean of the pirates which infested it, and taken possession of Tangier, which had been ceded to England by the Portuguese, on the occasion of the marriage. The Spanish ambassador, furious at the failure of his manoeuvres, resolved to revive, at the Court of Charles II., the ancient pretensions of Spain to take precedence of all other crowns. On the day when the Danish minister, M. de Brahe, entered London, a skirmish took place in the streets between the attendants of M. de Wateville, the Spanish ambassador, and those of M. D'Estrades, the ambassador from the Court of France. The bystanders, though taking no part in the dispute, were in favour of the Spaniards. More than fifty persons were killed or wounded. M. D'Estrades' coachman was thrown from his seat, the traces of his horses were cut, and M. de Wateville immediately drove on before him. This event so enraged Louis XIV. that M. de Fuensaldagna, the ambassador from Spain to the French Court, was instantly dismissed thence. Charles II. also took the side of France in the quarrel.

Lady Derby wrote:

> I have just been told that the Spanish ambassador has received orders from the king not to appear again at court, and that it is on account of what passed in the dispute between him and the French ambassador, he having taken some of His Majesty's subjects into his pay without his knowledge. They say that the king, his master, does not sanction his proceedings, which is, perhaps, the reason why the king (Charles II.) has forbidden him the court.

Philip IV. did in fact refuse to sanction the course taken by M. de Wateville; he recalled him from London, and promised that in future his ambassadors should abstain from appearing in ceremonies where their pretensions might come into collision with the rights of the French ambassador.

Louis XIV. says in his *Memoirs*:

> I do not know that anything more glorious for France has ever happened since the beginning of the monarchy, it is a kind of homage that leaves no doubt in the minds even of our enemies, that ours is the first crown of Christendom. This tumult in London was looked upon as a misfortune; it would now be a misfortune if it had not happened.

Affairs were prospering with both the royal allies; Louis XIV. exulted in his superiority over all the thrones of the earth, and rejoiced in the possession of a son to inherit this glorious crown. In London prayers were beginning to be offered for the new Queen of England, "in the chapel at Whitehall, and afterwards in all the churches of the kingdom, mentioning her by her Christian name." The countess wrote on the 14th of November 1661:

> Both our queens cannot be mentioned together, and it has been settled therefore in this way, that her name is to come first in the prayers.

But Lady Derby was now reduced to the necessity of leaving London, she says:

> I cannot subsist much longer, it is time to retire. I write this in such haste that I hardly know what I say, having a thousand things to do, with little help and little heart. I feel that I am very unfit for the business of this world.

And she adds soon after:

> The chancellor earnestly assures me of his friendship, and I think he intends to do what he can for me with the king, so that I have every reason to hope the best. I resign myself to the will of God. In spite of her unfitness for mundane affairs, Lady Derby had not forgotten to write thus to her sister-in-law on the 31st of October, while speaking of the envoys sent by Charles II. to congratulate Louis XIV. on the birth of his son:— They have with them Mr. Hyde, a younger son of the chancellor, who is a great favourite with Their Royal Highnesses; I write to your son to beg that he will make known to him how much I respect his father and mother. I am sure he will not refuse to grant me this favour, and that you, dear sister, will not fail to remind him of it.

She wrote from Knowsley on the 24th of January, 1662, very much interested in a preacher, who had just come from France:—

> The king says that M. Morus is the finest preacher he has ever heard; I know that he is a great friend of yours, as M. Duret is of mine, and one that I highly esteem. M. Morus lodges at Somerset (House or Street?) I believe the French Church is strongly opposed to him, but that has not prevented his preaching before the king, and Their Royal Highnesses, at St. James's, which he did on Sunday the 12th of this month, with great success. I own that I am very much disappointed at not being able to hear him, and regret exceedingly my change from London; but I assure you that nothing but extreme necessity would have

driven me away.

And again on the 1st of April:—

> We are very much surprised at the news you have sent of *Madame's* accouchement; she is young enough to have many sons and daughters, if she goes on as she has begun. I am astonished that the queen, her mother, had not made all the necessary preparations. *mademoiselle*, then, has lost her title.
> The king has again sent me his promise, by Lady Ormond, and I am assured that I need have no further doubt as to this matter, in which I resign myself to the will of God. It is my sole desire to be able to serve Him, and to forward the fortunes of my younger children, for both they and I are in a sad condition. It was pure necessity that drove me from London, which is certainly a fine place; and, above all other reasons, I regret it on account of M. Morus. If God should ever give me the means of returning there, I will do my utmost to be of service to him. Besides what I should wish to do out of friendship to you, I own that I have an extreme desire to hear him preach. They say that Prince Rupert is going to live in England; no doubt he will find it to his advantage, for he is very much liked. I wish him a good and virtuous wife, and one who is known to you.

At Thouars, and at the Hotel de la Trémoille, great preparations were being made for the marriage of the only daughter of the house. She was no longer young; she must have been at least thirty; her mother and her aunt had carefully examined the pretensions of a great number of suitors, but their offers had all been refused by her; this time, however, she said yes. On the 3rd of June, 1662, Lady Derby wrote:—

> My youngest son met M. Morus on the day that the king gave his assent to the bills in Parliament, and from him he heard of the marriage of *mademoiselle* your daughter. I wrote to him to beg that he would send me the particulars, but to my great regret he was gone when my letter arrived. I know this Prince by name only (Bernard de Saxe Weimar, Duc de Jena), but you may believe, dear sister, how much pleased I am to hear of it, and that I wish your daughter as much happiness and contentment as if she were my own. Do me the honour, dear sister, to send me the particulars by M. de Rosemont, for I am extremely anxious to hear them.

✶✶✶✶✶✶

Note:—The Duc de la Trémoille's man of business, to whom Lady Derby wrote with this curious address:—"*Monsieur, Monsieur de Rosemont, Logé chez le Sr Froisart, couturier en la Place du Pont St Michel, vis-a-vis de Samourier, patissier, à Paris.*"

✶✶✶✶✶✶

I know well that the marriage of an only daughter must have overwhelmed you with business, and I cannot expect you to write. May God give you as much happiness as with all my heart I pray you may have. When I know that the marriage is over, I will not fail to write to you more fully. You have heard, no doubt, about the king's marriage, and how much pleased he is with the queen his wife, to whom my daughters went to pay their respects yesterday; they think Her Majesty is very agreeable. The king is very much in love with her; but her women are not liked. The husband of one of them entreated the king not to kiss his wife when he saluted her, which they say he very willingly promised as she is not at all pretty.

The queen, I believe liked her journey very much, having never before been in a carriage, but only in a litter. She was a whole month at sea, and was very ill. She has never worn anything on her head either at night or in the day, a custom which she still continues. They say she is very strict in her religion, and she is to have priests and other subjects of the king about her, which will make her more so. May God preserve to us our religion. I am positively assured that the king will do me the honour to keep his promise to me; it is known to everybody, and if *Monsieur* your brother would interest the Duke of St. Albans (formerly Lord Jermyn, a favourite of Queen Henrietta Maria), in my favour, the queen, his mistress, would not oppose it.

All people of consequence tell me that I may count upon it, and if it were not for the hope of being able to serve God, I should not wish for it so much. I hope also, through God's grace, that I may be enabled to serve Their Majesties by the care and fidelity with which I should devote myself to them. M. Morus, I hear, is certainly coming back; he stands very well, they say, with the Duke of St. Albans. If I get this appointment, I hope to be of service to him.

Lady Derby wrote again on the 3rd of October, on the subject of a horse which she was commissioned to buy for the Duchesse de la Trémoille, adding:—

> At our court nothing is spoken of but amusements, in which our queen takes little pleasure. The queen, her mother-in-law, was never gayer or more happy. Do me the honour to let me hear if *Madame*, your daughter, has left you, and how she has been received at her new home. I pray to God for her happiness.

Lady Derby's next letter is written from Brierton, on the 25th of November:—

> Your letters of the 23rd and 26th reached me at a place a day's journey from Knowsley, the house of a good friend of mine, a daughter of the Earl of Norwich,—better known to you by his name of Goring. I think I was wrong to leave London against my own feeling and that of all my friends, at a time, too, when I might have improved my affairs; but I was forced to it by absolute necessity, not having enough to support me, and being in continual misery about the payment of my debts. All sorts of people refused to supply me with the most necessary things. What troubles me most is the thought that I might be of use to you if I were there. When I took leave of His Majesty, he repeated the promise which I told you of before.
>
> The chancellor, though very ill of the gout, gives me many assurances of his friendship, and has promised to speak to the king for me that my pension may be secured for several years, which would enable me to make arrangements for the payment of my debts, for which I am very much pressed. I hear from one who is a good judge that this will be done. I am sure you must have heard that the Parliament has begun to sit again, and that the king's speech gave great satisfaction to his people and faithful subjects. We all hope he will remember those who have always been loyal to him and his father. His Highness the Duke of York has returned from Dunkirk. (Charles II. had just sold Dunkirk to Louis XIV. for four hundred thousand pounds.)
>
> There are still many conspiracies, and some very strange letters have been found in the possession of a Presbyterian minister. May God preserve His Majesty. I told the prime minister what you informed me; he answered, that they had had the same intelligence before. I am infinitely obliged to your son for the care that he promises to take of Mr. Hyde. I do not understand

how M. de la Tour can say that I did not tell him you had written to me in his favour: I assured him that I would do all I could to serve him. I think he was displeased because I have not placed a little French boy in the service of my daughter Dorchester: her husband does not wish her to have a page, for he does not like French customs.

Lady Derby hoped in vain, for, though the chancellor was favourable, and the king had given his promise to make her governess to his children, these children still remained unborn. Soon after, the violence of popular feeling obliged the Chancellor Clarendon to leave England. When the countess next wrote from Knowsley, on the 6th of February, 1663, she was recovering from an illness:—

> If the winter is as severe with you as it is here, it is wonderful how your health can improve. I have been very much indisposed for more than a month; but God has been pleased to restore my health, and I hope He will give me grace to employ it better than I have hitherto done. My illness prevented me from telling you that His Royal Highness has been pleased to appoint your nephew Stanley to be his first and sole gentleman of the bedchamber, which is a great thing for him; and, what is of more consequence still, the honour was conferred upon him without any solicitation by His Royal Highness, to whom and to the duchess he is alone indebted.
>
> His younger brother has obtained a cornetcy in the King's Guards; His Majesty did him the honour of assuring him that this was only a beginning; and I hope it may be so..... I have only to add my prayers that God may grant you many happy years, with every blessing you can desire. Permit me to say the same to *Monsieur* my brother.

Here ends the correspondence of Charlotte de la Trémoille, Countess of Derby, with her sister-in-law, Marie de la Tour d'Auvergne, Duchesse de la Trémoille. From this time till her death, which took place at Knowsley, on the 31st of March, 1664, Lady Derby wrote no more. We have no details of her last moments; we know not even if her children were with her, or if her sister-in-law, who did not long survive her, knew of her illness. Of the death of the Countess Charlotte no other record remains, except the Latin words inscribed by the clergyman at Knowsley in the parish register of burials, after the names and titles of the deceased, "*Post funera virtus*."

Such an epitaph might well be written over Charlotte de la Trémoille. At once haughty and humble, her character bore no resemblance to the portrait that Sir Walter Scott has drawn of her in his *Peveril of the Peak*. It was unjust to attribute to her the fate which, after the Restoration, befell Captain William Christian. He was found guilty of insurrection and of treason, for having surrendered to the Parliamentary Commissioners the Isle of Man, together with the widow and children of the Earl of Derby, his liege lord. But it was Lord Derby's successor, that son so long estranged from his parents on account of his marriage, and ever after regarded coldly by his mother, although forgiven by his father,—it was Charles, Lord Strange, afterwards eighth Earl of Derby, who, in January, 1662, out of respect to his father's memory, caused William Christian to be shot.

This was done by virtue of a local sentence, which, in August, 1663, was declared illegal by the Privy Council of Charles II., as contrary to the Act of Indemnity. Lord Derby maintained that he had proceeded according to the laws of the Isle of Man, which was a separate and independent kingdom; but he was not in favour at court, and his arguments were held to be invalid. Not only was his right to the exercise of sovereign justice denied, but the king's ill will went so far that he refused to sanction a bill which had been passed by both Houses of Parliament for restoring to the family the estates of James, Earl of Derby, confiscated in 1651, on the repayment by his son of the inconsiderable sums which had been given for them.

Long afterwards, at the commencement of the eighteenth century, James, tenth Earl of Derby, who had succeeded to the title on the death of his brother William without heirs male, and who spent the last years of his life in retirement at Knowsley, devoted his leisure to the rebuilding of the house, over the entrance of which he caused the following inscription to be engraved :—

> This was erected by James, Earl of Derby, Lord of Man and the Isles, grandson of James, Earl of Derby, by Charlotte, daughter of Claude, Duke of Trémoille, who was beheaded at Bolton, October 15th, 1651, for strenuously adhering to Charles II., who refused a Bill unanimously passed by both Houses of Parliament, for restoring to the family the estates which he had lost by his loyalty to him.

In spite of the brilliant proofs of passionate devotion which she had given to her husband, Charlotte de la Trémoille seems during her latter years not to have shared in her son's hereditary hatred and revenge. Heroic by nature, she sought no opportunities of displaying her heroism, nor was she ambitious of critical positions or important adventures,—yet none of these could have been found—none ever were found—to which her high heart and firm will were not equal, and that spontaneously, without either effort or premeditation.

Endowed with the noblest qualities of her era, of her race, and of her station, resolute to perform all duties, ready for all sacrifices, capable of any heroism, but too proud to make a merit of these things, she accepted, from a sense of honour as much as from conscientiousness, the trials of her destiny. Pious by education as well as by conviction, she nevertheless lacked that deep and steadfast fervour which was a distinguishing feature of French Protestantism in the age which preceded her own. Her piety, though earnest and sincere, did not occupy itself with minute subtleties; she was simple in her faith as in her heroism, and no more thought of troubling herself with scruples than she would have hesitated to accept the fate of a martyr, if her conscience or her honour had required it.

After having borne so noble a part in the struggles and sufferings of a great revolution, when these stern times were succeeded by a reign of less severity, and the Restoration of Charles II. revived in England the manners and magnificence of a court that soon became as profligate as it was frivolous, Charlotte de la Trémoille, with an ease and elasticity of nature, characteristic rather of France, her native country, than of England, the land of her adoption, looked on at these things without anger. Untouched by either the frivolity or the corruption of the court, or, perhaps, not recognising sufficiently its evils and dangers, she played the part of a court lady as naturally as in the time of the Civil War she had done that of a heroine.

Living in a foreign country and in the midst of foreign manners which she frankly adopted, called upon to endure, and enduring nobly, the most unexpected trials, she nevertheless retained something of the prejudices, habits, and tastes of her own country, and of the rank in which she was born. She was pre-eminently a "*grande dame*" and a noble lady; frank and resolute, loyal and faithful; a woman of whom the great houses from which she was sprung and to which she was allied might well be proud,—one who was worthy to bear upon her arms the two mottoes which had governed her life:—

"*Je maintiendrai,*" and "*Sans changer.*" (The mottoes of William the Silent, Prince of Orange, and of the Earls of Derby.)

A Journal of the Siege of Lathom House in Lancashire

The following journal of a celebrated siege, on which the novel of *Peveril of the Peak* has conferred new and additional interest, exists in MS. among the Harleian Collection in the British Museum, and has never previously been presented to the public. From the expression "our retreat" in the account of the sally on May 25, the author was probably one of the officers engaged in that service, who composed the narrative in the intervals of action, or before the spring of $164^{5/6}$ (*sic*), when Lathom, which is described as entire in one of the last paragraphs, was demolished. At all events he was an inmate of the mansion, and a man acquainted with classical literature, who retained the provincialisms of Lancashire, but had formed a regular style by habits of composition.

This leaves a narrow circle for conjecture, and it may be allowed to point out as the probable author Captayne Edward Chisenhall of Chisenhall, representative of an ancient family, promoted subsequently by Rupert to the rank of colonel of infantry, and in 1653 author of a learned controversial work, intitled *Catholike History*. The transcript of the before-mentioned Harleian MS. (2043), from which the present publication is printed, forms part of an extensive, and (as it is believed) *complete* collection of tracts relating to the progress of the local struggles in Lancashire during the Great Rebellion, preserved in the library of a gentleman of that county, by whom the present portion of it was presented to the publishers.

A BRIEFE JOURNALL OF THE SEIGE AGAINST LATHOM

The Earle of Derby in the rise of this rebellion having on his own charges brought up 3,000 of his best men (the Lord Mullineux his regt. and St Gilbert Gerard's out of Lanc., Sir Tho. Salisbury's out of Wales), and armes to the king's standard, with purpose to have attended his sacred Maty in person, was att the request of the truely noble Sir Gilbert Haughton and others sent backe for Lancashire by His Majestie's expresse command, where with naked men or thinly armed hee sustained the fury of the rebells, and kept the field against them for 7 monethes together, storming severall of their townes, and defeating them in sundry battles, himself in every assault and skirmish chargeing in the front to encourage his souldiers with exemplary resolucion when the multitude of the enemy exceeded his number by the advantage of 2 or 3 to 1, till his lord unhappily called to crush the thriveing sedition in Cheshire, withdrew his horse into that county.

The enemy now spyeing an opportunity for action in his absence, drew out their garrisons, and with theire whole strength assaulted the towne of Preston, which not yet fortyfyed and suddenly surprized, notwithstanding the endeavours and resolute resistance of Sir Gilbert Haughton, the maior, and other gentlemen, was lost to the enemy. Upon his lord's return he found himselfe straitned to a narrow compasse; yet opposing loyal thoughts to dangers, and labouring to keepe life in the busines by speedy action, hee withdrew into the field, and marched above 20 myles into the enemyes' countrey, taking Lancaster, and regayneing Preston by assault, when the rebells with a numerous army were within 6 houres march pursuing him.

After this his lord giving 2 or 3 dayes to refresh his souldiers, toyld out with 3 dayes restles service, the enemy got fresh supplies, from Yorkshire, Cheshire, Staffordshire, and Derbyshire, soe that now again swelled into a numerous body, they attempt an assault of Wigan, which with little service was unfortunately lost, ere his lord could come to its releeffe; whereof Her Majestie, then att Yorke, haveing intelligence, sent expresse comand to his lord not to engage his army in any service, till she sent him ayde, which his lord expected a fortnight every day; but being disappointed in his hopes, and the enemy growen insolent by his stillnes, hee was moved by the Lord Mullineux, Sir Thomas Tildsley, and other gentlemen with him, to repayre to the queen in person, to hasten the promised supplyes, when (after a fortnight's attendance) fell out that unfortunate surprize of the Lord Goreing in Wakefield, which utterly disinabled Her Majestie to spare him any releefe, which the Governor of Warrington (Col. Norris) understanding, after 5 dayes siedge, gave up the towne (the greatest key of the County) to the enemy, and all his lord's forces then with the Lord Mullineux and Colonell Tildsley marched down to York.

Att the same time her Majestie received intimation of the Scottish designe for the invasion of England, with signification of their intention to shipp from the north of Ireland for the Isle of Man, and soe for England, wherefore it was the queene's pleasure expressly to command him for the island, to prevent theire passage that way. Att his arrival there he found the whole countrey in sedition and insurrection, some turbulent spirits, tutored by theire brethren the Scotts, haveing taught the commons the new tricke of rebellion, under the masque of defensive armes for the preservation of theire religion and libertyes; and indeed this subtill poyson had soe wrought in that litle bodye, that the whole countrey was swelled to one tumour, which by all symptoms had broke out in 3 dayes with the death of the bishoppe and governour, and the losse of the island.

To prevent this rupture his lord presently raised the horse of the countrey, apprehended the persons of theire seditious agents, doeing execucion upon some, imprisoning others, and strikeing a general terrour into all, which suddenly callmed the madnes of the people, and drew a face of quyett upon the countrey.

Yett to remove the ground of this disease required both skill and tyme, as well to prevent a relapse of the countrymen, as an invasion of the Scotts, who still promise for conscience-sake to abett them in theire rebellion, it being the good fortune of that ungrateful nation to be esteemed angells for troubling and poysoning all waters.

His lord by the queene's command haveing spent much tyme in this unhappy busines, is at last called backe by His Majestie to attend his Parliamt att Oxford, and att his returne to England is welcomed with the newes of a siedge against his ladye, which had been long in consultation, and now is matured for action.

Upon the surrender of Warrington, May 27, 1643, a summons came from Mr Holland, Governor of Manchester, to the Lady Derby, to subscribe to the propositions of parliament, or yield up Lathom House; but her ladishippship denyed both—shee would neither tamely give up her house, nor purchase her peace with the losse of her honour. But being then in noe condition to provoke a potent and malitious enemy, and seeing noe possibility of speedy assistance, shee desired a peaceable abode in her own house, referring all her lord's estate to theire dispose, with promise onely to keepe soe many men in armes, as might defend her person and house from the outrages of theire common souldiers, which was hardly obtayned.

From this time she endured a continued siedge, onely with the opennes of her gardens and walkes, confined as a prisoner to her owne walls, with the liberty of the castle-yard, suffering the sequestracion of her whole estate, dayly affronts and indignityes of unworthy persons, besides the unjust and undeserved censures of some that wore the name and face of friends; all which shee patiently endured, well knoweing it noe wisdome to, quarrell with an evill she could not redresse.

Therefore, to remove all pretences of vyolence or force against her, she restrayned her garrison souldiers from all provocation and annoyance of the enemy, and soe by her wisdome kept them att a more favorable distance, for the space of allmost a whole year. Rigby all this tyme, restles in his malice, sought all occasion to disturb her quyett, sending out his troopes to plunder her next neighbours, and surprize such of the kinges good subjectes, as had fledd unto her for safety.

In the beginning of February, her garrison-souldiers had a skirmish with a troope of his horse commanded by Captayne Hyndley, wherein they rescued some of her friends, takeing prisoners Lieutenant Dandy, first wounded, his Cornet, and some troopers. By his unjust report of this action, and some other slight visitations within muskett-shot of her house, hee wrought on Sr Tho. Fairfax and the rest of the Parliament forces to his owne purpose.

On Saturday, the 24th of February, it was resolved in a councill of the Holy State att Manchester, after many former debates and consultations to the same purpose, that Mr Ashton of Midleton, Mr Moore of Banckhall, and Mr Rigby of Preston, (3 Parliament Colonells,) should with all speed come agst Lathom, of which her Lap had some broken intelligence on Sunday Mornyng, and therefore dispatcht a messenger to her secret friend, one acquainted with their determinations, to receave fuller satisfaction, in the meane time useing all diligence and care to furnish her house with provision and men, which was a hard worke, considering shee had been debarred of her estate for a whole yeare.

Yett in these straites she used not the least vyolence to force releeffe from any of her neighbours, though some of them were as bad tenants as subjects, but with her owne small stocke, and the charity of some few freinds, by the industry of her carefull servant Mr Broome, provided herself to bear the worst of a cruell enemy. The messenger returned on Monday. Shee had assurance of their designe, who were then on their march as farre as Bolton, Wigan, and Standish, with pretence to goe for Westmerland to carry on the multitude blindfold against a house that theire fathers and themselves, whilst their eyes were open, had ever honoured, reputing Lathom, in more innocent tymes, both for magnificence and hospitality, the onely court of the northerne parts of this kingdom, when the good men would in meere love vent theire harmles treason, "God Save the Earle of Derby and the King."

But theire factious ministers, very dutyfull sonnes of the Church of England, made the pulpitt speake theire designe aloud, one whereof, Bradshaw, to the dishonour of that house (Brazen-nose) which had give him more sober and pious foundations, tooke occasion, before his patrons at Wigan, to prophane the fourteenth verse of the fifteenth chapter of Jeremy, from thence by as many markes and signes as ever hee had given of Antichrist, proving the Lady Derby to bee the scarlett whore and the whore of Babylon, whose walls he made as flatt and as thin as his discourse. Indeed, before he dispatchet his prophecy hee thumpet 'em downe, reserveing the next verse to bee a triumph for the victor.

Feb. 27, 1643-4. On Tuesday the enemy tooke their quarters round the house, at the distance of a myle—2 or 3 att the furthest.

Feb. 28. On Wednesday, Capain Markland brought a letter from Sr Thomas Fairfax, and with it an ordinance of Parliament, the one requiring her ladishippship to yield up Lathom House upon such honourable condicions as hee should propose, and the other declareing the mercy of the Parliament to receave the Earle of Derby would hee submit himselfe, in which business Sr Tho. Fairfax promises to bee a faithfull instrument. To which her ladishipp gave in answer:

> She much wondered that Sir Tho. Fairfax wold require her to give up her lord's house without any offence on her part done to the Parliament: desireing in a busines of such weight, that struck both att her religion and life, that soe nearly concerned her soveraigne, her lord, and her whole posteritie, she might have a weekes consideracion, both to resolve the doubts of conscience, and to advice in matter of law and honour."

Not that her ladishipp was unfixt in her owne thoughts, but indeavouring to gayne tyme by demurhes and protraccions of the busines, which happly the good knight suspecting, denyed her the tyme desired, moveing her ladishipp to come to Newparke, a house of her lords a quarter of a myle from Lathom, and to come thither in her coache (no meane favour, beleeve it), where himselfe and his colonells would meete her for a full discourse and transaction of the busines.

This her ladishipp flatly refused, with scorne and anger, as an ignoble and uncivill mocion, returneing only this answer:

> That, notwithstanding her present condicion, she remembred both her lord's honour and her owne birth, conceaving it more knightly that Sr Thomas Fairfax shold waite upon her, than shee upon him.

Thursday (Feb. 29) and Friday (March 1) were spent in letters and messages, his generallship att last requireing free accesse for 2 of his colonells, and assurance of safe returne, unto which her Lapp condescended. On Saturday Mr Ashton and Mr Rigby vouchsafed to venture their persons into Lathom House, being authorised by the generall to propound the following condicions.

> 1. That all armes and ammunition of war shall bee forthwith surrendered into the hands of Sir Thomas Fairfax.
>
> 2. That the Countesse of Derby, and all the persons in Lathom House shall bee suffred to depart, with all theire goods to Chester, or any other of the enemyes quarters, or upon submission to the orders of parliament to theire owne houses.
>
> 3. That the countesse with all her meniall servants shall bee suffred to inhabite in Knowsley, and to have 20 musketts allowed for her defence, or to repaire to her husband in the Isle of Man.
>
> 4. That the countesse for the present, untill the Parliament be acquainted with it, shall have allowed her for her maintenance all the lands and revenues of the earle her husband, within the Hundred of Derby, and that the Parliament shall bee moved to continue this allowance.

These condicions her ladishipp rejected, as in part dishonorable, in part uncerteyne, adding withall, she knewe not how to treat with them who had not power to performe theire owne offers, till they had first moved the Parliament, telling them it were a more sober course, first to acquaint themselves with the pleasure of the Parliament, and then to move accordingly. But for her part, shee wold not move the good gentlemen to petition for her. Shee wold esteem it a greater favour to permitt her to continue in her present humble condition.

The 2 colonells being blancke in their treaty, spent their stay in wise instructions to her ladishipp and unjust accusations of her frie and servants, which shee not onely cleared, but nobly and sharplye returned upon their religious agents, soe that the grave men being disappointed, both of their witt and malice, returned as empty as they came.

Sunday was theire Sabbath. On Monday Mr Ashton came agayne alone with power to receave her ladishipp's propositions, and convey them to his generall (a notable and trusty employment), which came in these terms.

> 1. Her ladishippship desired a monethes tyme for her quyett continuance in Lathom, and then herselfe and children, her freinds, souldiers and servants, with all her goods, armes and ordinance, to have free transport to the Isle of Man, and in the meane tyme that she shold keepe garrison in her house for her owne defence.
>
> 2. Shee promised that neither dureing her stay in the countrey, nor after her comeing to the Isle of Man, any of the armes shold bee imployed against the Parliament.
>
> 3. That dureing her stay in the countrey, noe souldier should be quartered in the Lordshipp of Lathome, nor at Knowsley House.
>
> 4. That none of her tennants, neighbours and freinds then in the house with her, shold, assisting her, suffer in their persons or estates, after her departure.

In the first of these she struck at more time: in the second shee understood *the Parliament of the 3 estates at Oxford*, knowing noe other: in the third shee laboured to remove impediments that might hinder the victualling of her house: in the fourth shee gave a collour to her depart, and content to her souldiers, of whom in her treaty she showed an honorable care.

These propositions returned by Mr Ashton were interpreted to the right sense, being apprehended too full of policy and danger to bee allowed, as onely beating at more tyme and meanes, that her ladishipp might use that opportunity to confirm herself in her fastnes. And therefore in his answer Sir Thomas thus qualified them to a better understanding.

> 1. That the Countesse of Derby shall have the tyme shee desyred, and then liberty to transport her armes and goods to the Isle of Man, excepting the canon, which shall continue there for the defence of the house.
>
> 2. That her ladishipp by 10 o'clock tomorrow disband all her souldiers, except her meniall servants, and receave an officer,

and 40 Parliament souldiers, for her guard.

This, as the last residue of all their councells, with some terrible presages of the danger shee stood in, was delivered to her ladishipp by one Morgan, one of Sir Thomas his colonells, a litle man, short, and peremptory, who met with staidnes to coole his heat; and had the honor to carry backe this last answer, for her ladishipp could scrue them to noe more delayes.

That she refused all their articles, and was truely happy they had refused hers, protesting shee had rather hazard her life, than offer the like again. That *though a woman and a stranger, divorced from her friends, and robed of her estate, She* was ready to receive their utmost vyolence, trusting in God both for protection and deliverance.

Being now disappointed in their plot, who expected a quicke dispatch with the afflicted ladye by a tame surrender of her house, having scattered very fearfull apprehensions of their great gunnes, their morter-piece, their fireworks, and their engineers, after 'all their consults, they prepare for action, when they find her ladishipp as feareless of their empty terrors, as, carefull to prevent a reall danger, shee is willing to understand the power of the enemy, and studious to prevent it, leaving nothing with her eye to be excused afterwards by fortune or negligence, and adding to her former patience a most resolved fortitude. "*Ne minimo quidem casui locum relinqui debuisse.*"

The next morneing discovered some of the enemyes nightworkes, which were begun about musquet-shott from the house, in a stoopeing, declineing ground, that their pioneers by the nature of the place might be secured from our ordinances on the towers, and soe in an orbe or ringe-worke cast up much earthe everye day by the multitude of countrey people forced to the service.

March 7, 8, 9, 10. After three dayes, finding a fixednes and resolution in her ladishipp still to keep her house for the service of His Majestie against all his enemyes, on Sunday they imploy 6 neighbours of the best rancke with a petition to her ladishipp, haveing thrust a forme into theire hands, and prepared their heads with instructions, as by confession now appeares;

> That in duty to her ladishipp, and love to their countrey, they most humbly beseech her to prevent her owne personal dangers, and the impoverishing the whole countrey, which she

might do if shee pleased to slacken something of her severe resolution, and in part condescended to the offers of the gentlemen.

Theise her ladyeship received with all curtesy, discourseing unto them the nature of former treatyes, and the order of her proceedings, and this soe smoothly and comeingly, that the good men were satisfied, and had litle to say, but God bless the king and the Earle of Derby. For answer to their paper, shee told them, it was more fitt that they petition the gentlemen who robbed and spoyled their country, than her, who desyred only a quyett stay in her owne house, for the preservation not spoyle of her neighbours.

One of the sixe, of more ability and integrity than the rest, reported the whole busines of the answer, and theire entertainment, as a true subject to His Majestie and a faythful friend to her ladishipp, with which the noble colonells were moved to new propositions, in meer mercy, if you'll beleeve 'em, to her ladishipp and her children. The next day therefore Captayne Ashurst, a man that deserves a fairer character than the rest, for his even and civil behaviour, brought a new missive to her ladyeship, in theise terms:

1. That all former condicions be waived.

2. That the Countess of Derby, and all persons in the house, with all armes, ordinance, and goods, shall have liberty to march to what part of the kingdome they please, and yeild up the house to Sr Tho. Fairfax.

3. That the armes shold never be imployed agt the Parliament.

4. That all in the house excepting a 100 persons shold leave it, and the rest within ten dayes. The message read, her ladishipp perceaved they began to coole in their enterprize, and therefore to lend 'em some new heate, returned this answer by the captayne, that she scorned to be a ten dayes prisoner to her owne house, judging it more noble, whilst shee could, to preserve her liberty by armes, than to buy a peace with slavery.

Said shee:

And what assurance have I ever of liberty, or the performance of any condicion, when my strength is gone? I have receaved, under the hands of some eminent personages, that your generall is not very conscientious in the performance of his subscriptions, so that from him I must expect an unsinewed and faithles agreement. 'Tis dangerous treating when the sword is given to the enemies hand.

And therefore her ladyeship added:

> That not a man shold part her house, that shee wold keepe it, whilst God enabled her, against all the king's enemyes, and in breefe, that she wold receave no more messages without an expresse of her lord's pleasure, whoe shee now heard was returned from the Isle of Man, and to whom shee referred them for the transaccion of the whole busines, considering that frequent treatyes are a discouragement to the souldier besieged, as a yeildance to some want or weakness within, and soe the first key that commonly opens the gate to the enemy.

To seconde and confirme her answer, the nexte day, beinge Tuesday, a 100 foote, commanded by Captayne Farmor, a Scotchman, a faithfull and gallant souldier, with Lieut. Prethergh ready to second him in any service, and some 12 horse, our whole cavallerie, commanded by Lieut. Key, sallied out upon the enemy: and because the sequel of every busines dependeth upon the beginning, the captayne determined to doe something that might remember the enemye there were souldiers within.

He marcht up to their workes without a shoote, and then fireing upon them in their trenches, they quickly left their holes, when Lieut. Key, haveing wheeled about with his horse from another gate, fell upon them in their flighte with much execucion; they slewe about 30 men, tooke 40 armes, one drum, and 6 prisoners. The maine retreate was that day made good by Capt. Ogle, a gentleman industrious to returne the curtesie which some of theire party shewed to him when he was taken prisoner in the battell at Edgehill. The other passage was carefully secured by Captayne Rawstorne. Not one of ours that day was slaine or wounded.

By the prisoners wee understood the purpose of the enemy was to starve the house, the commanders having courage to pyne a ladye, not to fight with her.

The foure dayes following (13, 14, 15, 16) passed without much accion on either side, saveing that the garrison gave them some night alarums, which to some ministered an occasion of runneing away, and to others of be lyeing their owne courage, that they had repulst the garrison souldiers, and slayne thousands out of hundreds.

17th. On Sunday night the commanders under her ladishipp resolved to try their watches, and therefore, at 3 o'clock in the morning, Captayne Chisnall, a man of knowne courage and resolucion, Lieut. Prethergh, and Lieut. Heape, with one 30 musqueteers, issued out of the backe gate to surprize the enemy in their new trenches; but they discovering some of the light matches ran faster than the captayne or his souldiers could pursue, secureing their flight in a wood close by, where, not willing to engage his souldiers in unnecessary dangers, hee left 'em, onely killing 2 or 3, and chaseing the rest in flight.

Theise sallyes and allarums soe diseased the enemye that theire work went slowly on, haveing been 3 weekes and yet not cast up one mount for ordinance; but now for theire owne security, to keepe off our men with their cannon, they hasten the busines, with the losse of many mens lives, compellid to. doe desperate service. It moved both wonder and pitty to see multitudes of poore people soe enslaved to the reformers' tirranny, that they would stand the muskett and lose their lives to save nothing, soe neare are theise to the times complained of by the historian, when they would noe lesse feare men for theire vices, than they once honored them for their virtues

19, 20. On Tuesday night they brought up one peece of canon; Wednesday morneing gave us some sport. They then played theire canon 3 shootes, the ball 24. They first tryed the wall, whch being found proof, without much yeildance or the least impression, they afterwards shott higher to beate downe pinacles and turretts, or else *to please the women that came to see the spectacle.* The same day Sir Tho. Fairfax sent her ladishipp a letter that he had received from the Earle of Derby, wherein his lordshipp desired an honorable and free passage for his ladye and children, if shee so pleased, being loath to expose them to the uncertaine hazard of a long seidge, especially considering the roughnes and inhumanitie of the enemy, that joyned pride and malice, ignorance and crueltie against her: nor knoweing, by reason of his long absence, either how his house was provided with victuals and ammunition, or strengthened for resistance; and therefore desireous to leave only the hardy souldiers for the brunt, till it should please His Majestie to yeild him release, and to preserve his ladye and children from the mercy of cruell men, which indeed was the desire of all her friends.

But she had more noble thoughts within, which still kindled and encreased att the apprehension of danger; who, returneing an acknowledgement of that first curtesye of Sir Tho. Fairfax, after some discourse with the messenger, one Jackson, a sawcy and zealous chaplaine to Mr Rigby, gave backe this answeare. She willingly wold submitt herselfe to her lords commands, and therefore willed the generall to treate with him; but till she was assured it was his lordshipp's pleasure, she wold neither yeild the house, nor herself desert it, but waite for the event according to the good will of God. And with the like significacion she dispatcht a messenger to his lordshipp in Chester, which was sent out by an allarum to open a passage through theire gards and centries.

21, 22, 23, 24. The 4 dayes followinge were spent in allarums and excursions, without much busines of service.

25. On Monday they gave us 7 shott of their culverin and demi cannon, one whereof, by some checke in the way, entred the greate gates, which were presently made good by the opposition of beds, and such like impediments, to stay the bullett from rangeing the court.

28. On Thursday 5 cannons: this day the enemy, capable of any impression of feare, tooke a strong allarum, fighting one agt another, and in the accion 2 peices of canon att the ayre. *29.* The next day one of our men, vainely provokeing danger with his body above a tower, was shott to a present death. In the afternoone, they played 4 cannons, one whereof, levelled to dismount one of our ordinance upon the great gates, strucke the battlements upon one of our markes-men ready to discharge att the cannonneere, and crusht him to deathe.

31. On Sunday night 2 canons mounted to the lodgeing chambers, intending bylike to catche us napping, as our men had often caught them.

April 1. On Munday, in the day and night, 6 canon loden with chaine shott and barres of iron.

2. The next day they played their morter peice, 3 times loaden with stones, 13 inches in diameter, 80*lb* in weight. It was planted about halfe musket shott southwest from the house, on a riseing earthe, convenyently giveing the engineere a full perspect of the whole buildeinge. Their worke to secure it was orbiculer, in forme of a full moone, 2 yards and a half of rampier above the ditch.

4. On Thursday they shott one stone and one granadoe, which overplayd the house. Chosen men upon the guards, standing ready with greene and wett hides to quench the burneing, had their skill, for they wanted no malice, enabled them to cast fireworks.

5. Haveing hitherto met so unprosperous successe in their holy worke, the 2 collonels, Mr Ashton and Mr Moore, cast a shew of religion over their execrable work; and like those devoute men in the poetts, by publike and private suplications call God to assist them in their merciles practizes, to which purpose they issue out com'andes to all their ministers for a general and humble imprecacion in the following forme:

> To all Ministers and Parsons in Lancashire, well wishers to our successe against Lathom House, theise.
> Forasmuch as more then ordinary obstruccions have from the beginning of this present service against Lathom House interposed our proceedings, and yet still remaine, which cannot otherwise be removed, nor our successe furthered, but onely by devine assistance, it is therefore our desires to the ministers, and other well affected persons of this county of Lancaster, in publike manner, as they shall please, to commend our case to God, that as wee are appoynted to the simployment, soe much tending to the settleing of our present peace in theise parts, soe the Almighty would crowne our weake endeavours with speedy successe in the said designe.
> Ormskirk, Apr. 5, 1644.   Raph Ashton,
>   John Moore.

The 4 dayes following were on theire parts slept out in this pious exercise: on Wednesday our men resolved to waken them. About 11 o'clock, Captayne Farmor and Captayne Mullineux Rattcliffe, Lieut Penckett, Lieut Woorrale, with 140 souldiers, sallyed out at a postern gate, beate the enemy from all theire worke and batteries, which were now cast up round the house, nailed all theire canon, killed about 50 men, took 60 armes, one collours, and 3 drumes; in which accion Captayne Rattcliffe deserves this remembrance, that with 3 souldiers, the rest of his squadron being scattered with execucion of the enemy, he cleared 2 sconces, and slew 7 men with his owne hand. Lieut. Woorral, ingageing himselfe in another worke among 50 of the enemy, bare the fury of all, till Captayne Farmor releeved him, who, to the wonder of us all, came off without any dangerous wound.

The sally port was this day warded by Captayne Chisnall, who with fresh men stood ready for succour of ours, had they been putt to the extremity; but they bravely marched round the works, and came in att the great gates, where Captayne Ogle with a party of musketeers kept open the passage. Captayne Rawstorne hadd the charge of the musketeers upon the walls, which hee placed to the best advantage to vexe the enemy in their flighte: Captayne Foxe, by a collours from the Eagle Tower, gave signall when to march and when to retreate, according to the motions of the enemy, which hee observed att a distance.

In all this service, wee had but one man mortally wounded, and wee tooke onely one prisoner, an officer, for intelligence. In former sallyes some prisoners were taken, and by exchange releast, Colonells Ashton and Rigby promising to sett at liberty as many of the king's freinds then prisoners in Lancaster, Manchester, Preston, and other places proposed by her ladishipp; but most unworthily they broke condicions, it suiting well with their religion neither to observe faith with God nor men; and this occasioned a greater slaughter then either her ladishipp or the captaynes desired, because wee were in no condicion to keepe prisoners, and knew the commanders wold never release 'em but upon base or dishonorable terms.

The same night they played a sacre twice, to tell us they had cannon that wold speake, though our men had endeavoured to steele up all theire lippes. This whole night was with them one continued allarum, nothing but shoutes and cryes amongst them, as if the cavaleers had still been upon them. 12. On Friday they sent us two shottes from their morter peice, which our men had nailed and battered with smith's hammers, but it had too wide a mouth to bee stopt. This day a chance bullet from the sacre through the claye walls entred the window of my ladye's chamber, but was too weake to fright her from the lodgeing.

13. On Saturday theire demi cannon opened againe, but spake but once very lowe, some of the steele nayles yet sticking in her teeth, and the gunners also suspecting poyson in her belly. 15. On Monday they played their morterpeece 5 times with stones, and with granadoe, which fell shorte of the house in a walke neere the chappell-tower. Some pieces of the shell, 2 inches thick, flewe over the walls, and were taken up in the furthest parts of the house.

16. Tuesday morning they had a hott alarum, haveing not yet quitt themselves of the fright they took at the last sally. They played their cannon twice, and theire muskett half one houre together. In requitall whereof, about 11 o'clock they played their morter peece with stone, and perceaving it strucke within the body of the house, they cast a granadoe att the same levell, which fell into an old court, strikeing

above half a yard into the earth, yet rose again with such vyolence in the bursteing, that though its strength was much lessened, and deaded with earth, it shooke down the glasse, clay, and weaker buildings neere it, leaving only the carcase of the walls standing about it, yet without hurt of any person, saveing that 2 woemen in a neere chamber had theire hands scorcht, to putt them in mind hereafter they were in siedge at Lathom.

The morter peece was now more terrible than formerly, insomuch that the captaynes, to prevent the souldiers feares, lodged in the upprooms within clay walles, as not esteeming the force of the granadoe: and one thing more now happily lent more courage to our men, that one of their engineers, mounting the rampier to see the fall of the granadoe, was happily slaine by a marksman from one of our towers. On Saturday, they made 30 shootes of their demi canon and culverin, to batter a posterne-tower, some part whereof stoode without the mote and pallizadoes, yet soe fenced by a riseing ground that their ordinance tooke onely the battlements and a yard of wall, which was made good agayne the same night, with greater strength and safety for the musketeers then formerly.

It was some requitall for the breach of a few stones that theire cannoneere was slaine through the porthole by one of our men from the tower. Havinge either done with the canon or canoneere, they now begin with the morter peece, which that afternoone they played five times, in the night twice with stones and once with granadoe, which alsoe by turneing of the gunner fell short of the house.

On Easter Monday they must needs shew the people some pastime, and therefore gave us the bulletts, and them the noise of 9 canon and 2 periers, to heare the rabble shout. That night, two darke for accion, the captaynes sent out 2 or 3 firelocks, which strucke the whole night into alarums, soe that to their muskett they added one morterpeece, and 2 cannon with chayne and small shott. 23. The next day was the second wakes, when Rigby, must gratify the countrey for their 2000li with the battery of the Eagle Tower att Lathom, against which they playd their culverin and demi canon 23 tymes, which unhappily striking agt a staircase forced a large breach. 2 of the bulletts entred her ladyishipp's chamber, which last made her ladishipp seeke a new lodgeing, with this protest, that she would keepe the house, while there was building to cover her head.

This action must needs proceed eyther from pride or malice, it being noe furtherance to the takeing of the house to batter a tower that stood in the midst of it: but sure it was theire plot eyther to strike off one of the hornes of the Whore of Babylon, or els to levell one of her hills, the 7 towres in the devines sermon being easily found to bee the hills of Rome. It saved the tower some buffetts that day that 2 of theire gunners were discharged of theire employment by our marksmen from the top of the same tower which they were battering. The same night a strong alarum beate all their men to the canon, not to defend them, but themselves, which they bravely discharged, twice loaden with cartridge and chayne, against 2 lighted matches cast neere their workes in balls of clay.

24. On Wednesday they only gave us 3 periers and 2 canon. But now Mr Rigby, who undertooke the manage, and expected the glory of this enterprize, having wearyed his souldiers, wasted his powder, and emptyed himself of a good part of his exacted and plundered moneyes, finding her ladishipp nothing to yield to his greate gunnes, but daily to beate and baffle his souldiers, is now for present fire and ruine. Hee was provided a new stock of granadoes, and intends to spend his powder and malice in them.

25. Thursday, hee sends his last message, as hee calls it, a furious summons to her ladishipp to yeild upp Lathom House, all the persons, goods, and arms within it, into his hands, to receave the mercy of the Parliament, and to returne her finall answer the next day before 2 o'clock; which her ladishipp haveing read, with a brave indignation calls for the drum, and tells him, "a due reward for his paynes is to be hanged upp at her gates; but," says she, "thou are but a foolish instrument of traytors pride : carry this answi backe to Rigby," (with a noble scorne teareing the paper in his sight), "*Tell that insolent rebell, hee shall neither have persons, goods, nor house: when our strength and provision is spent, we shall find a fire more mercy full than Rigby, and then if the providence of God prevent it not, my goods and house shall burne in his sight: myselfe, children, and souldiers, rather then fall into his hands, will seale our religion and loyalty in the same flame;*" which being spoke aloud in her souldiers' hearing, they broke out into shouts and acclamations of joy, closeing all with this generall voyce, "Wee'll dye for His Majestie and your Honour-God save the King!"

The drum returned: her ladishipp and the captaynes fell into consultation of a further answer to that proud message. Something must be done, and now was the nicke and joynt of tyme, according to the observacion of the historian, "that the chaunges of tymes are the most fitt for brave attempts, and delayes on they are dangerous, where softnes and quyetnes draweth more danger then hazarding rashly"

The morter-peece was that that troubled us all. The litle ladyes had stomack to digest canon, but the stoutest souldiers had noe hearts for granadoes; and might not they att once free themselves from the continuall expectacion of death?—"'Tis a hard choice," says young Piso, "either to kill, or bee killd," and this was our present condicion—either sheepishly to receave death, when they would send it upon our heads, or manfully returne it upon theire owne. At last it was resolved, notwithstanding a battery, and ordinance planted against every passage, to sally out the next morneing and venture for all.

26. All things prepared, about 4 o'clock next morneing, Captayne Chisnall and Captayne Foxe, Lieut. Brethergh, Lieut. Penkett, Lieut. Walthew, and Lieut. Worral, are designed for the service. Captayne Ogle had the maine guard, to secure a retreate att the southerne gate; Capt. Rawstorne has the charge of the sally gate, to secure our retreate on the east side; Captayne Rattcliffe has the care of the marksmen and musketeers upon the walls, to attend the approche or vex the flight of the enemy. Captayne Farmer, with a reserve of fresh men, stands ready att the parade to releeve either captayne in state of necessitye.

All things thus disposed, Captayne Chisnall and 2 lieuts, issues out att the easterne gate, and before hee was discovered, gott under theire canon, marching straight upon the scouts, where they had planted their great gun. It cost him a light skirmish to gayne the fort: at last hee entred: many slayne, some prisoners, and some escaping. Now by the command of that battery the retreate being assured, Captayne Foxe seconds him with much bravery, beateing upon their trenches from the easterne to the southwest point, till hee came to the work which secured the morter-peece, which being guarded with 50 men, hee found sharpe service, forceing his way through muskett and canon, and beateing the enemy out of the sconce with stones, his muskett, by reason of the high worke, being unserviceable.

After a quarter of an houres hard service, his men gott the trench, and scald the rampier, where many of the enemy fledd, the rest were slayne. The sconce, thus won, was made good by a squadron of musketeers, which much annoyed the enemy, attempting to come upp agayne. The 2 maine works thus obtained, the 2 captaynes with ease walked the rest of the round, whilst Mr Broome, with a companye of her ladishipp's servants and some fresh souldiers, had a care to levell the ditch, and by a present devise, with ropes lifting the morter-peece to a low dragge, by strength of men drew it into the house, Captayne Ogle defending the passage against another companye of the enemye which played upon their retreate.

The like endeavour was used to gayne theire greate gunnes; but lying beyond the ditch, and being of such bulke and weight, all our strength could not bringe them off before the whole army had fallen upon us; however our men tooke tyme to poyson all the canon round, if any thing will doe the feate, Captayne Rawstorne still defending the first passe agt some offers of the enemy to come up by the wood.

This action continued an houre, with the losse of 2 men on our part, who, after they were mortally wounded, still fired upon the enemy, till all retreating. What number of the enemy were slayne is not easy to guesse. Besides the execucion done in theire trenshes, Captayne Farmours and Captayne Rattcliffes reserves, with the best marksmen, played upon them from the walls with much slaughter, as they quitt theire holds. Our men brought in many armes, 3 drums, and but 5 prisoners, preserved by Captayne Chisnall, to shew that he had mercy as well as valour.

One of theise was an assistant to their engineere Browne, who discovered to us the nature of theire trench, in which they had laboured 2 monethes, to draw away our water. Theire first designe was to drayne and open our springs, not considering theire rise from a higher ground southeast from the house, which must needs supply our deepe well, whereever they suncke their fall: this invencion faileing, they bringe up an open trench in a worme work, the earth being indented or sawed, for the securitie of their myners, and the ditch 2 yards wide and 3 deepe, for the fall of the water. But now neither ditches nor ought els troubled our souldiers, theire grand terror, the morter-peece, which had frighted 'em from theire meate and sleepe, like a dead lyon quyetly lying among 'em: everye one had his eye and his foote upon him, shouteing and rejoyceing as merrily as they used to doe with theire ale and bagpypes.

Indeed, every one had this apprehencion of the service, that the maine worke was done, and what was yet behind but a meere pastime. The house, though well fenced against the shott of canon, has much inward building of wood, an ancyent and weak fabrick, with which many mens lives was nakedly exposed to the periers, and by this dayes action preserved, of which in respect of all other occurrences in the siege, it was the greatest and most fortunate exployt.

Her ladishipp though not often overcarryed with any light expressions of joy, yet religiously sensible of soe great a blessing, and desireous, according to her pious disposition, to returne acknowledgements to the right authour, God alone, presently comands her chaplaynes to a publike thanksgiving.

The enemy, thus terrifyed with this defeate, durst not venture theire workes agayne till midnight; towards morneing removeing some of theire canon, and the next night stealeing away all the rest, save one peece for a memorandum. This one escapt nayleing, which the colonells durst not venture on its owne mount, but planted att a distance, for feare of the madmen in the garrison.

One thing may not heere bee omitted : that day that our men gave Rigby that shamefull defeate, had hee destined for the persecuteing of his utmost cruelty. Hee had invited, as it is now generally confest, all his freinds, the holy abettors of this mischiefe, to come see the house yeelded or burnt, hee haveing purposed to use his morter gunne with fireballs or granadoes all afternoone; but her ladishipp before 2 o'clocke (his owne tyme) gave him a very skurvy satisfying answer, soe that his friends came opportunely to comfort him, who was sicke of shame and dishonour, to be routed by a ladye and a handfull of men.

After this hee was hopeles of gayneing the house by any other meanes than starveing us out, or withdraweing the water, which our captaynes perceaving, presently suncke an eye, to meete 'em in theire workes, if they discover any mynes to blow the towers, or walls, in which we had diligent observers to harken to any noyce from their trench, that accordingly our men might direct their countermine.

From this tyme to the 25th May wee had a continued calme, Mr Rigbye's spirit being laid within our circle, soe that wee were scarce sensible of a siege, but only by the restraynt of our liberty. But our men continually vexed their quyet, either by the excursions of a few in the night, or by frequent alarums, which the captaines gave theire souldiers leave to invent and execute for theire recreation. Sometymes, in spite of their perdues, they would steal a corde about some tree neere the enemyes, and bringeing th' end round, would make it terrible with many ranks and files of light matches; sometymes dogs, and once a forlorne horse, handsomely stared with match, but turned out of gate, appeard in the darke night like young constellations.

But the enemy, soe diseased and beaten both in jest and earnest, many of them quitt theire charge, the rest cryed out for pay, ready to take any occasion to leave the plunder of Lathom House to others.

Colonell Rigby, perceaveing them ready to crumble into mutinyes endeavored to cement the breaches with some small pittance of theire pay, declareing it had cost him 2000li of his own moneyes in the siege, who was never knowne to bee worth one till hee became a publike robber by law; but you must remember hee had beene a lawyer, and a bad one.

All this cheape talke wold not keepe his souldiers from defection; many ran awaye, one whereof, escapt from the enemyes works att mid day, came to us, from whom we receaved this intelligence. Our men, not judgeing it safe to trust a fugitive enemy, wold not venture upon another sallye, imagining some treacherye might have beene weaved in all theise playne webbs, and covered by artifice of this strange convert: but Rigby heareing tell of his renegado, p'sently smelt a plot, and every day and night doubled his guards. His men, wearyed out with extraordinary duty, and himselfe perplexed with feares and jealousyes, was forced to call downe Colonell Holland from Manchester to his assistance. About this tyme wee discovered a cessation in theire myne work, the abundance of rayne soe slackinge and looseing the earth, that theire trench all fell in, with the death of 3 of theire myners.

May 23. On Thursday Captayne Edw. Moseley brought another summons to her ladishipp from his colonell. Mr Holland and Rigby, something fuller than the former—(it not beseeminge Mr Rigbyes greatnes to remit any thing of his former rigour)—that her ladishipp shold forthwth yeild upp her house, her armes and goods, all her servants and her own person and children, into theire hands, to bee submitted to the mercy of the parliament; which being read, her ladishipp smiled, and in a troubled passion challenged the captayne with a mistake in the paper, mercy instead of cruelty.

"Noe," sayes hee, "the mercy of the Parliament:" when her ladishipp quickly and composedly replyed, "the mercyes of the wicked are cruell: Not that I meane," sayes shee, "a wicked Parliament, of which body I have an honorable and reverend esteeme, but wicked factors and agents, such as Moore and Rigby, who for the advantage of theire owne interests labour to turne kingdomes into blood and ruyne. That unless they wold treat with her lord, they shold never have her, nor any of her freinds alive;" which the souldiers seconded with a generall acclamation. The captayne finding her still resolute in her first intention, in discourse with her Lapp and some others, gave a tacitt intimation (belike not without instrucions from the colonells), that her ladishipp may now have her owne first condicions to quitt the house; but shee returned the captayne with the first answer, that she wold never treate without commands from her lord.

The same night one of our spyes, sent out for newes, approcht the enemyes works, and takeing the opportunity of a single centrye, pistolled him, and entred the house with intelligence from his lord, that His Highnes Prince Rupert was in Cheshire, on his march for her ladishipp's releefe, which gave us joyfull occasion that night to pray for the princes happy and victorious approach.

24, 25. Fryday and Saturday were passed over in a hopefull ignorance, for whiles wee, knewe nothing, wee had good cause to hope well. It beinge the custome of the enemy to storme us with most hideous tales from theire trenches when they had the least foundation for a lye.

26. On Sunday nighte our centryes discovered a weakness in the enemy by the thinnesse of theire releefe, wherefore the captayne agreed to sally out the next morneing with 200 men.

Captayne Ogle and Captayne Rawstorne were allotted for the accion; but they, like good provident fellows, thrifty of theire owne lives, prevented the captayne this honour, who heareing of the prince's victorious entrance into the countrey, (by the defeate of Colonells Duckenfield, Mainwaring, Buckley, and others, who kept the passe at Stockport, the second key of the county,) stole away betwixt 12 and 1 o'clock in the night.

The next day Rigby drew upp his companyes, and what freshe supplyes hee could raise, in all about 3,000 (Mr Holland being returned to Manchester, and Mr. Moore to Liverpoole), unto Eccleston Greene, sixe miles from Lathom, standing there in a greate suspence which way to turne. Att last imagining the prince wold either march through Blackburnè or Lancaster for the releefe of Yorke, hee intends not to come in his way, but diverts to Bolton, formerly a garrison, and still fortifyed.

In this towne the prince intended to take upp his quarter, being truely certifyed by his scouts, that it was not without an enemy; but being happily prevented by Rigby and some other auxiliaries from Colonell Shuttleworth, to the number of 4,000 or 5,000 in all, His Highnes on Tuesday drew upp his army before the town, as truely happy of occasion to fight with the merciles besiegers of a princesse in misery, and forthwith with all gallantry and resolucion ledd up his men to an assault.

The Earle of Derby desireing to be one of the first avengers of that barbarousnes and cruelty expressed to his ladye, with a part of the princes owne horse charged a troope of the enemy, which braveringly issued out of the towne, to disorder and vexe our foote in the assault. Theise hee chact to the very walls, where he slewe the Cornett, and with his owne hand tooke the collours, being the first ensigne taken that day, which hee sent to His Highnes. Att his first passe into the towne, closely following the foote at theire entrance, his lordshipp mett with Captayne Bootle, formerly one of his owne servants, and the most virulent enemy age his ladye in the siege.

Him hee did honor of too brave a death to dye by his lords hand, with some others of his good countreymen, that had 3 monethes thirsted for his ladye's and his children's blood. The prince that day not only releeved but revenged the most noble ladye his cosen, leaveing 1,600 of her besiegers dead upon the place, and carrying away 700 prisoners.

For a perpetuall memoriall of his victory, in a brave expression of his owne noblenesse, and a gracious respect to her ladishipps sufferings, the next day hee presented her ladishipp with 22 of those collours, which 3 dayes before were proudly flourisht before her house, by the hands of the vallient and truely noble Sir Richard Crane, which will give honour to his Highnes and glory to the accion, soe long as there is one branch of that auncyent and princelye familye which His Highnes that day preserved.

A View of the Garrison, Theire Strength and Discipline.

Her ladiship comanded in cheeffe, whose first care was the service of God, which in sermons and solemne prayers shee duely saw performed: 4 tymes a day was shee com'only p'sent in publike prayers, attended with 2 litle ladyes her children, the Lady Mary and the Lady Catherine, for piety and sweetnes truelye the children of soe princely a mother: and if daringnes in tyme of danger may adde anything to theire age and virtues, lett them have this testimonye, that though truely apprehensive of the enemyes malice, they were nev' startled with any appearance of danger.

Her Captaynes.

Captayne Hen. Ogle, Captayne Edw. Chisnall, Captayne Edw. Rawsterne, Captayne Wm Farmor, Captayne Mullineux Rattcliffe, Capt. Richard Fox, assisted in their consultacions by Wm Farrington of Werden, Esq. who, for executeing the commission of array, and attending her ladishipp in her troubles, had suffered the seizure of all his personall estate, and the sequestration of all his lands.

The souldiers 300, proportioned to every captayne his number; theire duty was every second night 150 men upon the watch, excepting 16 select marksmen out of the whole, which all the day kept the towers. The sallyes were by, lotts. The captayne drawne by her ladishipp chose theire lieuts. Without the walls is a deepe ditch, fenced on each banke with stronge palizadoes; upon the walls 7 towers convenyently flancking one another: within, the walls are lined with earth and sodds, 2 yards thicke, by the industry of the souldiers in the siege.

The ordinance 6 sacres, 2 sling peeces, in every tower 1 or 2 murtherers to scoure the ditches.

Our greatest feare was want of powder, which had been suddenly spent, had not the captaynes dispensed it frugally, and prohibited the souldier from wast of shootes.

Every sally brought us in some new stocke, which the souldiers found in the enemyes trenches, to augment our magazine.

This feare made the captaynes sparing in theire sallyes and theire ordinance, who would els have prevented theire neere works.

In the whole siege we spent but 7 barrels, beside that we tooke from the enemy: in all the time they neither gave us assault nor alarum.

The provision wold have lasted 2 monethes longer, notwithstanding the souldiers hadd always sufficient, whom her ladishipp had a care often tymes to see served herselfe.

We lost but 6 men in the whole siege, 4 in service, and 2 by theire owne negligence, or over daringnes, appering above the towers.

À View of the Enemy.

Sr Tho. Fairfax commanded in cheeffe; under him Colonnel Ashton, Colonnel Holland, Colonnel Moore, Colonnel Rigby, by turns assisting one another.

The common souldier continually in leaguer betwixt 2,000 or 3,000, which divided in *tertias*, 700 or 800 watched every third day and night. Theire artillery, one demi canon, 1 culverin, a morterpeece, and 3 sacres.

Their works was an open trench round the house, a gard of ditch, and a gard raised with turfe, att the distance of 60, 100, or 200 yards from the walls.

Their sconces 8, raised in such places as might most annoy our men in the sallye, built directis lateribus, 2 yards in rampier and a yard in ditch, in some places staked and pallizadoed to keepe off a violent assault.

Their pioneers were first sheltred by basketts and hurdles, and afterwards by a kind of testudo, a wooden engine runneing on wheeles, rooft towards the house, with thicke plancks, and open to the enemy for liberty to cast up the earth.

They shott 107 canon, 32 stones, and 4 granadoes. They spent by confession of theire owne officers neare 100 barrels of powder, lost about 500 men, besides 140 maymed and wounded.

ALSO FROM LEONAUR
AVAILABLE IN SOFTCOVER OR HARDCOVER WITH DUST JACKET

THE WOMAN IN BATTLE by Loreta Janeta Velazquez—Soldier, Spy and Secret Service Agent for the Confederacy During the American Civil War.

BOOTS AND SADDLES by Elizabeth B. Custer—The experiences of General Custer's Wife on the Western Plains.

FANNIE BEERS' CIVIL WAR by Fannie A. Beers—A Confederate Lady's Experiences of Nursing During the Campaigns & Battles of the American Civil War.

LADY SALE'S AFGHANISTAN by Florentia Sale—An Indomitable Victorian Lady's Account of the Retreat from Kabul During the First Afghan War.

THE TWO WARS OF MRS DUBERLY by Frances Isabella Duberly—An Intrepid Victorian Lady's Experience of the Crimea and Indian Mutiny.

THE REBELLIOUS DUCHESS by Paul F. S. Dermoncourt—The Adventures of the Duchess of Berri and Her Attempt to Overthrow French Monarchy.

LADIES OF WATERLOO by Charlotte A. Eaton, Magdalene de Lancey & Juana Smith—The Experiences of Three Women During the Campaign of 1815: Waterloo Days by Charlotte A. Eaton, A Week at Waterloo by Magdalene de Lancey & Juana's Story by Juana Smith.

NURSE AND SPY IN THE UNION ARMY by Sarah Emma Evelyn Edmonds—During the American Civil War

WIFE NO. 19 by Ann Eliza Young The Life & Ordeals of a Mormon Woman During the 19th Century

DIARY OF A NURSE IN SOUTH AFRICA by Alice Bron—With the Dutch-Belgian Red Cross During the Boer War

MARIE ANTOINETTE AND THE DOWNFALL OF ROYALTY by Imbert de Saint-Amand—The Queen of France and the French Revolution

THE MEMSAHIB & THE MUTINY by R. M. Coopland—An English lady's ordeals in Gwalior and Agra during the Indian Mutiny 1857

MY CAPTIVITY AMONG THE SIOUX INDIANS by Fanny Kelly—The ordeal of a pioneer woman crossing the Western Plains in 1864

WITH MAXIMILIAN IN MEXICO by Sara Yorke Stevenson—A Lady's experience of the French Adventure

AVAILABLE ONLINE AT **www.leonaur.com**
AND FROM ALL GOOD BOOK STORES

ALSO FROM LEONAUR
AVAILABLE IN SOFTCOVER OR HARDCOVER WITH DUST JACKET

A DIARY FROM DIXIE by Mary Boykin Chesnut—A Lady's Account of the Confederacy During the American Civil War

FOLLOWING THE DRUM by Teresa Griffin Vielé—A U. S. Infantry Officer's Wife on the Texas frontier in the Early 1850's

FOLLOWING THE GUIDON by Elizabeth B. Custer—The Experiences of General Custer's Wife with the U. S. 7th Cavalry.

LADIES OF LUCKNOW by G. Harris & Adelaide Case—The Experiences of Two British Women During the Indian Mutiny 1857. A Lady's Diary of the Siege of Lucknow by G. Harris, Day by Day at Lucknow by Adelaide Case

MARIE-LOUISE AND THE INVASION OF 1814 by Imbert de Saint-Amand—The Empress and the Fall of the First Empire

SAPPER DOROTHY by Dorothy Lawrence—The only English Woman Soldier in the Royal Engineers 51st Division, 79th Tunnelling Co. during the First World War

ARMY LETTERS FROM AN OFFICER'S WIFE 1871-1888 by Frances M. A. Roe—Experiences On the Western Frontier With the United States Army

NAPOLEON'S LETTERS TO JOSEPHINE by Henry Foljambe Hall—Correspondence of War, Politics, Family and Love 1796-1814

MEMOIRS OF SARAH DUCHESS OF MARLBOROUGH, AND OF THE COURT OF QUEEN ANNE VOLUME 1 by A. T. Thomson

MEMOIRS OF SARAH DUCHESS OF MARLBOROUGH, AND OF THE COURT OF QUEEN ANNE VOLUME 2 by A. T. Thomson

MARY PORTER GAMEWELL AND THE SIEGE OF PEKING by A. H. Tuttle—An American Lady's Experiences of the Boxer Uprising, China 1900

VANISHING ARIZONA by Martha Summerhayes—A young wife of an officer of the U.S. 8th Infantry in Apacheria during the 1870's

THE RIFLEMAN'S WIFE by Mrs. Fitz Maurice—The Experiences of an Officer's Wife and Chronicles of the Old 95th During the Napoleonic Wars

THE OATMAN GIRLS by Royal B. Stratton—The Capture & Captivity of Two Young American Women in the 1850's by the Apache Indians

AVAILABLE ONLINE AT **www.leonaur.com**
AND FROM ALL GOOD BOOK STORES

www.ingramcontent.com/pod-product-compliance
Lightning Source LLC
Chambersburg PA
CBHW031617160426
43196CB00006B/171